Operating Model Canvas

Other publications by Van Haren Publishing

Van Haren Publishing (VHP) specializes in titles on Best Practices, methods and standards within four domains:

- IT and IT Management
- Architecture (Enterprise and IT)
- Business Management and
- Project Management

Van Haren Publishing is also publishing on behalf of leading organizations and companies: ASLBiSL Foundation, BRMI, CA, Centre Henri Tudor, Gaming Works, IACCM, IAOP, IFDC, Innovation Value Institute, IPMA-NL, ITSqc, NAF, KNVI, PMI-NL, PON, The Open Group, The SOX Institute.

Topics are (per domain):

IT and IT Management
ABC of ICT
ASL®
CATS CM®
CMMI®
COBIT®
e-CF
ISO/IEC 20000
ISO/IEC 27001/27002
ISPL
IT4IT®
IT-CMF™
IT Service CMM
ITIL®
MOF
MSF
SABSA
SAF
SIAM™
TRIM
VeriSM™

Enterprise Architecture
ArchiMate®
GEA®
Novius Architectuur Methode
TOGAF®

Business Management
BABOK® Guide
BiSL® and BiSL® Next
BRMBOK™
BTF
EFQM
eSCM
IACCM
ISA-95
ISO 9000/9001
OPBOK
SixSigma
SOX
SqEME®

Project Management
A4-Projectmanagement
DSDM/Atern
ICB / NCB
ISO 21500
MINCE®
M_o_R®
MSP®
P3O®
PMBOK® Guide
PRINCE2®

For the latest information on VHP publications, visit our website: www.vanharen.net.

Aligning operations and organization with strategy

OPERATING MODEL CANVAS

Andrew Campbell
Mikel Gutierrez
Mark Lancelott

Van Haren
PUBLISHING

Colophon

TITLE Operating Model Canvas
SUBTITLE Aligning operations and organization with strategy
AUTHORS Andrew Campbell, Mikel Gutierrez, Mark Lancelott
PUBLISHER Van Haren Publishing, Zaltbommel, www.vanharen.net
TEXT EDITOR Steve Newton (Galathea)
BOOK AND COVER DESIGNED BY Coco Bookmedia, Amersfoort - NL
NUR CODE 801, 982
ISBN HARD COPY 978 94 018 0071 6
ISBN EBOOK (PDF) 978 94 018 0072 3

EDITION First edition, first impression, March 2017
First edition, second impression, June 2017
First edition, third impression, with minor corrections, July 2017
First edition, fourth impression, with minor corrections, April 2018

Foreword

NIGEL SLACK, Emeritus Professor of Operations Management and Strategy, Warwick University, and author of best selling text books *Operations Strategy* and *Operations Management.*

There is an enduring dilemma that follows anyone charged with making strategy have a real impact. 'How do you think big while keeping your feet on the ground?' 'How do you translate the broad vision of where the enterprise wants to be into a set of practical and realistic plans and actions?' This is where the idea of the operating model fits in. It is a concept that has been gathering momentum in the strategy field – and for good reason. Operating models have the potential to provide a high-level design for any type of organization that both defines its structure and style and enables it to meet its business objectives. Done well, an operating model should provide a clear, 'big-picture' description of what the organization does, across both business and technology domains. It should provide a way to examining the business in terms of its key relationships, especially those between the business functions, processes and structures that are required for the organization to fulfil its mission. It should fit alongside the organization's business model in a way that helps convert strategy into a working model of how things need to be done in practice. A good operating model is a prerequisite for building effective change in the organization.

This is an important book for two reasons. First, it provides a first-class guide on how to put an effective operating model together. Andrew Campbell and his co-authors have taken the proven idea of a Business Model Canvas and created an Operating Model Canvas as a way of extending the number of operating elements that are considered from three (activities, resources, partners) to six (processes, organization, location, information, suppliers and management system). Of course there are many other ways of defining and presenting the idea of operating models. Every consultant has his or her own "model". But *Operating Model Canvas* is the first attempt, as far as I am aware, to document and share both the concept, a complete set of tools and worked examples. Second, the book is exceptionally well illustrated, with easy-to-follow steps and a wealth of engaging and insightful examples from all types of enterprise. I commend it to anyone involved in turning strategy into operational designs and choices.

RICHARD KOCH, author of the bestselling titles *Simplify* and *The 80/20 Principle*

I have followed Andrew's Campbell's work with pleasure for many years. Every time he takes on a topic, he contributes valuable new insights. This book is no exception.

Andrew and his co-authors start from a firm's value proposition – its distinctive advantages for customers – and then use their 'Operating Model Canvas' as a simple and practical way to work out *HOW* to deliver the value proposition the best way.

I see three huge advantages of this approach. One is that it actually does find the best feasible way to deliver the value proposition consistently.

The second advantage is that it helps managers in different areas get aligned so that the whole organization and its suppliers are trying to do the same thing.

And third, it provides a bridge for managers from the strategy to a portfolio of transformation projects, all pointing in the same direction – forward! Too often managers push their pet projects and huge value is lost by the firm and its customers. That will not happen with this approach.

I also love the messy look and feel of the book. The charts are drawn freehand by managers themselves, there are lots of post-it notes all over the place, the whole thing appears chaotic but is brilliantly cohesive. You can tell that the participants had a lot of fun – and you can too.

Endorsements

PATRICK VAN DER PIJL,
CEO Business Models Inc. and author of *Design a Better Business*

Designing a business is a difficult task. Books like *Operating Model Canvas* help cut through the complexity. It helps you to go one step deeper beyond the Business Model Canvas and Value Proposition. This book could be considered as part of a family of books like *Business Model Generation*, *Value Proposition Design*, *Design a Better Business* as we need to have conversations around the How. All are landscape. All are easy to read. All are full of tools and case examples. They should all be on your book shelf or the side of your desk.

YVES PIGNEUR,
co-author *Business Model Generation* and *Value Proposition Design*

Andrew Campbell and co-authors have focused on the left-hand side of the Business Model Canvas for creating an Operating Model Canvas. Their canvas consists of components such as locations, organization structure, people models, information systems and performance management systems. The book contains illustrations and worked examples, and has a nice landscape design. Let yourself be charmed by the thoughts, practical techniques and case studies proposed by the authors.

THOMAS H. DAVENPORT,
Distinguished Professor, Babson College, and author of *Competing on Analytics* and *Only Humans Need Apply*

If you liked Osterwalder et al.'s *Business Model Canvas* and *Value Proposition Design*, you'll also want to spend time with this one. All three books have a light and engaging tone and are co-created with practitioners. But *Operating Model Canvas* picks up where the earlier books leave off, taking the thinking about activities, resources, and partners to the next level. It's critical for making a business model work.

WILLIAM ULRICH,
President, Business Architecture Guild

Operating models have been written about for many years. The Operating Model Canvas moves the needle forward in this discussion by further framing operating model concepts in a canvas. As with most tools, readers should consider the canvas and related concepts as they continue their journey of streamlining and improving their business.

JOHN WEBB, Vice President & Program Lead Mars Operating Model, Mars Incorporated

I have just led a review and redesign of the global operating model for Mars Incorporated. Andrew Campbell was a significant help to me in this, and I learned a lot from applying some of the tools and processes that are in this book. I can see that the thinking has developed even further since then and this book would have been hugely helpful as I worked through the operating model scope and critical analyses with the Executive Committee.

I will certainly use this approach next time I have similar work to do. It simplifies what can be a complex and intimidating task, helps to put the work in the right context and provides tools that ensure rigor and focus.

If you have an operating model project to do, you need this book.

JOE SPADAFORD, Chief Operations Strategy Officer, Computershare

I have led many change and transformation projects that supported an overall business strategy. These are always difficult projects both in the design and the execution. *Operating Model Canvas* is a useful and pragmatic aid to this work, full of tools and examples and helpful ways of simplifying complexity. It provides a framework to consider the change elements holistically, giving you the opportunity to create an implementation plan that will more likely be successful.

FREEK DUPPEN, Senior Manager, Operating Model Development, The LEGO Group

Many people are going to find the insights in this book really valuable. Whether you are new to the topic or a seasoned practitioner, the book offers plenty to help you on your operating model journey: a clear framework for thinking about operating models, a basket of tools, and copious examples ranging from Zara to Snapfish and from a government department to an IT function. There are alternative ways to approach the concept of operating models, but I can highly recommend the approach in this book. It is easy to read, practically relevant, and touches upon all the important aspects.

DR GRAHAM EDWARDS, retired CEO, AECI

At AECI we got a lot of use out of the Business Model Canvas. Every business or proposed new acquisition had to present its Canvas to the Exco, and managers were subjected to a fairly rigorous grilling to ensure they really did understand their business model. If we had had the Operating Model Canvas, those sessions would have been more penetrating on operating issues. This book is another important step forward in management thinking.

MARK SMALLEY, Ambassador, ASL BiSL Foundation

Andrew Campbell has produced a very useful book that can be used in its own right or in combination with the Business Model Canvas. I had the pleasure of reviewing the book and learnt a lot in the process. For most people, the term operating model is poorly defined and loosely used. *Operating Model Canvas* does a good job in pinning it down in simple but well-grounded language. The guidance is practical and attractively presented. I used the principles and structure in my work for The Open Group's IT4IT Forum to create an IT operating model and I am pleased with the results. I have no hesitation in recommending this book.

MICHEL BERTHUS, Group Vice President - Head of Quality Management, ABB

Operating Model Canvas is both simple and powerful. It provides a simple framework (the Canvas) and some powerful tools (value chain map, organization model, supplier matrix, etc.). I cannot imagine anyone involved in working on organization design or operating models or even process improvement that will not gain a great deal from this easy to read and engaging book.

STEPHEN BUNGAY, author of *The Art of Action*

My work and teaching on strategy execution is about how organizations make things happen in line with their intentions. It focuses on the 'software' – how to set direction and align people so as to create unity of effort. But every company has made commitments to doing things in a certain way that is reflected and constrained by their 'hardware'. *Operating Model Canvas* addresses the question of how to change that hardware and design an organization with the right operational capabilities. I find the simplicity of the canvas, the wealth of examples in Chapter 2 and the quality of the tools explained in Chapter 3 both practical and powerful. The authors' innovative and engaging approach turns the hard work involved into fun, and redefines what a 'how to' textbook should be. It is a great companion to *The Art of Action*.

JEROEN DE FLANDER, author of the bestsellers *Strategy Execution Heroes* and *The Execution Shortcut*

Operating Model Canvas helps you in a practical and fun way to design the best possible operating model for your strategy. Highly recommended!

PROFESSOR GUNTER MÜLLER-STEWENS, Institut für Betriebswirtschaft, Universität St.Gallen

Strategies often fail to get implemented. We already have ways to convert strategies into scorecards and KPIs, but we have fewer tools to help convert strategies into portfolios of transformation projects. *Operating Model Canvas* fills this gap. Andrew Campbell and his co-authors seem to understand both strategy and operations and have created an ideal companion to the Business Model Canvas. It is an easy and fun read. And it encourages and supports the reader in applying the ideas on real projects.

MARC LANKHORST, Managing Consultant & Chief Technology Evangelist, BiZZdesign, and developer of the ArchiMate® standard for enterprise architecture modeling

Our company BiZZdesign does many projects that involve designing the business architecture and operating activities of a business or organization. The design of business models has been very successfully addressed by Alex Osterwalder and Ives Pigneur in their famous book *Business Model Generation*. But to make your business model work, you also need an operating model, describing how the elements of your organization together deliver its value proposition. The Operating Model Canvas proposed by Andrew Campbell, Mikel Gutierrez and Mark Lancelott extends the thinking behind the Business Model Canvas to provide a practical tool for designing such operating models. This book will help anybody involved in business design, target operating models, business architecture and operational improvements.

KIRILL DEREVENSKI, Strategic Business Architect, ex-Sodexo

I have carried out a number of jobs transforming strategy into operational results in mid-sized and large companies. I wish I had had Operating Model Canvas by my side. It is comprehensive, straightforward and accessible. It is written by people who understand strategy and who know how to connect strategy with operations to drive measurable results. It contains tools and methods that are effective and easy to apply while using the language that senior managers talk. A 'must have' to get your project right from the start, and to get it to a successful finish. A perfect operational 'nuts and bolts' companion to Business Model Generation, when you need concrete guidance on operating model design.

GRAHAM DALTON, Independent Management Consultant

I have used Andrew's OD tools over a hundred times, both at PwC and as an independent management consultant. They make sense to clients and give great insight and clarity.

This new contribution brings similar clarity to the complex topic of operating models.

Andrew's book is very visual and easy to read; and the great client examples bring the topic to life.

This book and its Operating Model Toolbox will be invaluable to consultants and executives alike, guiding them in how to align their organization and operations with their strategic aims. I was part of a team that developed PwC's approach to operating model work and I wish I had had this book to help me.

AMY KATES, Kates Kesler Organization Consulting and author (with Jay Galbraith) of *Designing Your Organization*

As organization designers, we help leaders make smart decisions about 'organization models'. A prerequisite to this work is a clear 'operating model'. The operating model articulates the business framework and how the organization components will relate to one another. A clear operating model makes selecting among organization options much easier.

Andrew Campbell brings a designer's eye to demystifying the steps for creating an operating model. This book is filled with tools, examples, and a wide variety of case studies. It will be an essential guide for anyone working on organizations.

NAOMI STANFORD, Organization Design Practitioner, author, speaker

Andrew Campbell, more typically known for his strategy and organization work, has focused his attention on the task of turning strategy into operations. He and co-authors explain, through illustrations and examples, the six elements of the *Operating Model Canvas* - value delivery chains, organization, information systems, locations, suppliers and management systems - in a beautifully clear and fun way that takes the pain out of operating model development and implementation. It's a substantial contribution designed in an engaging way showing the working steps as they actually progress and giving helpful tips, guidance and resources along the way. A great addition to any organization designer's toolkit.

Contributing authors

Important contributors (alphabetical):

Marcus Alexander, London Business School
Stephen Baishya, Consultant
Martin Bartram, Royal Bank of Scotland
Nicola Bateman, School of Business and Economics, Loughborough University
Marcia Blenko, Bain & Co
Stephen Bungay, Ashridge Strategic Management Centre
Christoph Burtscher, Yodel
Alan Crawley, Optima Partners
Kirill Derevenski, Strategic Business Architect
Joao Dolores, Sonae
Freek Duppen, Lego
David Favelle, ValueFlowIT
Chris Fox, StrategicLearningApp.com
Allan Gasson, Independent (ex Deloitte)
Geoff Grace, AXA
Alex Graham, Egremont
Ben Gray, Guild Consulting
Ben Groom, Capgemini
Jonathan Hammond, Knadel
Steven Han 韩松林, China
Amy Kates, Kates Kesler
Marc Lankhorst, BiZZdesign
Carl Lloyd, Royal Bank of Scotland
Peter McClure, Vodafone
Dev Mookerjee, Ashridge
Gillian Morris, Jaguar Land Rover
Rupert Morrison, Concentra
Guenter Muller-Stewens, Universitat St Gallen
Peter Murchland, Enterprise Architect
Mark Palmer, OEE Consulting
Joseph Paris, Opex Society
Anish Patel, Patel Miller
Anca Raines, PA Consulting
Richard Rawling, Nous Group
Howell Schroeder, Schroeder Forbes
Mark Smalley, IT & ASL BiSL Foundation
Joseph Spadaford, Computershare
Jonathan Tidd, OEE Consulting
Conrad Thompson, PA Consulting
William Ulrich, Business Architecture Guild
John Webb, Mars
David Winders, Lecturer and Business Architect
Nicolay Worren, Norwegian University of Life Sciences

Examples provided by:

The authors, and
Marc Baker, Ofqual
Andrew Freiman, Department of Work and Pensions
Roberto Gil, Velatia
Alex Graham, Egremont
Adam Laurie, DEV CON
Jamie Lopez, Faes Farma
Wendell Mitchell, Guardian Group
Howell Schroeder, Schroeder Forbes
Deborah Strazza, John Lewis Partnership
Alex Szekely, Wilson Perumal
Ricardo de los Rios, IESE
David Winders, Lecturer and Business Architect

Our course 'Designing Operating Models' at Ashridge Executive Education has been a huge learning experience for us. Here are some of the participants (about a third - random order).

Sebastian Pordomingo, Akzo Nobel
Dean Genade, Sanlam
Jonathan McDonnell, British Red Cross
Rob Adsley, XI Catlin
Wendell Mitchell, Guardian Group
Andrew Milbourne, Cambridge English
Collette Roche, Manchester Airport
Scott Schoenbrun, SPX
Sardip Sandhu , Walgreens Boots Alliance
Deborah Strazza, John Lewis
Ian Todd, Independent Police Complaints Commission
Phil Merrell, Willis Towers Watson
Carol Madeley, Belron
Tammy Tawdros, Ashridge
Else Marie-Brekke, DNVGL
Louise Wade, Project Delivery Excellence
Carlos Alpizar, Grupo Cuestamoras
Hannah Crossley, Egremont Group
Geoff Grace , AXA Insurance
Andrew Blundell , Walgreens Boots Alliance
Martin Bartram, RBS
Alhaidary Maher Monsour, CMA
Laura Worboyes, Amlin Investments
Jeremy Faint, NHS
Paul Hill, Manheim
Eric Smith, Calmac
Frances Hall, Corbar Consulting
Charlotte Eimer, BBC Monitoring
Stephen Ogundere, Consultant
Damian Pearson, Ernest and Young
Abdulaziz Aladwani, ELM Consulting
Alan Crawley, Optima Partners
Helen Own, Pasque Consulting
Eric Thiam Sebates, Imperial Tobacco
Janice Paterson, NIHR Clinical Research Network
Vikki Harmon, Grant Thornton
Christian Harm, Kion Group
Mike Fisher, Matthew Clark
Hester Gudmunsen, ACCA
Laura Lee Oliver, Red Apple Consulting
Karen Moore, University of Sydney
Paras Sood, SAB Miller
Kate Bendon, K8B Consulting Ltd
Adrian Twyning, British Gas
Imm Law, Royal Mail
Fiona Evans, Zoological Society London
Ben Groom, Capgemini
Michael Donaldson, Standard Life
Charlotte Wedd, Manchester Airport Group
Andy Aitkenhead, Kuoni Travel
Yana Meltser Shaer, HSBC
Vanessa Ryan, Royal Mail
Steve Curry, NHS
Sandra De Sousa, MMI Holdings
Jan Luyten, DSM
Sumit Mistry, Salesforce
Rachel Honey, John Lewis
Sam Airey, Weightmans
Mike Lynn-Jones, Lowell Group
Matthew McClelland, The Nursing and Midwifery Council
Andreas Kroepfli, Swiss Federal Department of Finance
Nigel Paling, Manheim
John Hall, Swagelok Manchester
Fred Creighton, World Duty Free
Jeeti Chauhan, Shell
Sam Lewens, myBBC
Naresh Mongroo, Guardian Shared Services
Devand Singh, Cambridge English
Maher AlHaidary, The Capital Market Authority
Chantal van der Ginste, Delaware Consulting
Olutoyin Orefuwa, TransmissionFour Consulting
Mohammed Omar Baqais, ELM
Oliver Landgraf, Consultant
Mary Kennedy, Consultant
Kathleen Versland, Deutsche Bank
Mark Bellamy, PA Consulting

Course website: www.ashridge.org.uk/dom

About the Authors

ANDREW CAMPBELL

is a Director of Ashridge Strategic Management Centre, a research and education center focused on the strategic management of organizations. Andrew directs research projects, runs management programs and advises client companies. He is program director of Advanced Organization Design and Designing Operating Models. Andrew has authored 10 books on strategy and capability, including Designing Effective Organizations and Strategy for the Corporate Level, and has published numerous articles in the Harvard Business Review and other management publications. He blogs at ashridgeonoperatingmodels.com and tweets @operatingmodels. Before joining Ashridge, Andrew was a Fellow of the Centre for Business Strategy at London Business School. Before that, he spent six years with McKinsey & Co in Los Angeles and London.

MIKEL GUTIÉRREZ

is Industrial Projects Director of Gamesa, the worlds largest producer of turnkey wind farms. He is responsible for the delivery of all Gamesa wind farms worldwide, from signing the contract, until the energization of the park. Previously he was CEO of Asebal, a company producing galvanized steel for road and solar businesses. He steered Asebal from a domestic, almost bankrupt Spanish company to a strong business, selling in more than 20 countries. Before that, he was General Manager of Ormazabal Germany and Director of Business Process Improvement of the parent company Ormazabal Group, a producer of equipment for the power industry. His functional roles have included sales, business improvement, IT, strategy, organization design, product design and processes. He studied mechanical engineering and has worked in Spain, France, Germany, Denmark and the USA.

MARK LANCELOTT

is a Director of Business Design at PA Consulting. He specializes in business design, helping businesses design new operating models that integrate structure, people, process and systems. He also leads the implementation of change together with executives, managers and staff in client companies. He has worked in many sectors including the finance, industry, government and charity sectors. He is currently interested in how to simplify organizations by tackling unnecessary complexity. Mark worked at Barclays for 10 years. He is active in the Business Architecture Guild, and European Organization Design Forum (EODF), blogs regularly and tweets (@marklancelott) on operating models and organization issues.

Contents

CHAPTER 1

CH1

OPERATING MODEL CANVAS

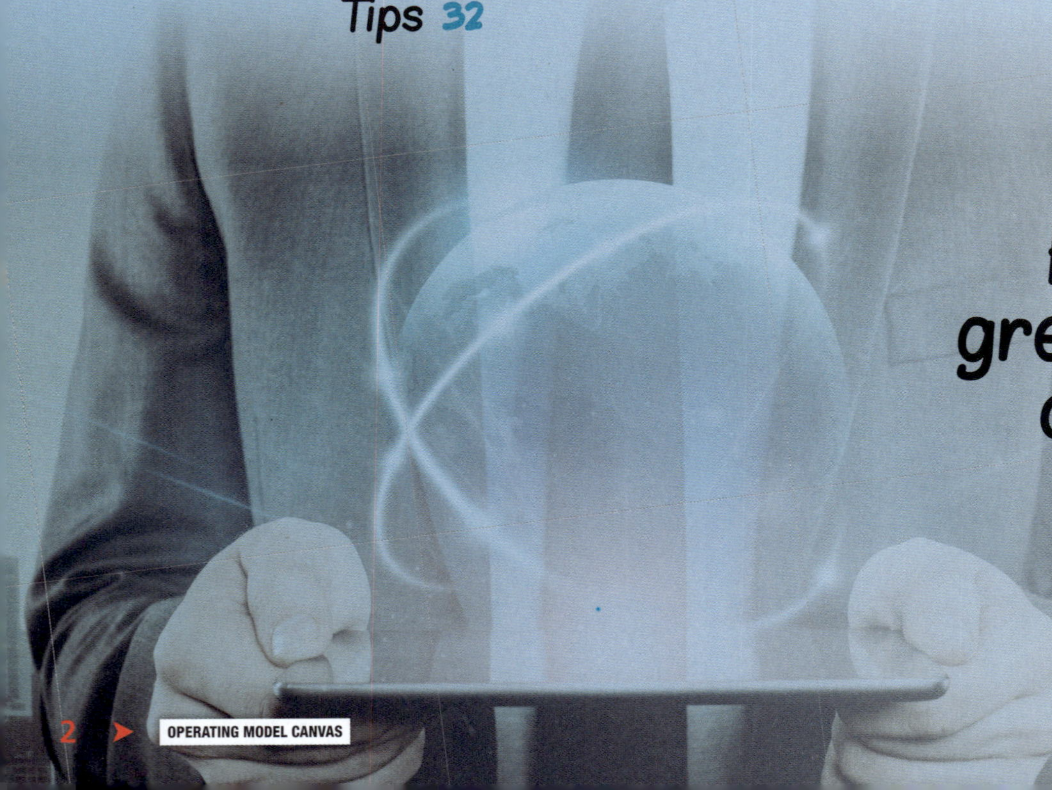

How to deliver great value to your customers and beneficiaries

AN OPERATING MODEL IS ...

.. a **VISUAL** representation (i.e. a model)

.. in the form of a **DIAGRAM OR MAP OR CHART** or collection of diagrams, maps, tables and charts

.. that show the **ELEMENTS OF THE ORGANIZATION**, such as activities, people, decision processes, information systems, suppliers, locations, and assets,

.. that are important for delivering the organization's **VALUE PROPOSITION(S)**

.. and how these elements **COMBINE** to successfully deliver the value proposition(s)

CH1

THE JOURNEY TO SUCCESS HAS FOUR PARTS:

- **THE STRATEGY PART:** deciding what the organization will do
- **THE OPERATING MODEL PART:** designing the organization so that it is able to execute the strategy
- **THE BUILD OR TRANSFORMATION PART:** creating the target operations and organization
- **THE DOING-THE-BUSINESS PART:** running the organization so that the strategy is achieved

This book is about the operating model part: the design part. It is not about the strategy, transformation or doing-the-business parts

Different authorities define operating model differently. There is no standard definition. This is our definition.

Other authorities include a mission, vision and values step before strategy. We include this as part of strategy.

HIGH-LEVEL OPERATING MODELS

This book is about high-level operating models. It focuses on the link between strategy and operations and between business models and operating models.

One page Operating Model

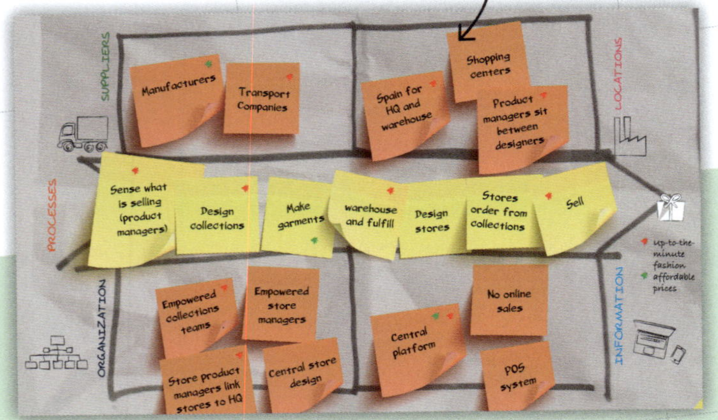

Explained and illustrated in Chapters 2 and 6

Ten page Operating Model

Explained and illustrated in Chapters 3, 4 and 5

DETAILED OPERATING MODELS

For an organization to function, many hundreds of design decisions need to be made. Our belief is that these decisions - the detailed operating model decisions - are better made if there is a high-level operating model guiding them.

One hundred page Operating Model

One thousand page Operating Mannual

Not covered in this book

WHEN DO YOU NEED TO WORK ON

WHEN YOU ARE STARTING SOMETHING NEW

- Helps test the practicality of what you want to do
- Helps you understand costs, resources and timing, and hence develop a better business case
- Helps you align your team and your stakeholders
- Helps ensure you focus on the important

WHEN YOU ARE CHANGING STRATEGY

- Helps test the practicality of what you want to do. Often leads to better strategies.
- Helps you understand costs, resources and timing, and hence develop a better business case
- Helps your people understand the new strategy
- Helps ensure your implementation plan is complete

WHEN YOU HAVE PERFORMANCE PROBLEMS

- Helps you find the root causes
- Helps you see the connections between symptoms and causes
- Helps ensure your implementation plan is complete
- Helps your people see why all the changes are needed

YOUR OPERATING MODEL?

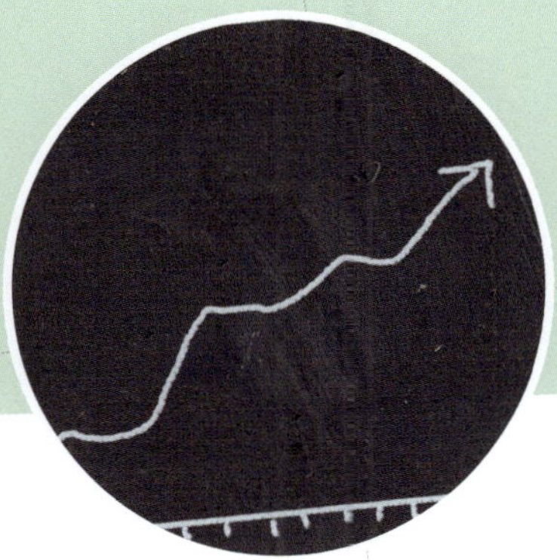

WHEN YOUR TEAM IS NOT ALIGNED

- Helps those with different views explain their thinking
- Provides the senior team with a shared blueprint of what they are trying to build together
- Provides a line of sight between purpose and activity

WHEN YOU ARE FINDING IT HARD TO IMPLEMENT YOUR PLANS

- Enables you to check that your plans are practical
- Helps those who are dragging their feet explain their position
- Often results in re-sequencing the implementation plan

WHEN YOU ARE IMPLEMENTING MAJOR CHANGE

- Enables you to check that your project sequence is practical
- Helps explain the plan and the business case
- Helps those who are concerned about the plan to explain their position
- Helps align the leaders of different projects

THIS BOOK WILL HELP YOU ...

Who are you?

CH1

- A **manager in operations** or **in any function** who wants to design how the operation works
- A **CEO** or **COO** or **entrepreneur** who wants to review his or her organization and plans
- A **lean practitioner** or **process excellence manager** who wants to be more strategic
- A **manager in strategy** or **planning** who wants to make the plans more practical
- A **project manager** or **change specialist** working on a transformation project
- A **leader** who wants to make sure her team members are all on the same page
- A **business partner in HR, IT** or **Finance** who wants to improve the business
- A **business development manager** who wants to design a new business
- A **Business Architect, Enterprise Architect** or **Operations Strategist**
- A **manager** tasked with cutting costs or improving service or quality
- A **customer experience** or **user experience specialist**
- A **manager in charge** of post **merger** integration
- A **consultant** helping organizations improve
- **Anyone** responsible for performance

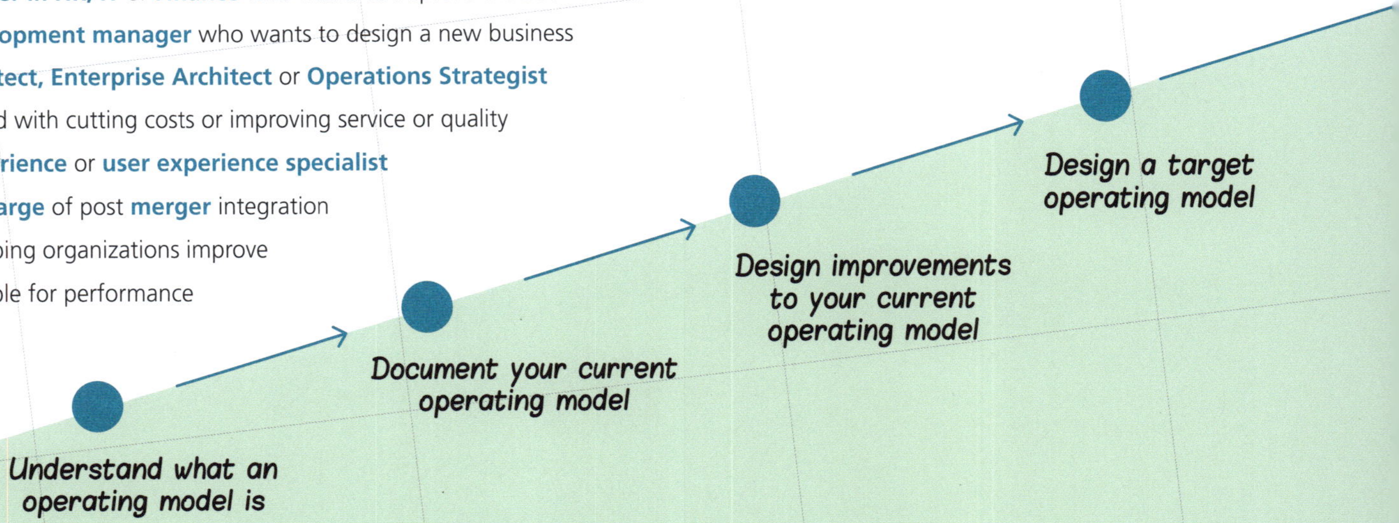

Improve the dialogue with those resisting or concerned about change

Better align managers from different functions, countries and cultures around a common view of what they are jointly trying to do

Discover ways of improving your strategies

Achieve your strategic objectives

Be more successful

Yes, operating model work can result in better strategies: more practical, more connected with capability, more profitable

THIS BOOK WILL HELP YOU

STRATEGIES ENGAGE 5% ...

CH1

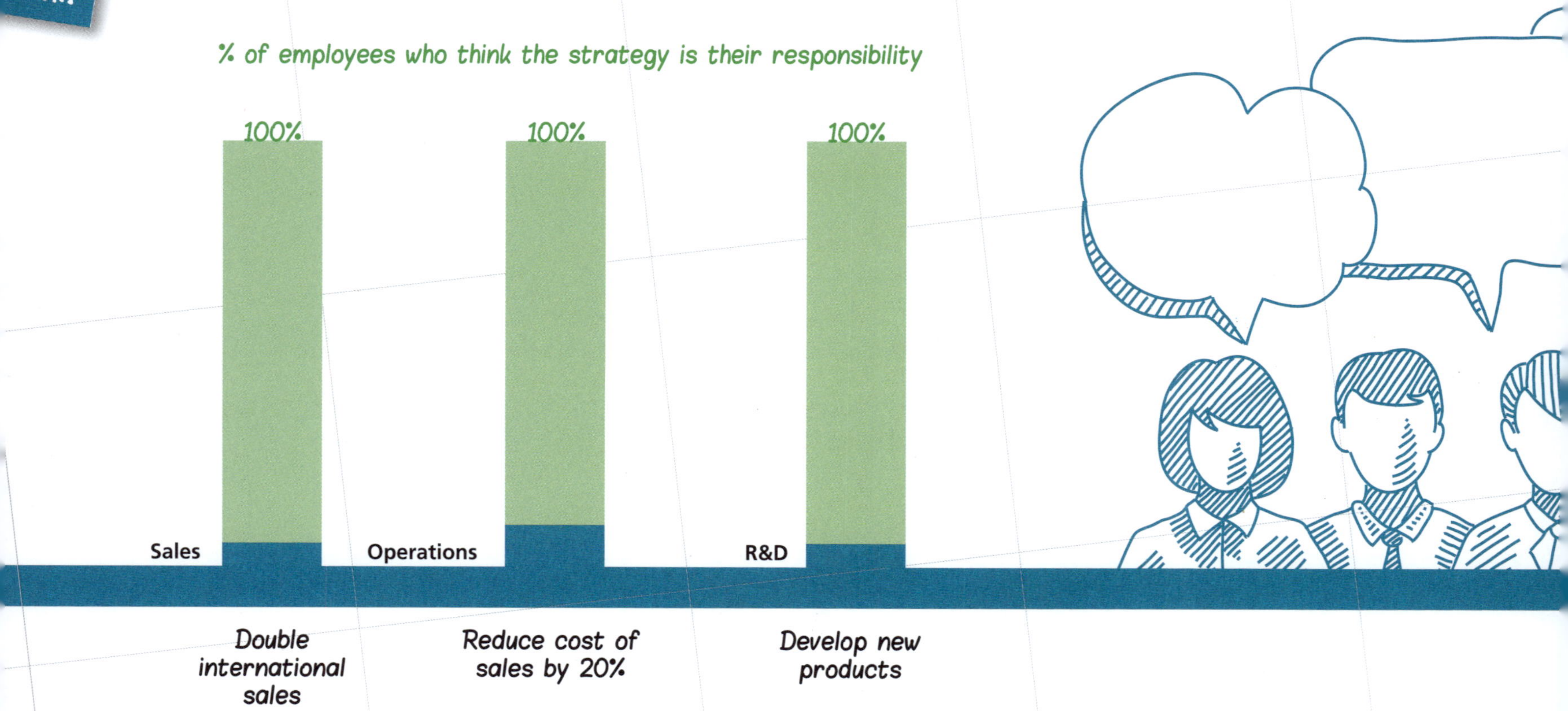

... OPERATING MODELS ENGAGE 95%

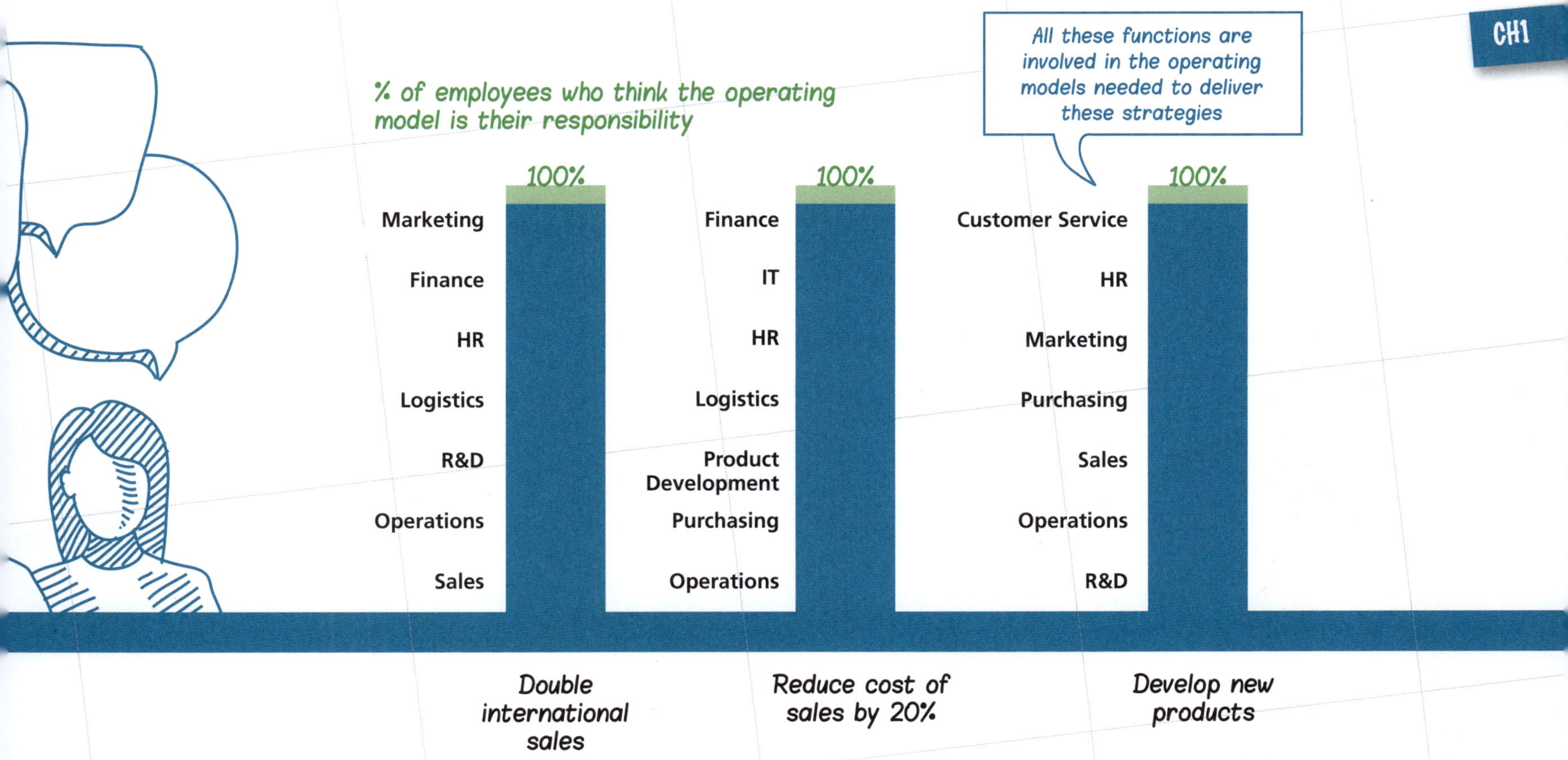

HOW TO USE THIS BOOK

The Operating Model Canvas is a tool that will help you think about and make changes to your operations.

It is a simple tool. You may be able to grasp the tool and start using it by reading this chapter and the first few pages of Chapter 2 - "The Operating Model Canvas - Examples".

However, you will gain the most from this book if you first identify a challenge or opportunity you have in your current situation. As you read, try creating a Canvas for your organization. Write a few post-it notes that capture some of the things you think are important about your organization (i.e. important to delivering the value proposition) and stick them on the Canvas. Then look at the examples provided (Chapter 2). Then look at the tools (Chapter 3) and try using some to understand your challenge and develop ideas for resolving it. Then explore the two big case studies (Chapters 4 and 5).

Have fun!

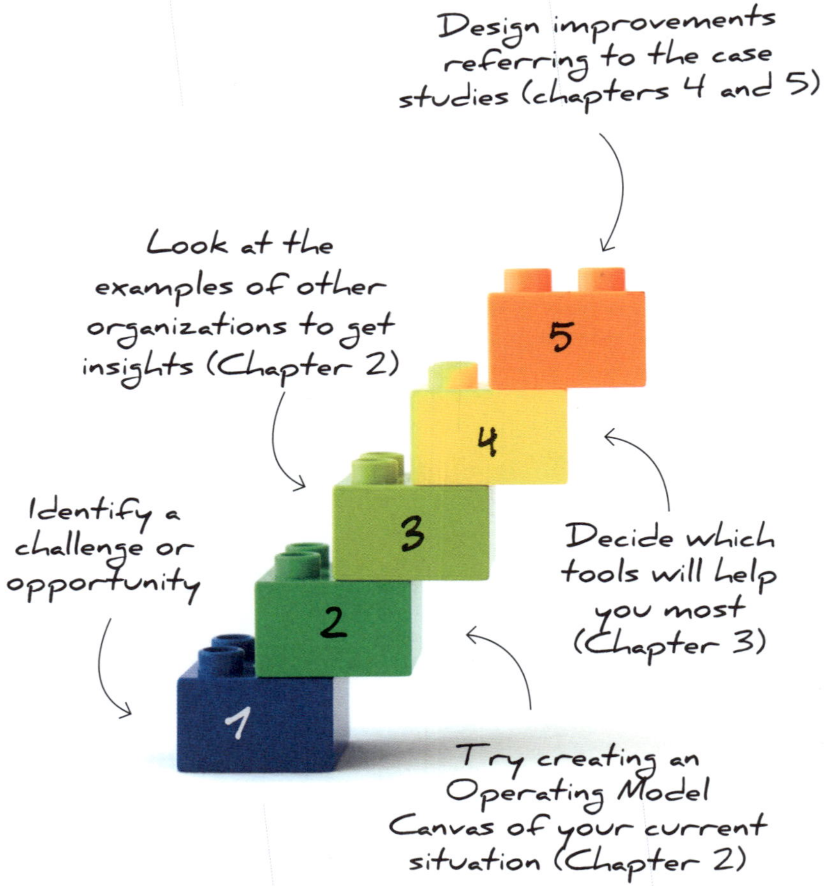

CHAPTERS

THE OPERATING MODEL CANVAS IS A ONE PAGE OPERATING MODEL

THE CANVAS IS FULLY EXPLAINED IN CHAPTER 2

The **OPERATING MODEL CANVAS** does not include the Financial Model. But, of course, the operating model does drive most of the organization's costs.

OPERATING MODEL CANVAS

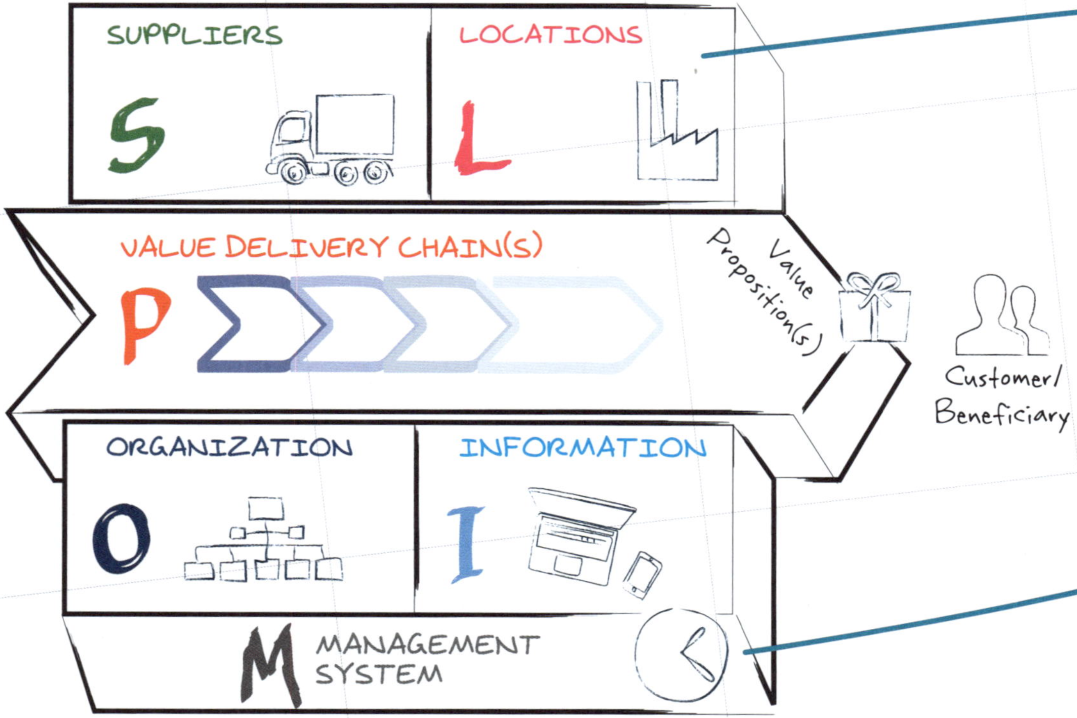

The link is roughly
P = Key Activities
S = Key Partners
O + L + I + M = Key Resources

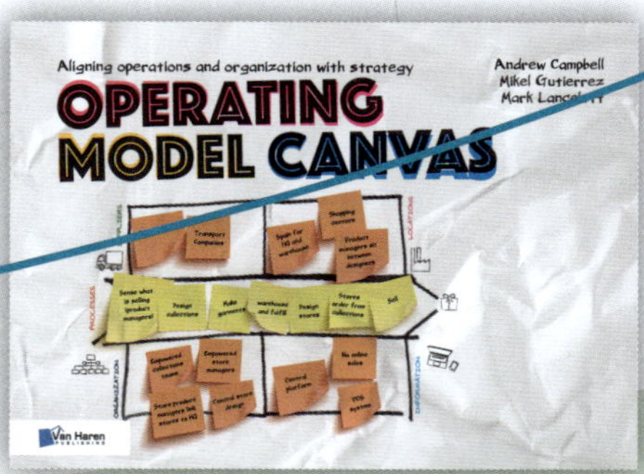

IT COVERS THE BACK END OF THE BUSINESS MODEL CANVAS

BUSINESS MODEL

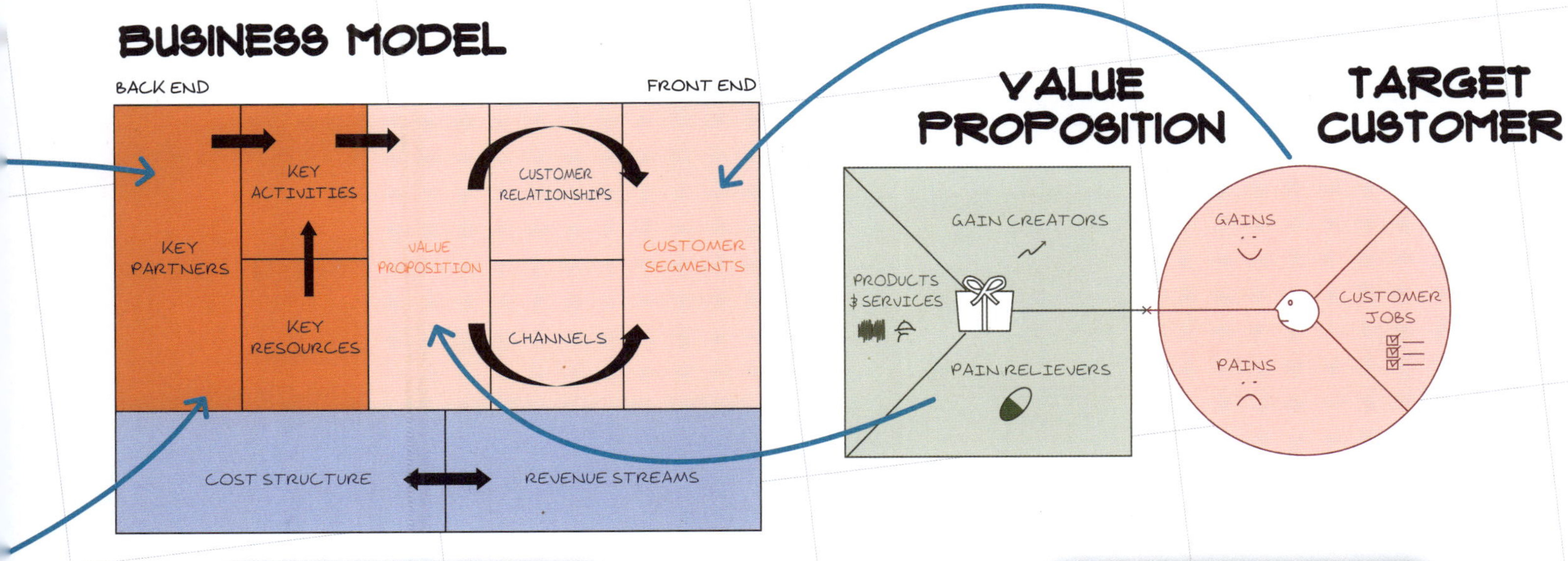

Are **CHANNELS** and **CUSTOMER RELATIONSHIPS** part of an operating model? Yes in so far as they involve **KEY ACTIVITIES** or **KEY PARTNERS**

WHAT IS THE ...

CH1

The Business Model Canvas is a framework developed by Alex Osterwalder, Yves Pigneur and co-authors to describe the main elements of a business. It describes how an organization creates, delivers and captures value, what value is being delivered and to whom.

You do not need to be familiar with the Business Model Canvas to understand and work with the Operating Model Canvas, but you will find it useful.

The book Business Model Generation, published in 2010, provides more information and there are on-line resources at strategyzer.com/bmg

KEY PARTNERS

External organizations who provide important inputs to the organization. They may be suppliers of raw materials or distribution services or IT support. Equivalent to the suppliers box in the Operating Model Canvas.

KEY ACTIVITIES

The most important work steps needed to deliver the value proposition. Equivalent to the processes arrow in the Operating Model Canvas.

KEY RESOURCES

The most important assets, such as people, technology, machinery, brand, buildings and locations. Equivalent to the locations box (which includes assets), the organization box (which includes people) and the information box (which includes data assets) in the Operating Model Canvas.

CUSTOMER SEGMENTS

The different groups of people the organization is trying to serve.

VALUE PROPOSITIONS

The offer to the customers or beneficiaries of the organization.

CHANNELS

How the organization communicates with and distributes to customers or beneficiaries.

CUSTOMER RELATIONSHIPS

How customers are acquired, engaged with and retained.

The four items in this column are about market strategy – what to offer to whom through which channels. They have implications for the Operating Model Canvas.

... BUSINESS MODEL CANVAS?

The Business Model Canvas

Designed for: *Designed by:* *Date:* *Version:*

Key Partners	Key Activities	Value Propositions	Customer Relationships	Customer Segments
	Key Resources		Channels	

Cost Structure	Revenue Streams

HOW DOES THE OPERATING MODEL CANVAS LINK TO ...

CH1

THE OPERATING MODEL CANVAS HAS SIX ELEMENTS:

- the work that needs to be done to deliver the value proposition (**VALUE CHAIN**);
- the people who do the work and how they are organized (**ORGANIZATION**);
- where the people will be located and the assets they need to help them (**LOCATIONS**);
- what information systems the people need to help them (**INFORMATION**);
- the suppliers who support the work (**SUPPLIERS**); and
- the management system used to run the organization (**MANAGEMENT SYSTEM**).

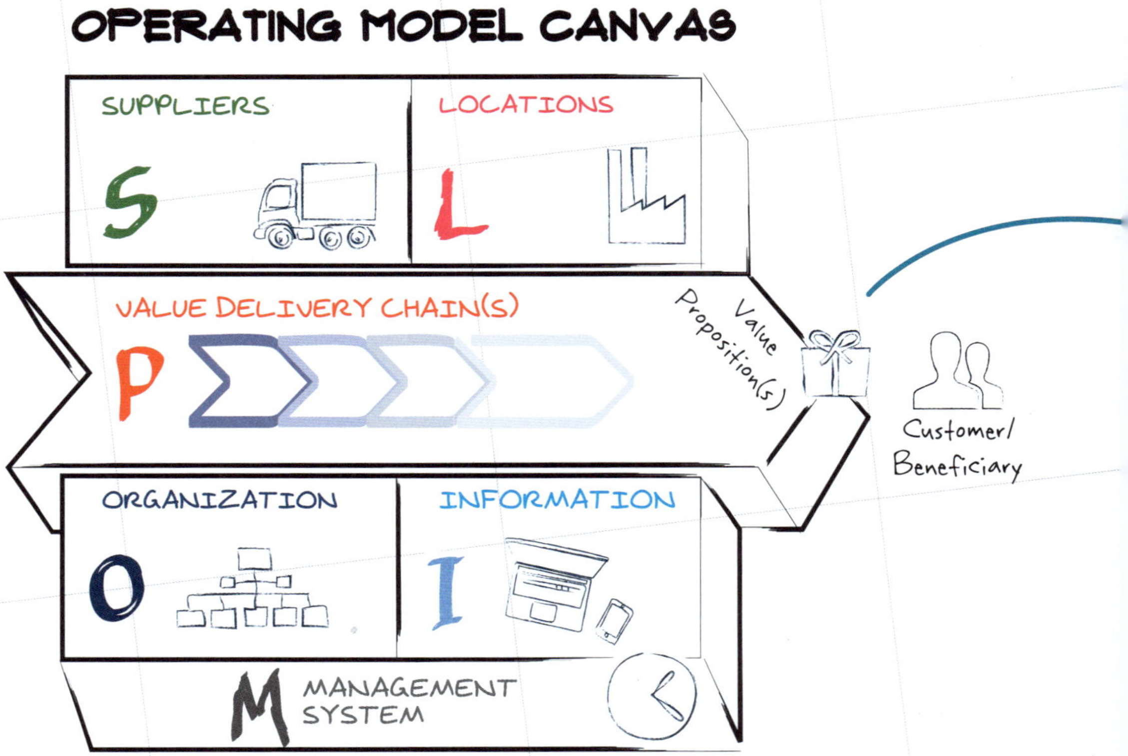

... AN ENHANCED BUSINESS MODEL CANVAS

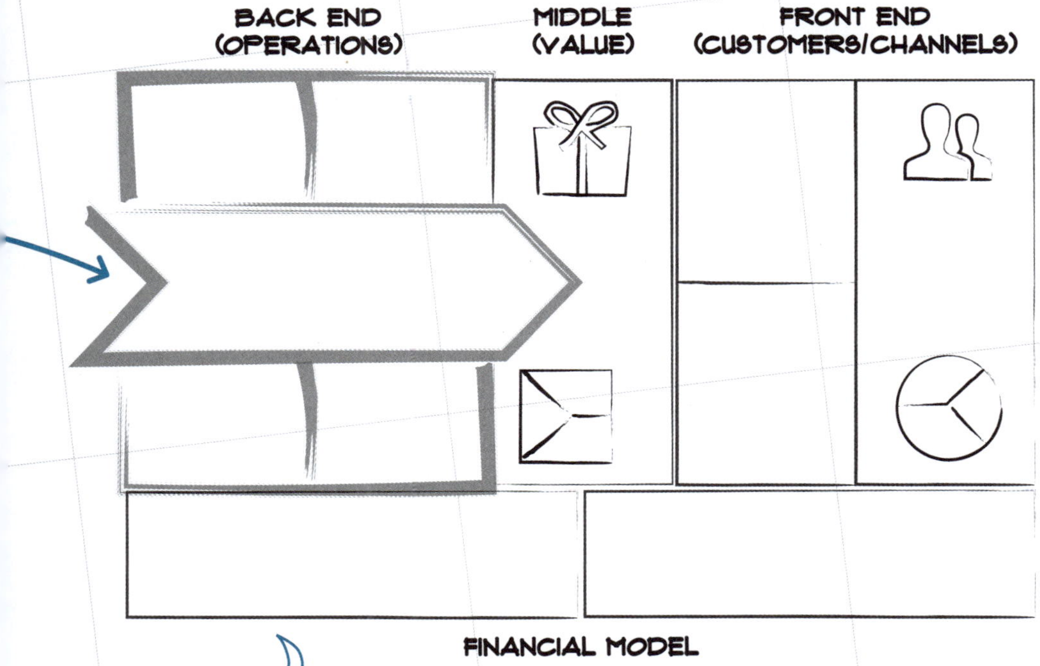

The Operating Model Canvas has icons for value proposition and customer. These are treated as inputs to the operating model design rather than as part of the design challenge. The book "Value Proposition Design" shows how to design these inputs.

The Operating Model Canvas with SIX elements is a more powerful "back-end" than the three elements - Key Activities, Key Resources and Key Partners - of the Business Model Canvas.

FROM STRATEGY ...

UNDERSTAND ENVIRONMENT

Customer preferences

Market & economic trends

Competitor performance

Supplier capabilities

Technical, legal, environmental, and political factors

All good strategy is founded on a deep understanding of the environment, economic trends, consumer trends, technology possibilities, etc ...

DEVELOP STRATEGY

A strategic plan explains who the organization will serve, what will be "offered" and how the "value" will be created.

Strategies need to be converted into a business design. This is best done by working on the elements of the business model: value proposition design, operating model canvas and financial model. This work can result in adjustments to the strategy.

... TOWARDS TRANSFORMATION

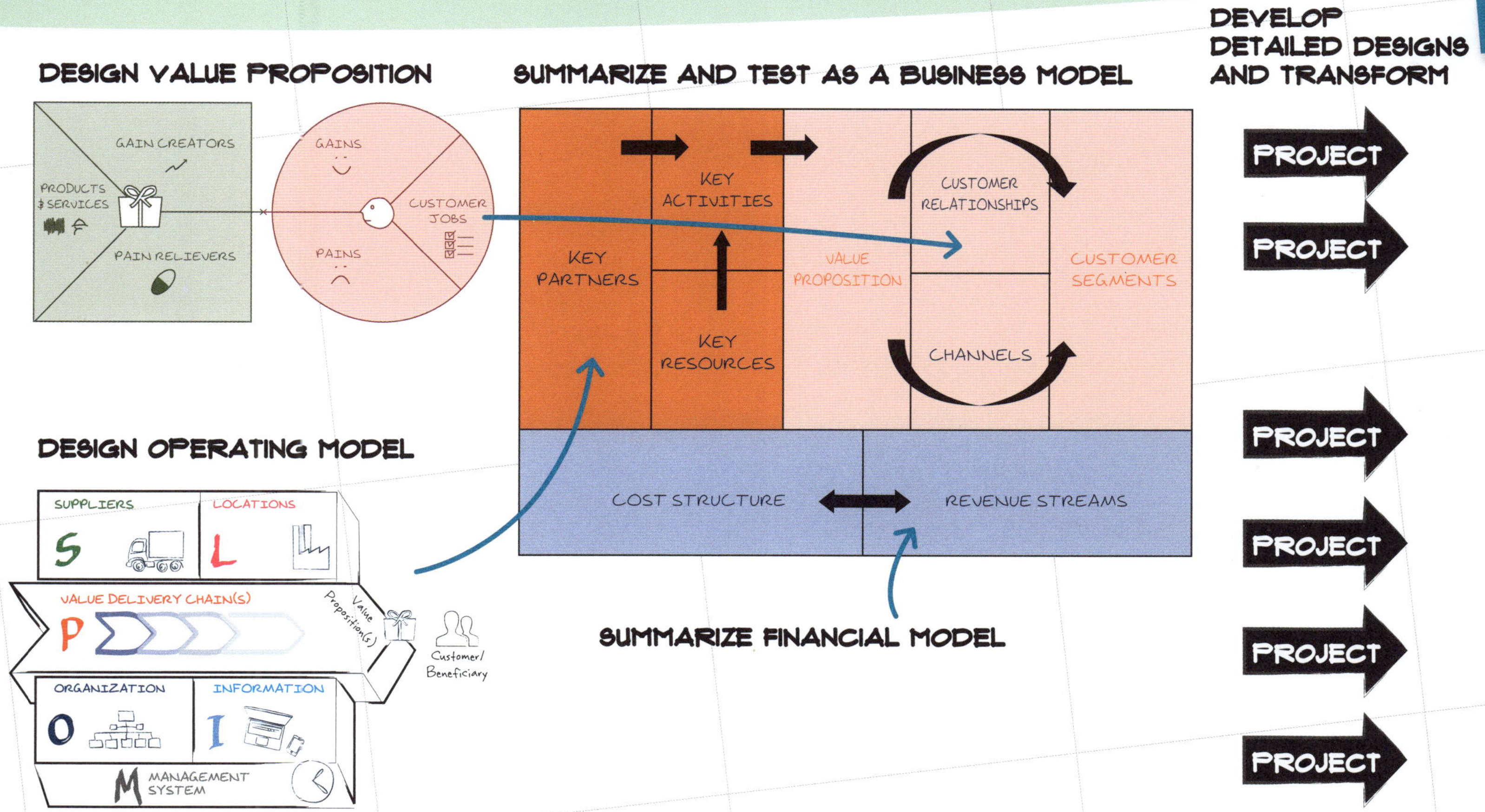

DESIGNING THE OPERATING MODEL ...

CH1

This book is about how to design (at a high-level) the "to be" or "target" or "future" operations.

IDENTIFY a reason to change

DESIGN the high-level 'to be' operating model

Design the **TRANSFORMATION** journey and work on lower-level operating model details

… NOT THE TRANSFORMATION JOURNEY

But the Operating Model Canvas can also be used as a guide during transformation; as a way of communicating both the 'as is' and 'to be'; and to help stakeholders build engagement around changes at any level of detail.

START TRANSFORMING from 'as is' to 'to be'
….
while designing more details and running the 'as is' organization

Transform from 'as is' to 'to be'
….
WHILE RUNNING a mix of 'as is' and 'to be'

Run the 'to be' organization
…
WHILE IMPROVING IT

IDENTIFY another reason to change

TYPICAL ACTIVITIES IN AN ...

Initiate

- Clarify issues
- Clarify stakeholders
- Clarify scope
- Define team
- Define governance
- Plan project
- Agree plan

Diagnose

- Understand strategic objectives
- Understand front end of business model
  - Target segments/geographies
  - Channels/relationships
  - Product/service value propositions
- Understand current operating model
- Understand sources of advantage/excellence
- Understand problems/issues/challenges
- Develop case for change

Design Principles

- Clarify strategic objectives
- Define design principles
- Test and get agreement

These are the typical steps that you might see in any proposal for operating model work.

... OPERATING MODEL DESIGN PROJECT

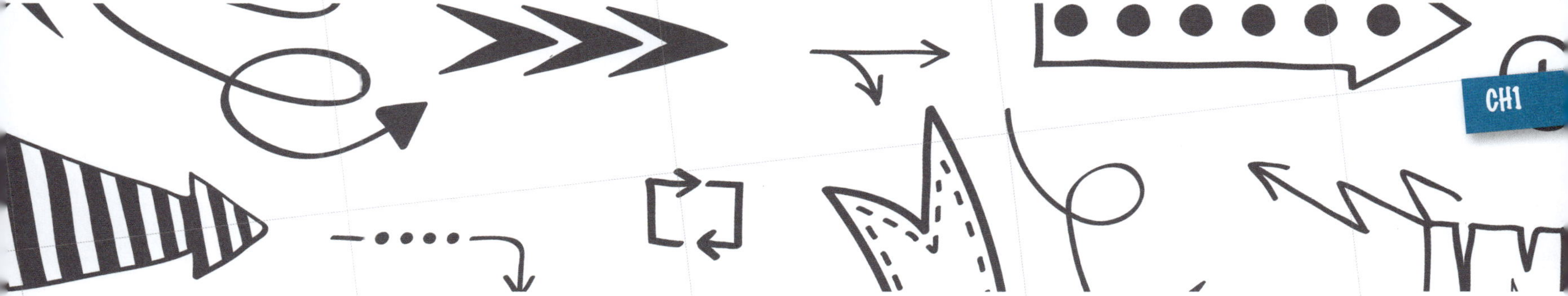

Develop Options

- Define critical choices
- Develop options
  - Organization options
  - Location options
  - Information options
  - Supplier options
  - Management system options
- Check alignment

Evaluate

- Check against design principles
- Test against other criteria
  - Cost/capital expenditure
  - Ease of implementation
  - Political support
  - Constraints
  - Risks
  - Etc.
- Check against principles of a good operating model (see page 132)

Plan changes

- Revise case for change
- Review communication/engagement plan for each stakeholder group
- Plan pilot
- Do gap analyses
- Plan rollout projects
- Create governance for implementation
- Allocate resources

Don't be put off doing operating model work or assume that it is so much work that it has to be done by a consultant. You do not have to go through all of these steps to do useful work. High-level design options can be created in 6 hours or 6 days or 6 weeks. Designs that are detailed enough to get commitment may take weeks. If it takes 6 months, you are doing detailed operating model work – not high-level work.

BUT DESIGN WORK IS A JOURNEY ...

WHO SHOULD BE IN THE DESIGN TEAM?

People who are open, creative and good in workshops. A mix of experiences and perspectives: customer, operations, environment, finance, HR. No more than can get round a table to discuss

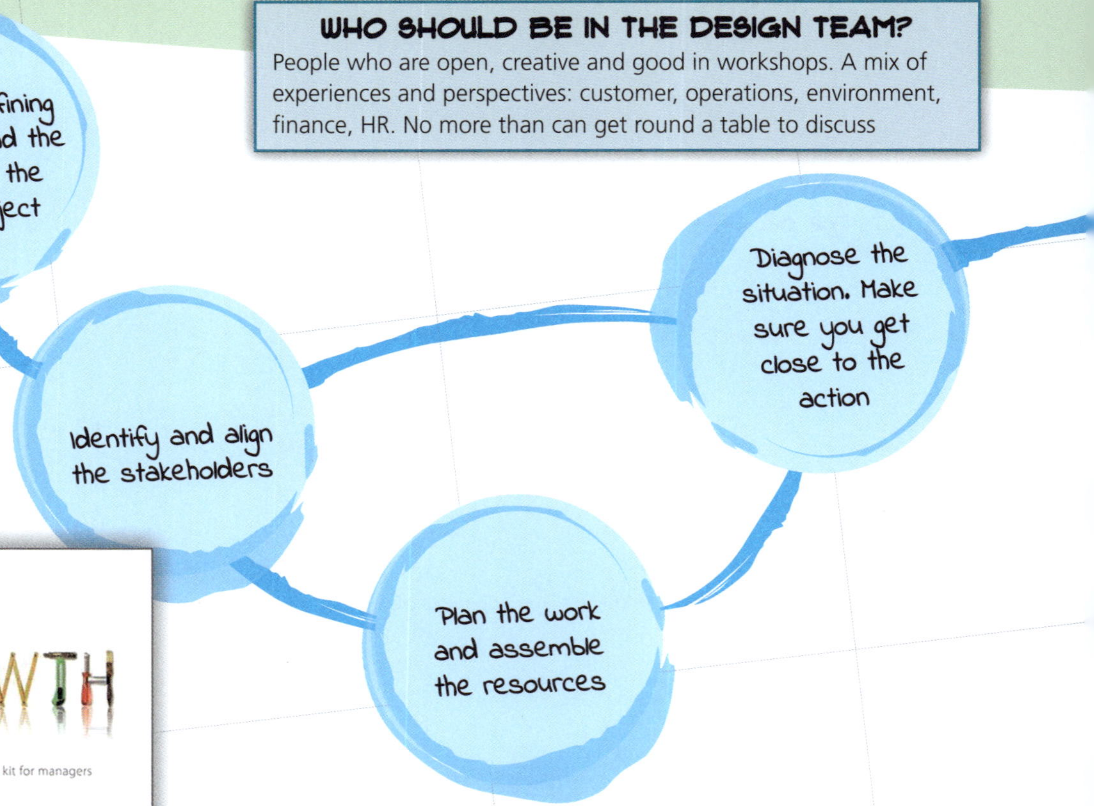

For more on the design journey

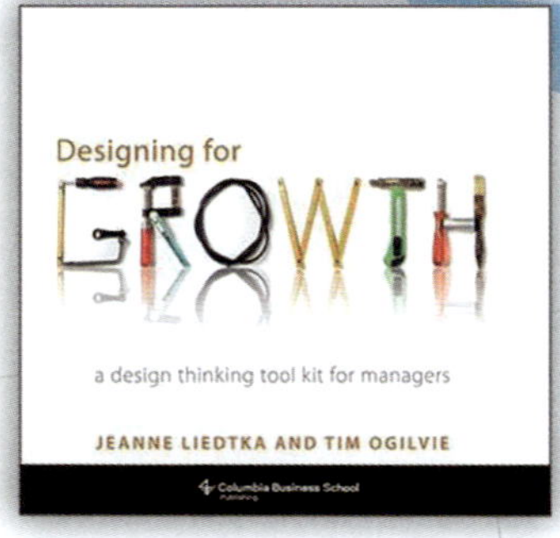

For help with design thinking

... RATHER THAN A SET SERIES OF STEPS

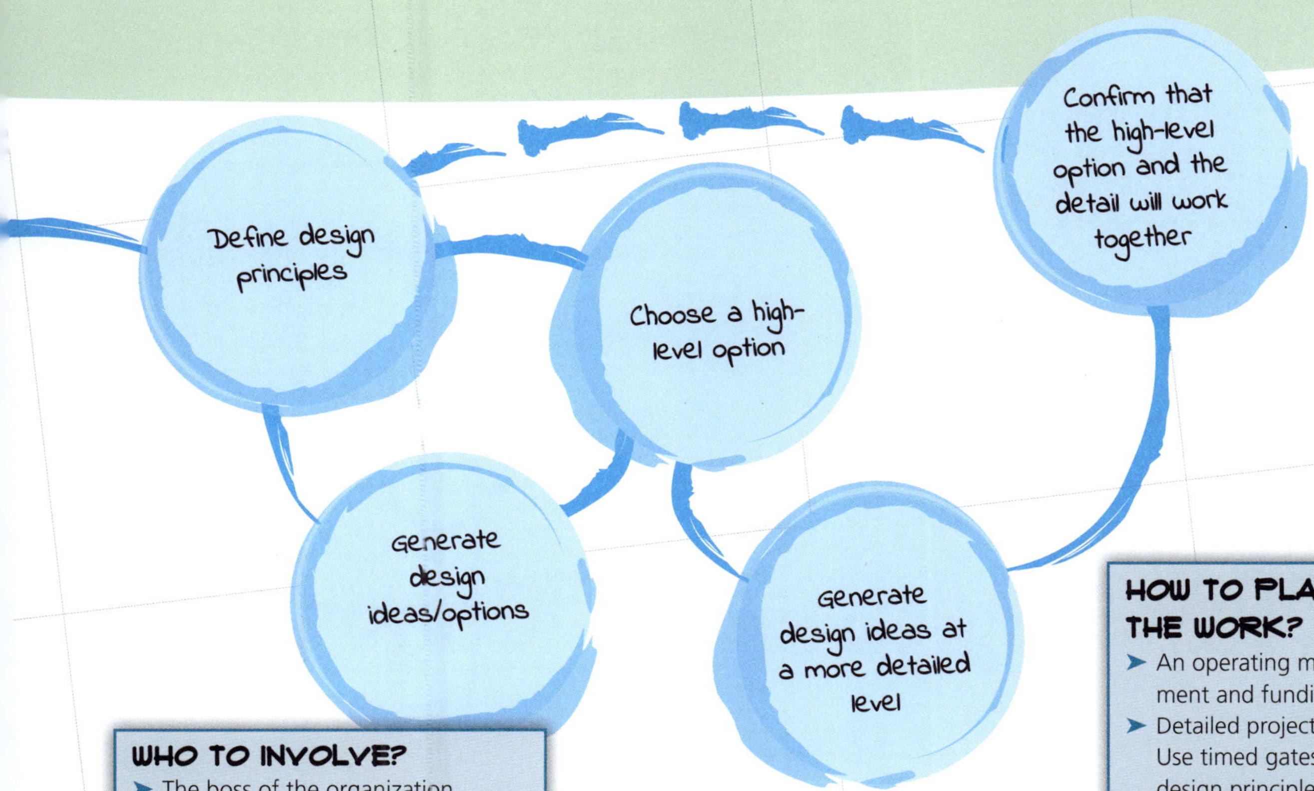

WHO TO INVOLVE?

- The boss of the organization.
- Stakeholders, especially customers.
- Those who will make it happen
- High flyers and influencers who will give energy to the changes

HOW TO PLAN AND CONTROL THE WORK?

- An operating model, sufficient to get commitment and funding, takes weeks not days.
- Detailed project management is unproductive. Use timed gates for steps like diagnostic, design principles, options.
- Stakeholder availability often sets the drumbeat because stakeholder working sessions need to be hours not minutes.
- The process should be intense.

DESIGN IS A MESSY PROCESS UNTIL ...

... A PREFERRED OPTION EMERGES

Design work is not just an intellectual problem solving activity. It is a critical part of the change process. It drives new and better ways of operating. It must build, with stakeholders, a compelling case for change that creates understanding, acceptance, adoption and ultimately commitment to new ways of working.

Early on in a design project, the focus is on clarifying the problem, the scope and the design principles. Often it feels like work is being done without any progress being made towards a solution. But, messiness is good. It ensures that we look at the problem from different angles.

Clarity arrives slowly as the problem becomes clear and ideas start to emerge that might form part of the solution. Messiness helps to get unusual ideas onto the table.

At some point a preferred option becomes clear. Now the design work can go forward with confidence.

There is still a lot of work to do on the design details and on change plans. But now every bit of work is improving the design and moving you closer to being able to start implementing.

13 POSSIBLE WORK STEPS FOR ..

Generating design ideas/options is not a paint-by-numbers process. Each project will be unique. Sometimes the focus will be organization; sometimes location; sometimes processes and decision rights. So do not treat the following 13 steps as gospel. They are provided as an aid not a straightjacket.

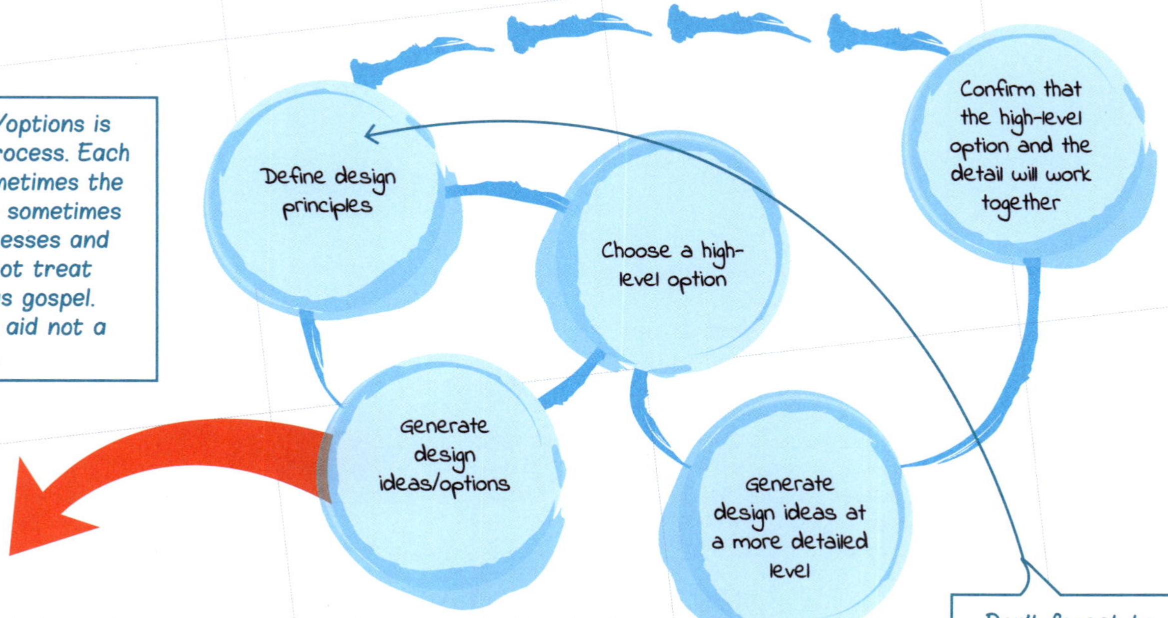

Don't forget to make sure you have some design principles before you start designing *(see page 140)*

1. **DRAW** a value delivery chain for each "segment" (a group of customers looking for the same value proposition) and highlight where there are problems and what are or could be sources of advantage/excellence
2. **CONSIDER** what "activities" will be combined or linked across value chains and which will be kept separate or outsourced
3. **CONVERT** the resulting value chain map into an organization model
4. **ADD** support functions (HR, IT, etc) to the model and highlight "challenges" (issues, constraints, difficult links and sources of advantage). Use the challenges to give focus to the rest of the design work.

... GENERATING A DESIGN OPTION

Think of yourself as a carpenter with a bag of tools. Each job you do is different requiring you to use different tools and in a different order. Chapter 3 describes the tools.

CH1

5. **DEVELOP** a decision grid for the big decisions
6. **DEVELOP** people models for important skill groups
7. **THINK** about where people and important assets will be located
8. **IDENTIFY** owners of key cross organization or cross location processes
9. **DEVELOP** a high-level IT blueprint: what core applications and who owns them
10. **IDENTIFY** those suppliers that need a collaborative relationship with the organization
11. **REVIEW** the “challenges” and “design principles” to make sure all have been addressed
12. **DEFINE** a scorecard including projects and KPIs
13. **DESIGN** the management calendar of planning and performance review meetings

Don't worry if some of these steps are not clear. They will become clear as you work through the book.

DESIGN

USE A GUIDING FRAMEWORK

The Operating Model Canvas is a good one!

MAKE SURE YOU HAVE A SPONSOR

Design needs clear leadership to set direction, deal with politics and make decisions.

BE CLEAR ON THE LEVEL OF DETAIL

Avoid committing to too much detail. Good design is often about confronting a few critical high-level issues.

DECIDE HOW DESIGN DECISIONS WILL BE MADE

By whom, where, and when? Are options required, and what criteria will be used?

BE CLEAR ON THE CASE FOR CHANGE

Link to changes in strategy or problems that can't be solved through continuous improvement.

TIPS

GET THE RIGHT TEAM

Look for insight, experience, influence, open minds, comfort with ambiguity, analytical smarts and people who simplify.

MANAGE TO GATES NOT PLANS

Design work cannot be planned. But it can be late. So manage with timed gates.

NO RIGHT ANSWER

Don't search for perfection. Look for a practical solution that will work.

DON'T OPEN THE MELON UNLESS YOU ARE READY TO EAT IT

If you say you are thinking of changing the organization, everyone stops working and starts worrying about their positions.

DON'T HAVE THE DECISION MAKER AT THE MEETINGS

If the decision maker is at the meeting, it will reduce openness and creativity.

Note: Mark does not agree with this tip!

EMBRACE OPTIONS

Options are healthy. Look for extremes. Get opinions from a wide range. Don't limit your thinking.

CHAPTER 2

CH2

Operating Model Canvas

- Examples

What is the ...

CH2

The Operating Model Canvas is a framework that describes the main elements of the operations of an organization. It describes how an organization creates and delivers value.

The Operating Model Canvas provides a high-level blueprint that can be used to guide lower-level design decisions.

The Operating Model Canvas is a tool that can be used in discussions between managers and in structured workshops. It helps expose issues for debate and ensures the debate considers the whole organization. It helps designers see the whole before they design the details.

PROCESSES

Processes describe the main work that the organization needs to do to deliver value to its customers or beneficiaries. Frequently there are multiple 'process chains', which we will call 'value delivery chains' because we want to keep things at a high level. We need a value chain for each different group of customers for whom we have a different value proposition. Processes are at the center of the framework to ensure attention is given to the main work steps needed to create and deliver value.

ORGANIZATION

How the value chains are converted into an organization structure (as a single value chain, as units each with its own value chain, or as a matrix). How the support activities, such as finance and HR are added to the structure. The important 'skill groups' and the people model for each skill group. The important decisions needed in the running of the organization and how they are made. The important linking processes and who owns each.

INFORMATION

The important applications and information that are needed to support the work, and who owns each.

LOCATIONS

Where the work is located and what assets are needed at these locations to support the work.

SUPPLIERS

The suppliers that need to be collaborative partners, and the nature of the collaboration.

MANAGEMENT SYSTEM

The processes that managers use to plan, set targets, make decisions and measure performance.

... Operating Model Canvas?

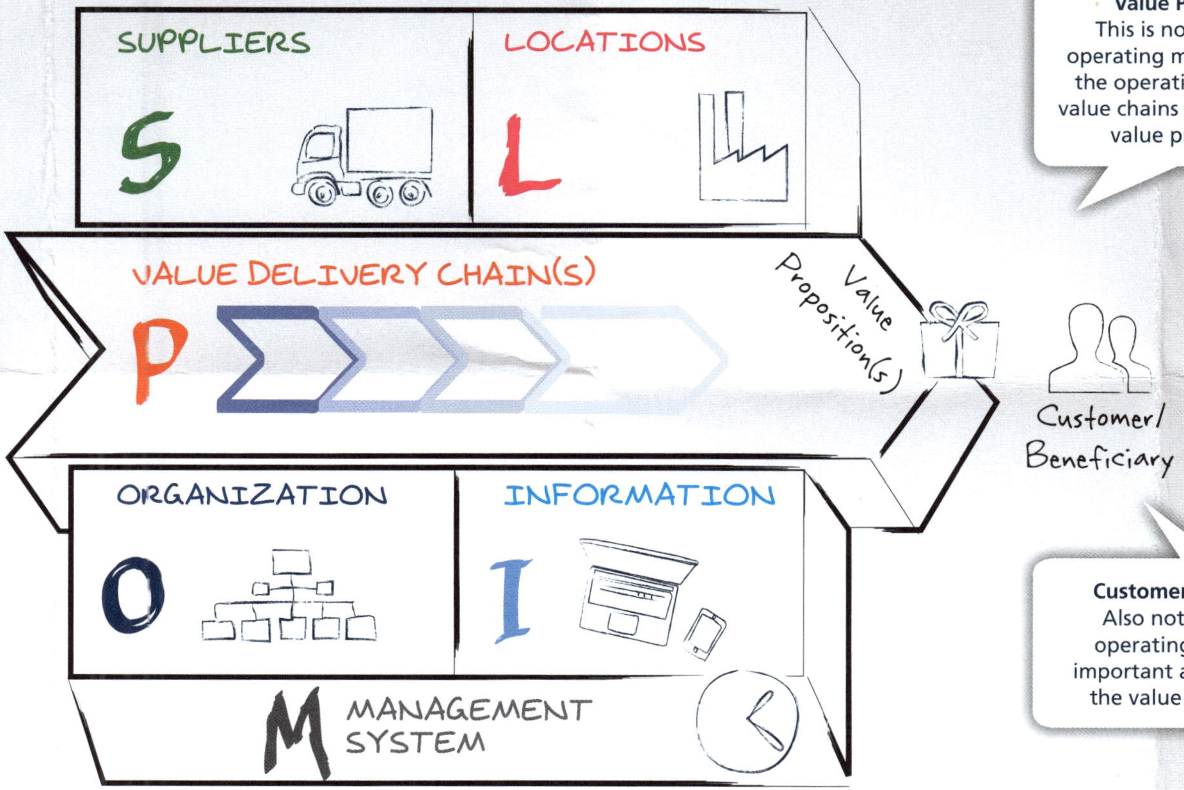

Value Proposition
This is not part of the operating model but drives the operating model. The value chains must deliver the value propositions

Customer/Beneficiary
Also not part of the operating model, but important as recipients of the value propositions

CH2

POLISM

THE SIX ELEMENTS OF THE CANVAS CAN BE REMEMBERED USING THE ACRONYM POLISM – PROCESSES, ORGANIZATION, LOCATIONS, INFORMATION, SUPPLIERS AND MANAGEMENT SYSTEM.

PROCESSES

How the organization creates and delivers the value proposition to the customers or beneficiaries. Often an organization is serving multiple customer segments, each with slightly different value propositions. A 'value chain map' lays out the different chains of steps needed to deliver the different value propositions. A good value chain map is at the heart of a good operating model.

ORGANIZATION

How the value chain map is structured (as a single value chain, as units or as a matrix). How the support activities, such as finance and HR are added to the structure. The important 'skill groups' and the people model for each. The important decisions needed and the role of each senior position in these decisions. The important processes that cross multiple parts of the organization and who owns each.

LOCATIONS

Where the work is located and what assets (buildings, machinery, intellectual property, etc) are needed at these locations to support the work. Locations can include which city or country to operate in, on which floor of a building to locate different departments, how to lay out a factory or where to position different categories of stock in a warehouse.

The management system is often considered to be additional to the core elements of the Operating Model Canvas because it underpins the core elements and addresses the management of the transformation part as well as the 'doing-the-business' part.

INFORMATION

What information and IT applications are needed to support each process, which applications need to be part of an integrated enterprise system, which applications need to be bespoke rather than standard modules, and who are the "business owners" of the data and of each application (i.e. who decides what data is captured and what jobs the application should do).

SUPPLIERS

Which suppliers to set up as collaborative partners, and the nature of the collaboration with each.

MANAGEMENT SYSTEM

What calendar of processes and meetings managers use to plan, set targets, make decisions, drive improvement and manage performance. Also what scorecard is used to measure progress.

PROCESSES

Level 1 (one page)	Operating Model Canvas
Level 2 (ten pages)	High-level value chain map
Level 3 (100 pages)	More detailed value chain maps
Level 4 (1000 pages)	Detailed process maps for all processes

Levels 1 and 2 are high-level operating model work. Levels 3 and 4 are detailed operating model work.

The Operating Model Canvas can be used at Levels 3 and 4, when designing high-level operating models for functions or departments.

There are many levels of detail ... when doing design work

CH2

ORGANIZATION STRUCTURE	LOCATIONS	INFORMATION	SUPPLIERS	MANAGEMENT SYSTEM
Operating Model Canvas	Operating Model Canvas	Operating Model Canvas	Operating Model Canvas	Operating Model Canvas
High-level organization model	High-level locations footprint	High-level IT blueprint: applications and owners	High-level supplier matrix	High-level management calendar/scorecard
Org. models for lower levels, decision grids, people models	More-detailed locations footprint	IT architecture	More-detailed supplier matrix	High-level attendees, agendas, KPIs
Job descriptions for all positions, detailed decision grids, etc.	Square meters of space, site plans, floor layouts, etc.	IT security policies, service levels, staffing rotas, etc.	Chosen suppliers, supplier agreements, etc.	Detailed agendas, reporting forms, etc.

CH2

How to use ...

The Canvas is a template you can draw on a page, a flip chart or a white board

The symbols are used to help us remember where to position different thoughts

... the Operating Model Canvas

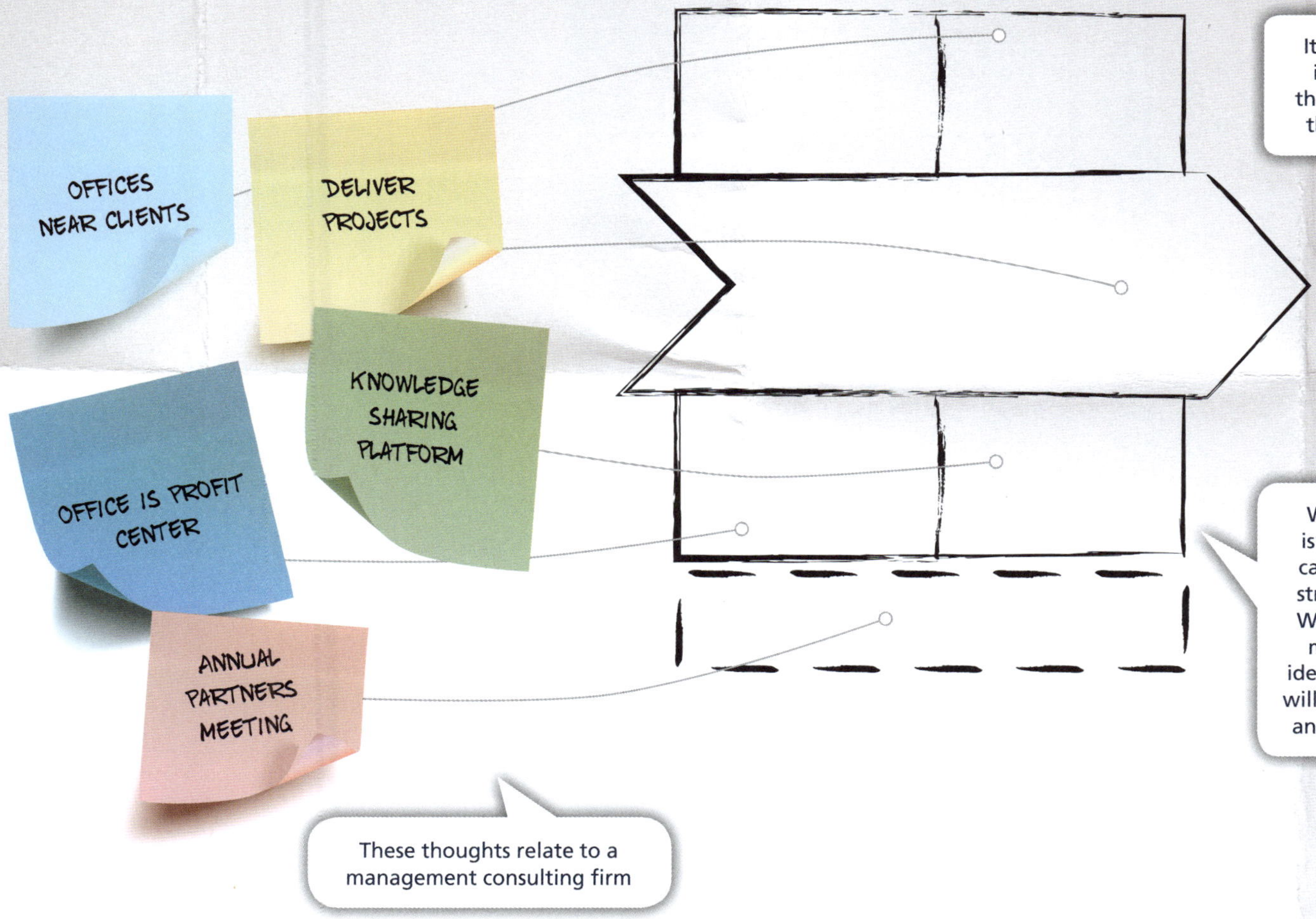

It is best to use post-it-notes to capture thoughts and position them on the Canvas

When describing an 'as is' operating model, you can capture current facts straight onto the Canvas. When designing a 'to be' model you can capture ideas, recognizing that you will need to check them out and probably revise them.

These thoughts relate to a management consulting firm

The Operating Model Canvas is ...

CH2

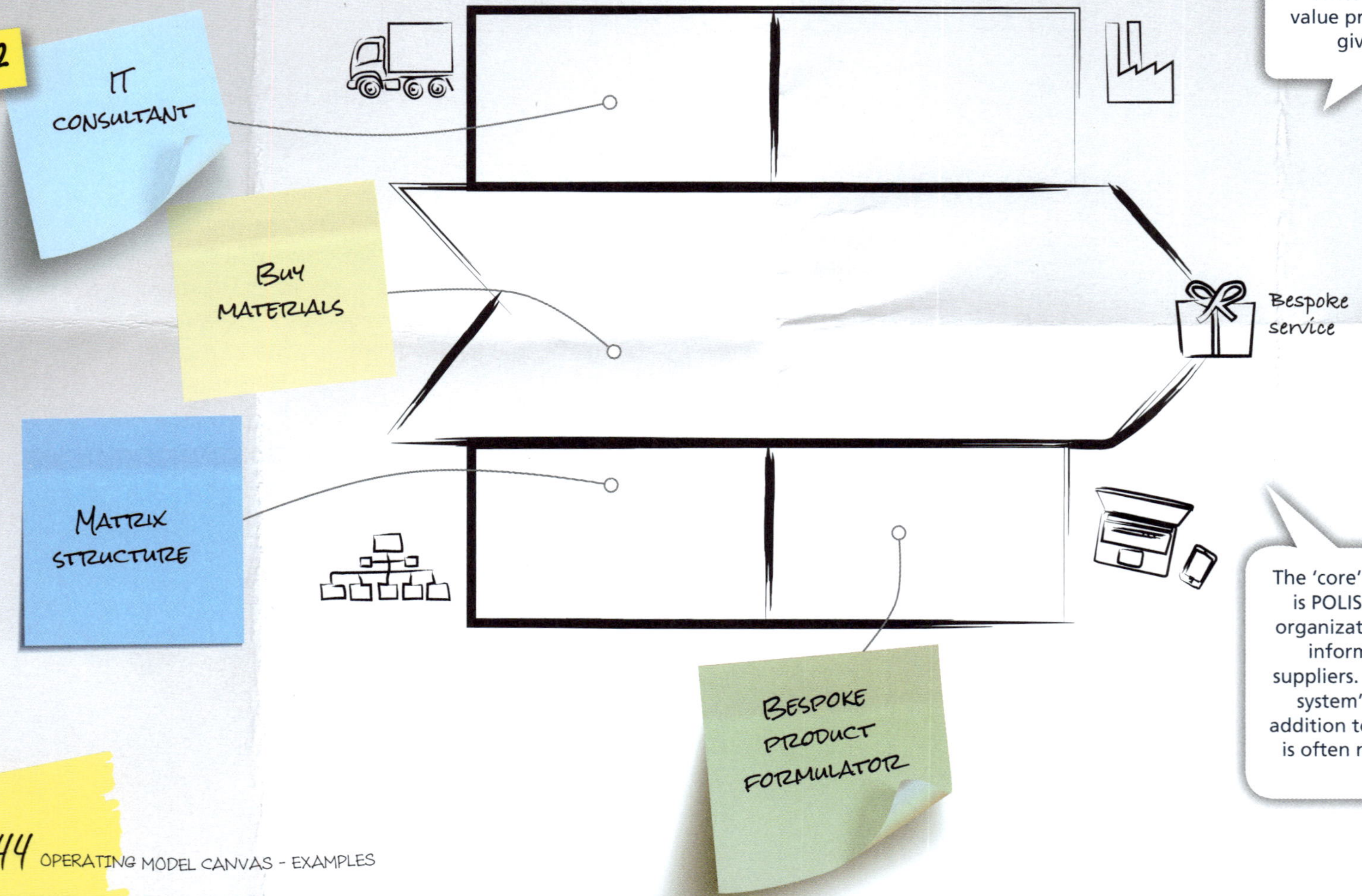

Write down the value proposition to give focus

The 'core' of the canvas is POLIS – processes, organization, locations, information and suppliers. 'Management system' is a helpful addition to this core, but is often not displayed.

.. focused on the value proposition

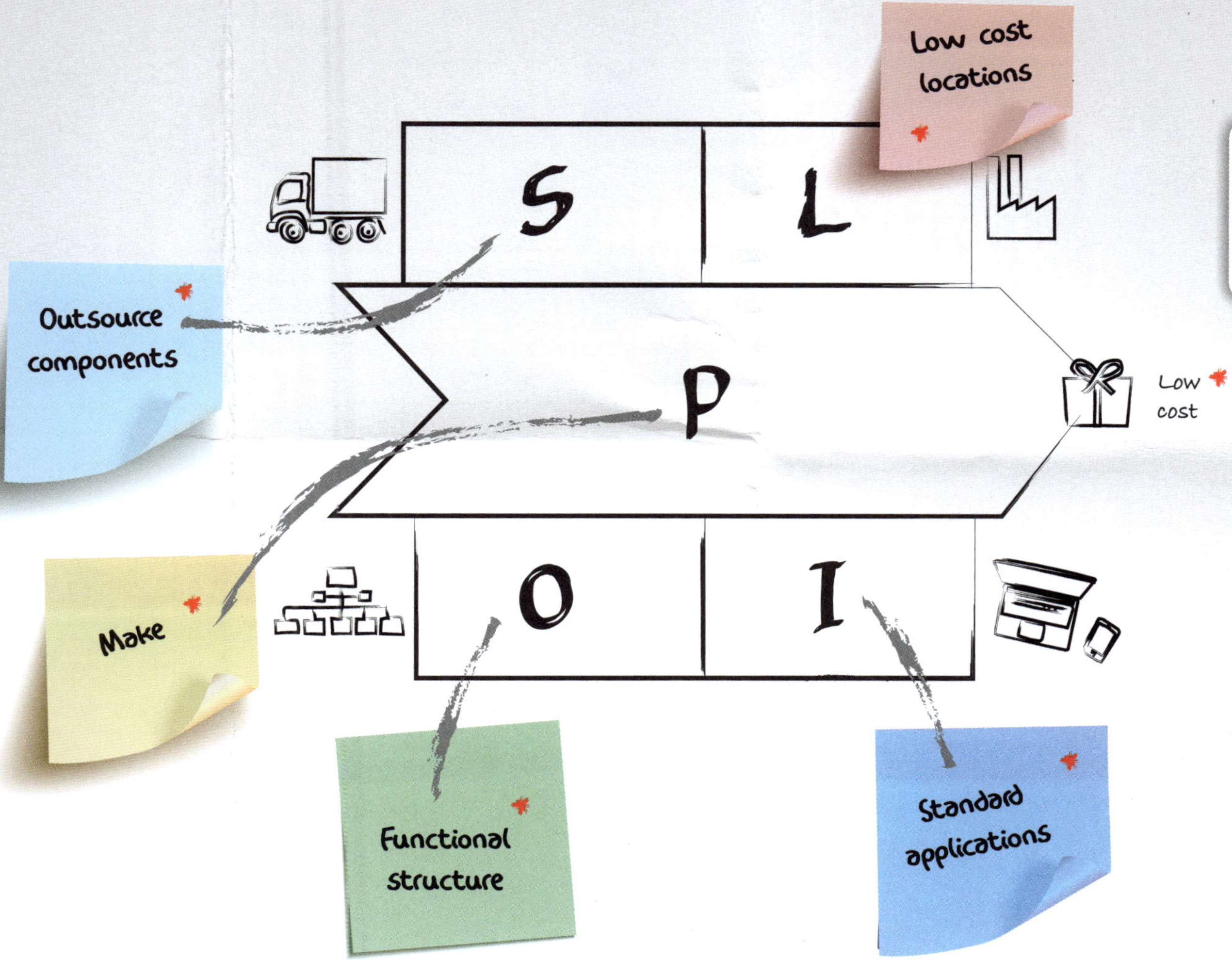

Choose what to put on the Canvas based on what is important to deliver the value proposition.

CH2

* Links the value proposition - 'low cost' - to the elements of the operating model that make low cost possible.

CH2

Before you fill out a Canvas ...

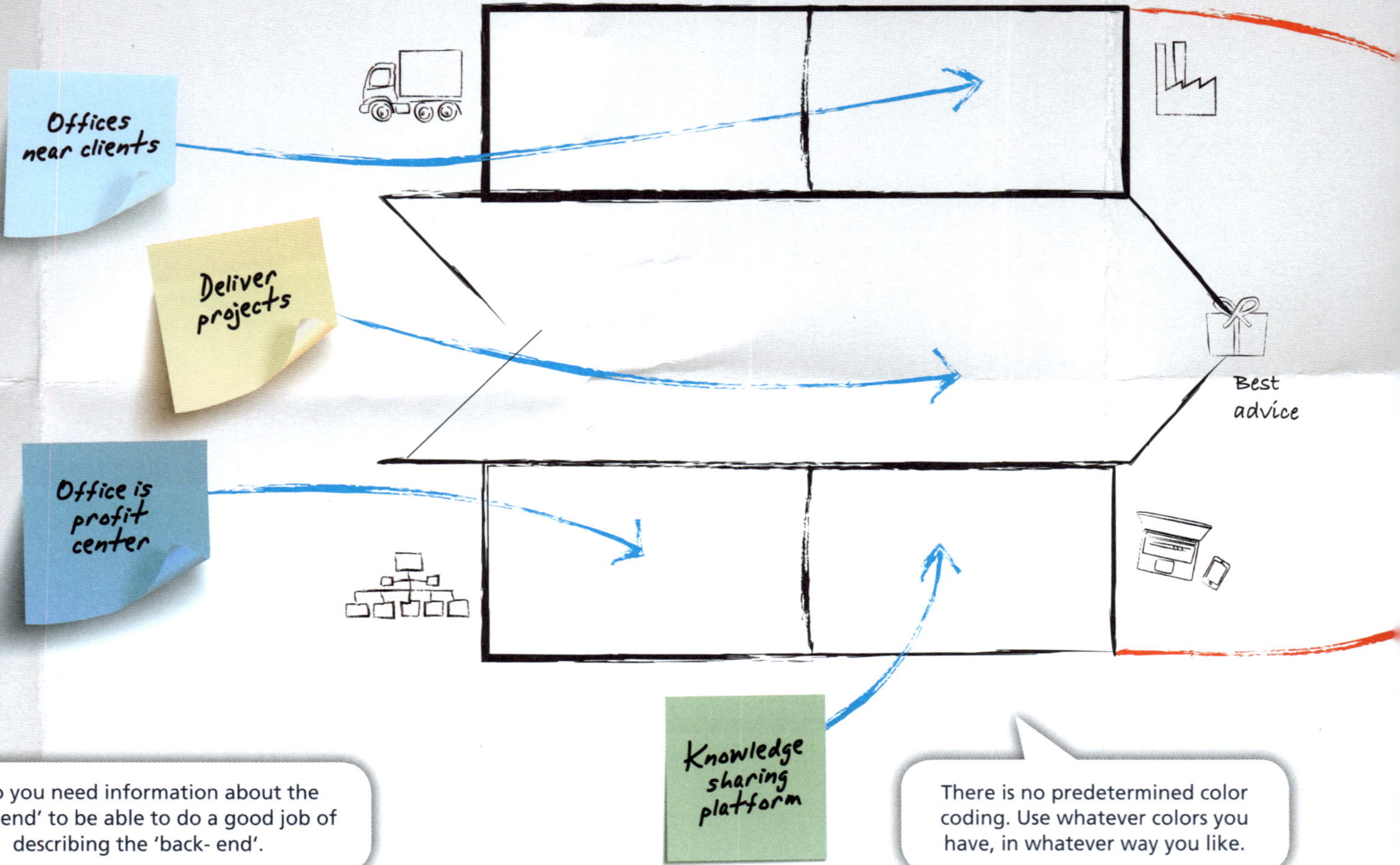

Remember that the Operating Model Canvas is the back-end of the Business Model Canvas, whether you are describing the 'as is' or starting to imagine a 'to be' ...

... so you need information about the 'front end' to be able to do a good job of describing the 'back- end'.

There is no predetermined color coding. Use whatever colors you have, in whatever way you like.

... you need to understand the front-end

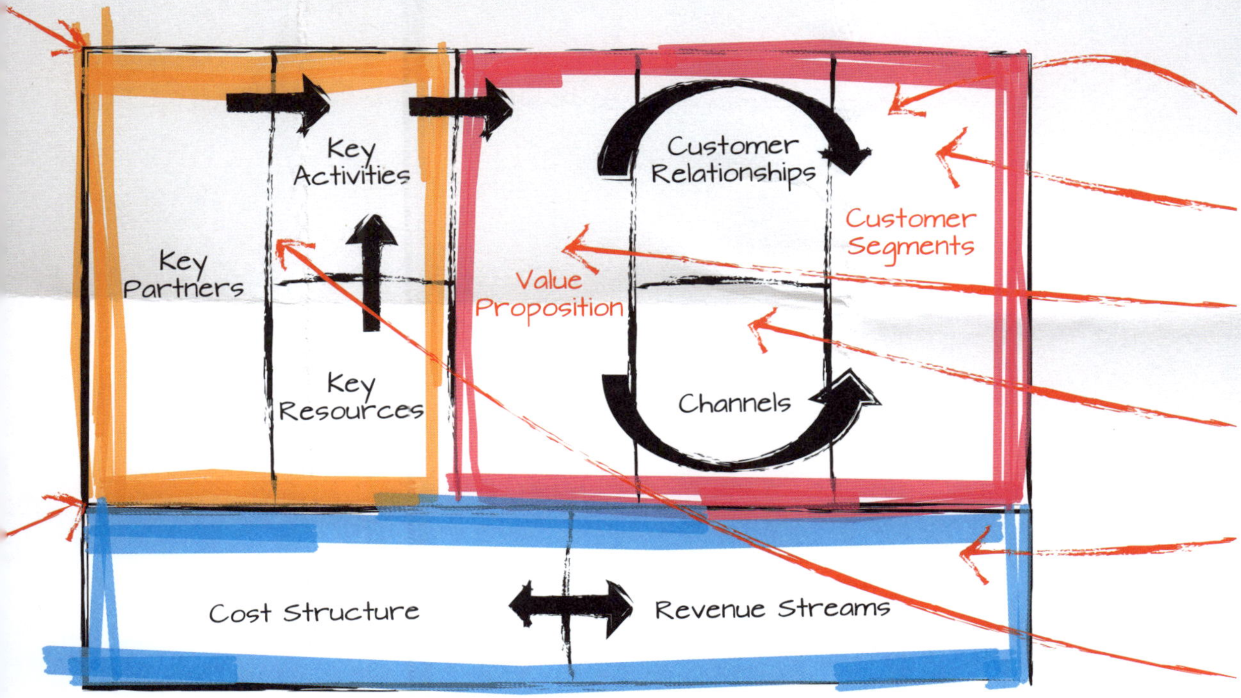

What you need to know about strategy to create a good Operating Model Canvas?

CH2

1. Target customers or beneficiaries and how these are segmented.
2. Geographies where customers are served
3. The value proposition (products and services) to each customer segment and how these propositions differ
4. Channels, such as distributors or direct sales, for communicating and building relationships with customers.
5. Which activities create the major costs and which revenue streams are the most profitable
6. Sources of advantage or excellence: what the organization needs to do really well to deliver the value propositions

CH2

Business examples

The Operating Model Canvas can be used to understand the operations of a whole business, even where the business has multiple product lines and multiple geographies.

The examples included here are descriptions of the "as is" operating model. Different examples show the differences between different businesses.

CH2

You can use an ‘as is’ Canvas as the basis for some penetrating diagnostics

- is the organization “good at” all of the activities important to the value propositions?
- are there difficult links between steps in the value chains?
- does the structure reflect the value chains?
- are there distinct people models for specialist areas?

See pages 132 and 133 for a longer list of diagnostic questions.

The Operating Model Canvas for ..

CH2

UBER

Uber is one of the world's most successful technology companies. The company is the world's largest taxi service without actually employing any taxi drivers. It matches passengers (riders) with drivers through a mobile phone app. However, the operating model involves a lot more than a platform.

Starting in 2010, Uber operates in more than 250 cities and had a market capitalisation in 2016 of over $50 billion.

Uber offers different levels of service. UberBlack is a limousine service, whilst UberX is a low cost service.

PROCESSES

In a chosen city, Uber negotiates with regulators for access; recruits suitable drivers (the drivers are all self-employed); issues drivers with a smartphone and Uber's software; trains drivers in how to use the software; markets the app to riders in the city; matches riders with drivers; enables drivers and riders to rate each other; and processes payments. The drivers take the rider to the rider's required destination. As far as is legally permitted in each jurisdiction, Uber takes no responsibility for the quality of the taxi ride.

SUPPLIERS

Drivers are the main suppliers to Uber, in addition, of course, to technology suppliers. But Uber's success depends on other stakeholders as well. Uber launches with 'influencers' such as attendees at tech conferences who are likely to tweet about the experience. Uber is dependent on social media. Uber also needs good relations with city regulators or good lawyers when regulators resist the service.

ORGANIZATION

Each city is a business unit. All the business units draw on strong central functions – finance, technology, human resources, marketing, legal, etc. The functions provide services and promote best practice sharing across geographies.

LOCATIONS

Uber focuses on big cities where its initial investment will pay back with subsequent traffic.

INFORMATION

The central technology function, the platform that Uber uses and the app software that connects riders and drivers, as well as allowing dynamic pricing, group rides and ratings, are the company's prime sources of advantage.

The 2016 legal ruling in the UK that drivers are employees not contractors may require a change of model in the UK.

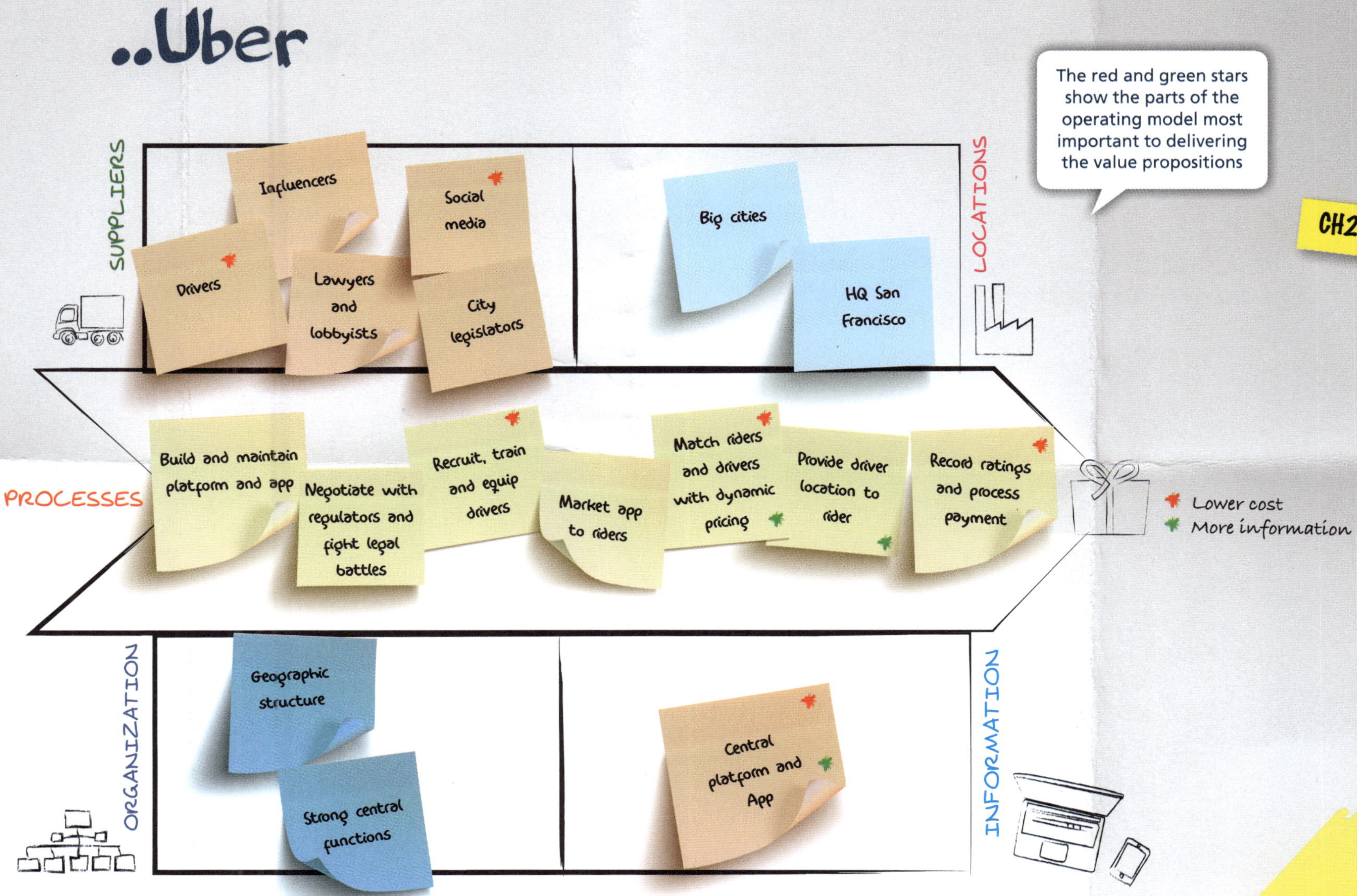
..Uber
The red and green stars show the parts of the operating model most important to delivering the value propositions
SUPPLIERS
Influencers
Social media
Drivers
Lawyers and lobbyists
City legislators
LOCATIONS
Big cities
HQ San Francisco
PROCESSES
Build and maintain platform and app
Negotiate with regulators and fight legal battles
Recruit, train and equip drivers
Market app to riders
Match riders and drivers with dynamic pricing
Provide driver location to rider
Record ratings and process payment
Lower cost
More information
ORGANIZATION
Geographic structure
Strong central functions
INFORMATION
Central platform and App

The Operating Model Canvas for...

ZARA

CH2

Zara, located in Northern Spain, was one of the first providers of 'fast fashion'. Recognizing that fashions change quickly, the company developed a tightly linked design, manufacturing and retailing system based on replenishing stores twice per week from central distribution centers, mostly located in Spain. A garment manufactured in India will most probably travel to Spain before being sent to a store in China.

SUPPLIERS

Zara has many clothing suppliers, but it does many tasks in-house that are typically done by suppliers. It manufactures 50% of its own garments. It develops its own IT software. It sends its own teams to refurbish stores.

PROCESSES

Zara's processes are the subject of many business school case studies. The journey starts when product managers check store data and visit stores to understand better what is selling and what is changing, Then designers create collections – often five or six per year rather than the industry standard of two. These are manufactured (50% in Zara's own factories, some linked to the main distribution center by railway), warehoused and then shipped (often by air) against store orders received twice per week.

LOCATIONS

Zara stores are in the leading shopping centers and streets. Distribution is mostly centralized in Spain. Product managers, who interact with stores, are placed in the middle of the design room to ensure good communications with designers.

ORGANIZATION

The basic structure is functional. But individual stores are profit centers, and each store manager is empowered to choose what to sell. Design teams are also empowered to design what they consider will sell and are measured on the margin they contribute. But many decisions are centralized, such as store locations and store design. The concept is to decentralize the 'fast fashion' decisions to those closest to the market and to centralize every other part of the operating model.

INFORMATION

IT support is a critical ingredient in Zara's success: the previous head of IT became the CEO. Store managers have hand held devices for helping decide what to order. Point-of-sale information transmits directly to the central office. Data on what was sold, what is being manufactured, what is in transit and what is in the distribution center is updated daily, if not hourly.

...Zara

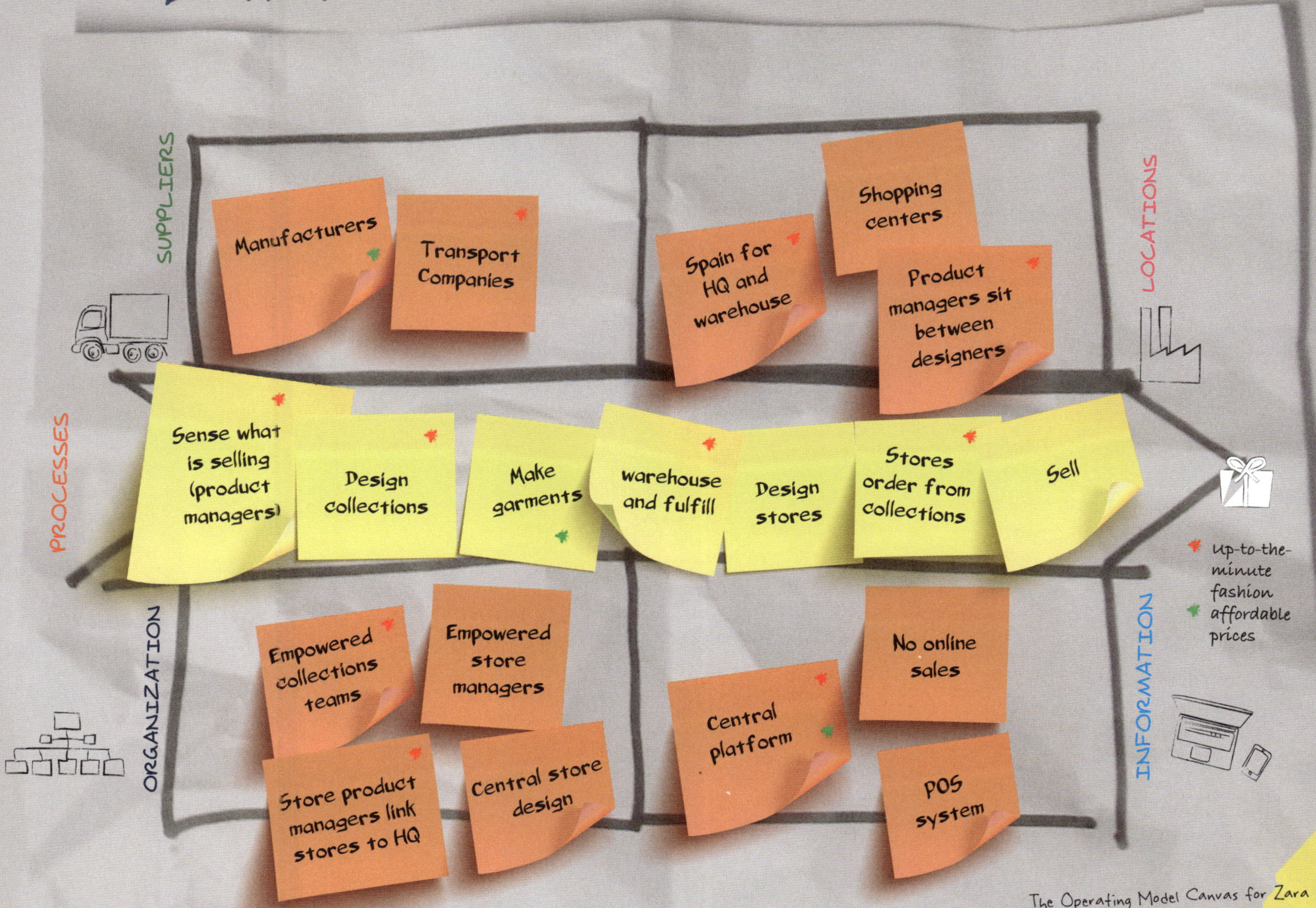
SUPPLIERS
Manufacturers
Transport Companies
LOCATIONS
Spain for HQ and warehouse
Shopping centers
Product managers sit between designers
PROCESSES
Sense what is selling (product managers)
Design collections
Make garments
warehouse and fulfill
Design stores
Stores order from collections
Sell
ORGANIZATION
Empowered collections teams
Empowered store managers
Store product managers link stores to HQ
Central store design
INFORMATION
Central platform
No online sales
POS system
up-to-the-minute fashion
affordable prices

The Operating Model Canvas for...

McKinsey&Company

CH2

McKinsey & Co is a global firm that provides 'top management' advice and consulting support.

McKinsey has offices in more than 60 countries, and, since its founding in the 1950s by Marvin Bower, has maintained its position as the premier management consulting firm. McKinsey & Co has retained its position despite strong challenge from rival 'top management' consultants such as Boston Consulting Group and Bain & Company, as well as much larger firms with capabilities in IT consulting and operations such as Accenture.

PROCESSES

The consulting business is about winning and delivering projects. While each project is a different value chain often involving completely different work steps, from the perspective of the firm as a whole there is one value chain – hire consultants, train and develop the consultants, develop knowledge and tools useful to clients, win projects and deliver projects. One area of differentiation is the way McKinsey builds relationships, making better use of research and alumni relationships.

ORGANIZATION

McKinsey has a matrix structure. Offices are profit centers, but power and decision making is divided between office leaders (e.g. New York), industry sector leaders (e.g. Financial Services), practice leaders (e.g. Organization) and major client directors (e.g. Volkswagen). McKinsey aims to attract the best and brightest from business schools and other sources; seeks to offer the best training; controls its people resources centrally; and runs a policy of promotion or exit ('up or out').

SUPPLIERS

McKinsey rarely uses external suppliers to help the firm deliver projects. However it does have important suppliers of training for its consultants and of IT systems for running the firm.

LOCATIONS

The firm has offices in 63 countries, normally in major cities that are attractive to consultants and close to major companies. Most project work is done on client premises.

INFORMATION

There are important central databases for knowledge management, client information and people. The business is run through an ERP system.

MANAGEMENT SYSTEM

McKinsey measures profit by project, by office and by client. However, quality of work and client satisfaction are more important. Partner election processes are elaborate.

... McKinsey & Co

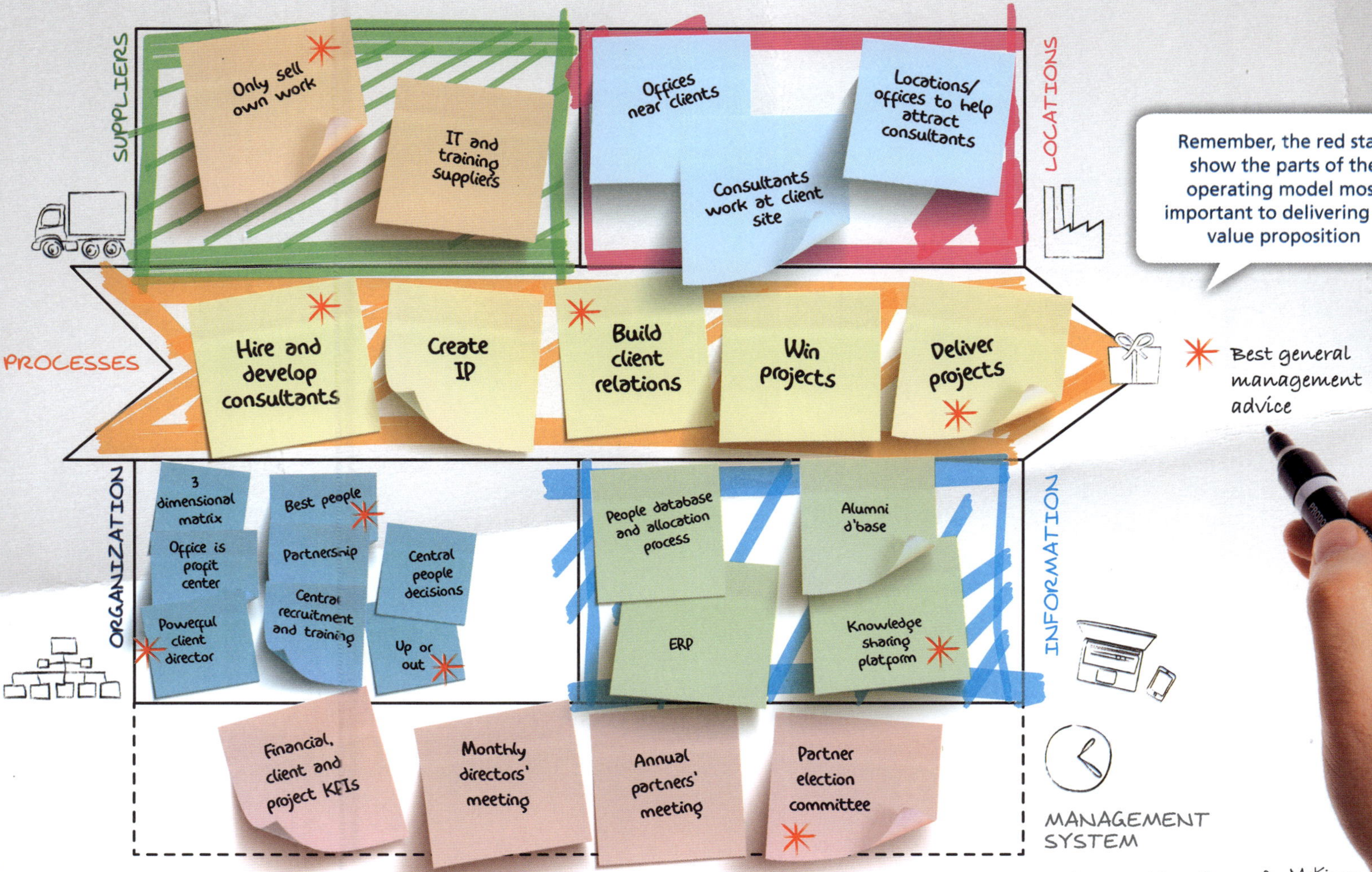

Remember, the red stars show the parts of the operating model most important to delivering the value proposition

The Operating Model Canvas for...

CH2

Van Haren Publishing (VHP) is a specialist publisher of IT and management books based in Zaltbommel, Netherlands, aiming at being "the worlds leading publisher on best practices, methods and standards".

The business publishes practically useful books and other formats at reasonable prices, serving training organizations, higher education and middle managers.

SUPPLIERS

VHP relies on many suppliers: authors, text editors, designers, printers, distributors, online retailers, physical retailers, social media platforms, etc.

PROCESSES

The publication process starts when VHP contracts with an author (team) to publish a book. The author (team) writes the book, mostly with strong guidance. The text is then first reviewed by specialists (peer review) and subsequently edited by a text editor, created in a Desk Top Publishing (DTP) office and printed and bound by a printing house. Derived from this is the eBook, in several formats. At VHP all of these steps are outsourced. The company then prices, markets, sells and distributes the printed and electronic versions, pays its suppliers and collects revenues.

ORGANIZATION

Only seven people work for VHP. Three of these are executives: Ivo van Haren (owner and marketing); Bart Verbrugge (publishing director, also responsible for production); Miriam Blom (owner and finance/HR). The other team members are broadly split between production and marketing.

LOCATIONS

The business is located in Zaltbommel because that is the preferred location of the founders, but also because The Netherlands is one of the places in the world where there is a concentration of people developing tools and standards for the IT industry.

INFORMATION

The main information asset of the business is a database of past and likely future readers (and hence purchasers) of the type of books that VHP publishes. This makes it possible for the business to sell 30% of its books through its own website.

MANAGEMENT SYSTEM

As a small business, Van Haren Publishing is run informally. There is a formal meeting of the whole team once per week, and a formal executive meeting every other week. The performance focus is on sales.

... Van Haren Publishing

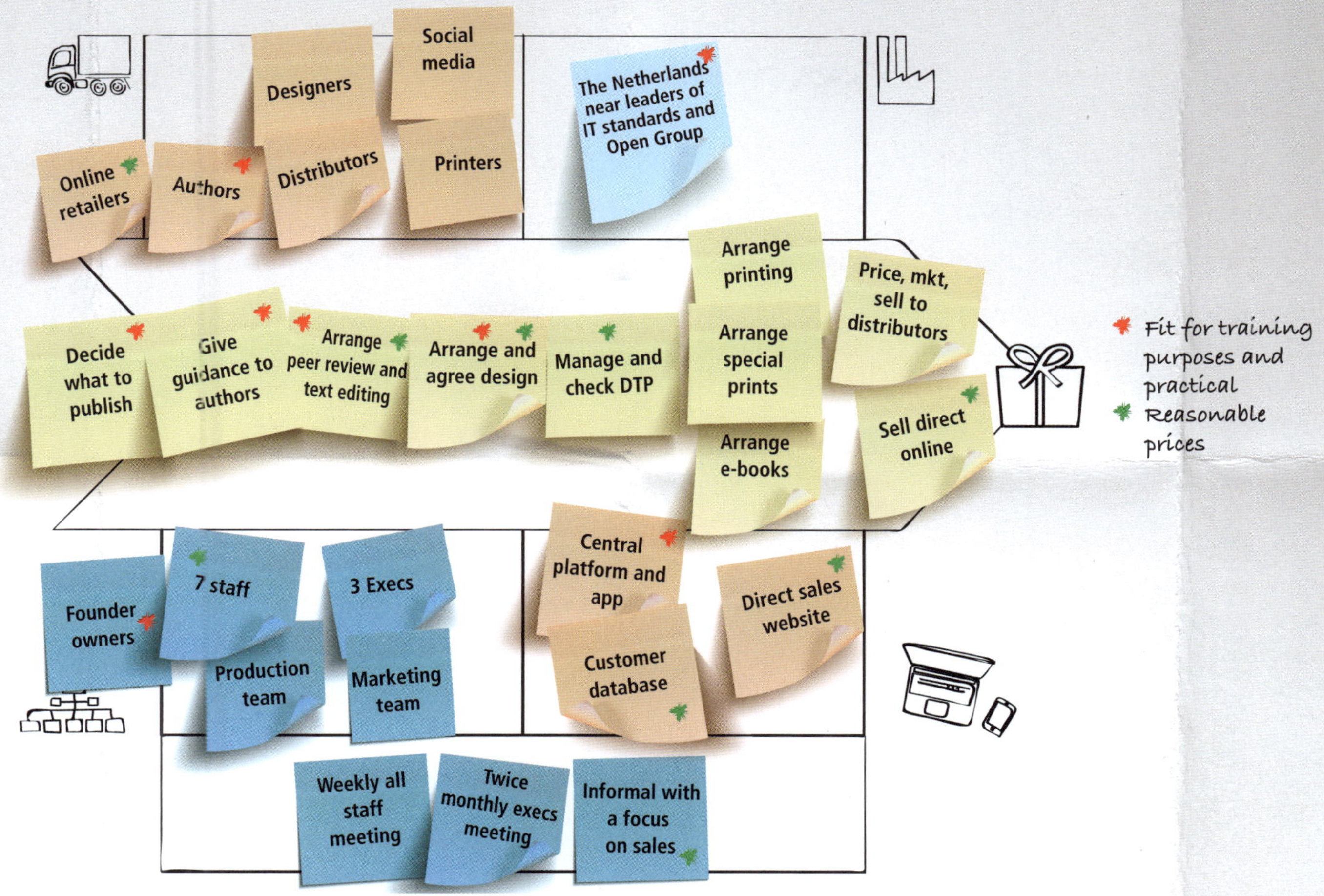

CH2

The Operating Model Canvas for...

CH2

Asset finance involves lending money secured against the asset – for example a forklift truck.

An asset finance company develops relationships with equipment manufacturers (vendors) and provides finance to their customers (lessees). The benefit to the vendor is that more customers can buy their equipment. The benefit to the lessee is that they do not have to pay for the equipment all at once.

Often the lessee thinks he or she is being financed by the vendor because the asset finance company acts as the finance arm of the vendor.

PROCESSES

The process starts with a vendor relationship. The asset finance company then needs to secure finance and tax arrangements to support the vendor. Once the vendor makes a sale that needs financing, the finance company approves the lessee for credit, administers the contract, services the contract and monitors the asset.

SUPPLIERS

The asset finance company needs support from IT suppliers because of the bespoke nature of the IT systems. It also needs good relationships with lawyers and repossession agents. Personal relationships are critical to ensure smooth working.

LOCATIONS

Treasury needs to be located near the sources of finance. Admin needs to be in low cost locations. Sales are located with the vendor. The executive team needs to be in adjacent offices to ensure frequent, balanced dialog.

ORGANIZATION

Organization design is important because of the tensions between sales (let's do the deal), administration (keep it simple) and risk (we must be sure we can get our money back). So the three most powerful people head up these three different functions.
It is important that there is a balance of power between these three functions so that sales grow without taking too much risk and without generating too much administrative complexity.

INFORMATION

The complexity of the product lines requires bespoke IT systems. Secure communications are also important to link decision-makers with local sales people. Data on defaults and portfolio risks are important.

MANAGEMENT SYSTEM

(NOT SHOWN OPPOSITE)

Controls and tight reporting processes are necessary to manage the risks being taken. A formal monthly review helps add formality to a fast moving business.

... an asset finance company

The Operating Model Canvas for an asset finance company

The Operating Model Canvas for

CH2

SnapFish is a global photo-personalisation and fulfilment business for creating personalised photo products such as prints, photo-books, cards and home décor items.

The company is based in California to be near to digital and technology innovators and sector leaders. Originally founded in the Bay Area of San Francisco, the company operates in EMEA, the US and Australasia.

Its value proposition is high quality personalisation and good value for money. The platform allows more options than competitors.

PROCESSES

There are two value chains, one for B2C customers and one for B2B customers. For B2C customers the chain starts with new ideas, which come from the Consumer team based on market insights. These are designed and released on the technology platform. Then the products are marketed, sold and fulfilled in each region. The B2B value chain involves understanding the business partner requirements, contracting, on-boarding and then fulfilling in the region.

INFORMATION

The core of the business is the in-house, designed & maintained technology platform

LOCATIONS

Headquarters is in California. Regional offices are in the EU and Australia.

ORGANIZATION

The three regions are set up as business units with a profit and loss accountability for B2C customers and B2B fulfillment. However, much of the work is centralized into a technology function, a global marketing function, and an operations function that looks after fulfillment and customer service. Partner Solutions manages B2B relationships in each region. The company is a region/function matrix.

SUPPLIERS

SnapFish is dependent on specialist technology suppliers as required by the platform. It is owned by its other major supplier, the printing company which provides the physical products e.g. photoprints, home-décor items, etc.

MANAGEMENT PROCESSES

The Executive Committee meets face to face each month and more frequently by conference call. The scorecard focuses on four aspects of performance – people, process, customer and financials.

... SnapFish

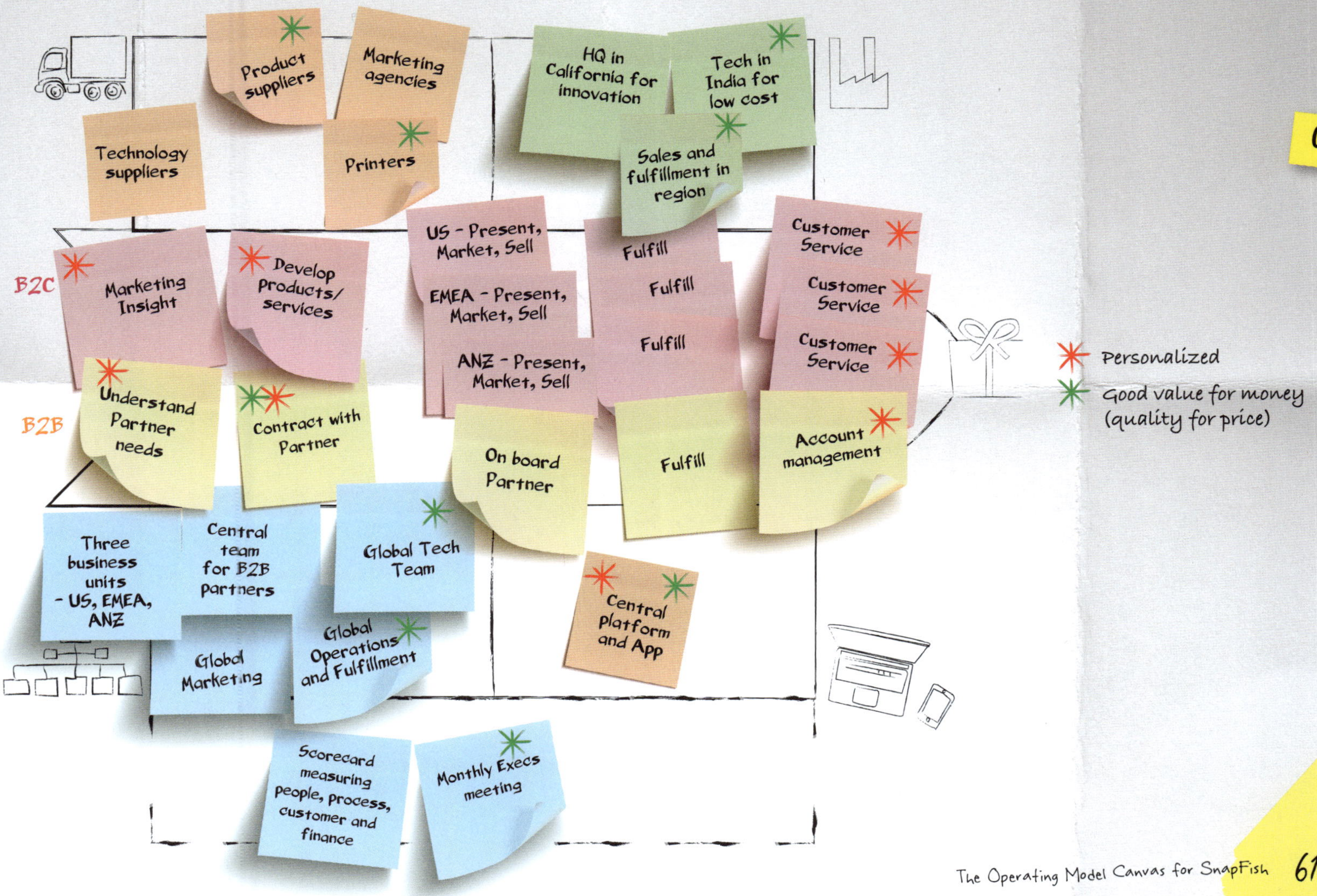
Product suppliers
Marketing agencies
Technology suppliers
Printers
HQ in California for innovation
Tech in India for low cost
Sales and fulfillment in region
B2C
Marketing Insight
Develop products/ services
US - Present, Market, Sell
EMEA - Present, Market, Sell
ANZ - Present, Market, Sell
Fulfill
Fulfill
Fulfill
Customer Service
Customer Service
Customer Service
B2B
Understand Partner needs
Contract with Partner
On board Partner
Fulfill
Account management
Three business units - US, EMEA, ANZ
Central team for B2B partners
Global Tech Team
Global Marketing
Global Operations and Fulfillment
Central platform and App
Scorecard measuring people, process, customer and finance
Monthly Execs meeting
Personalized
Good value for money (quality for price)

CH2

IT Solutions (flip chart example)

You do not have to use post-it-notes

Consulting company (flip chart example)

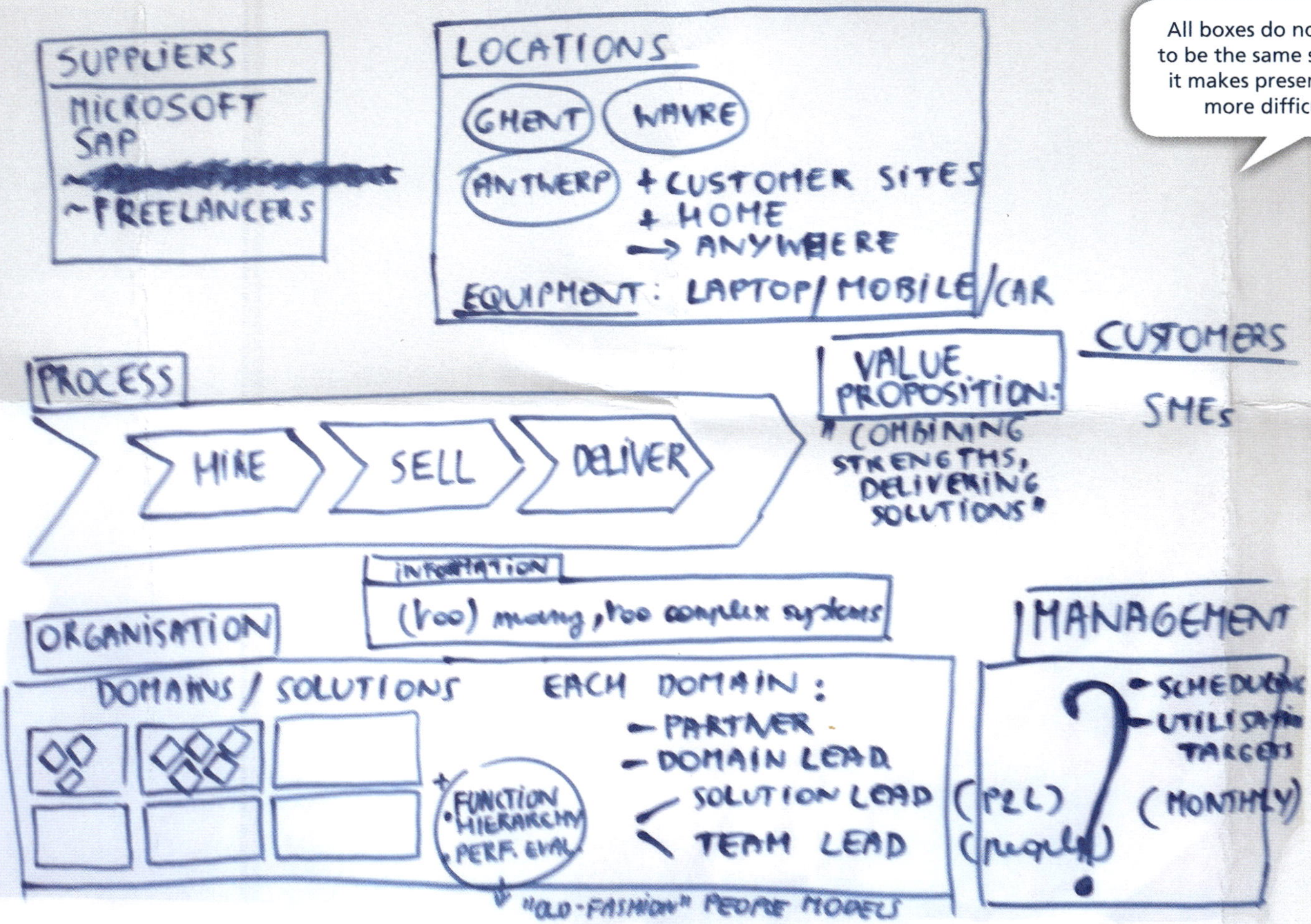

All boxes do not need to be the same size. But it makes presentation more difficult.

CH2

CH2

Functional examples

The Operating Model Canvas can be used to understand the operations of a function within a business.

The examples included are descriptions of the current situation. The collection shows the differences between different functions.

The Operating Model Canvas for...

CH2

Sunshine Financial Services (disguised) is a financial services group operating in a number of countries in Central America. The company has businesses in consumer finance, banking and insurance.

The IT function is centrally managed but with local IT units in each business. The objective is to provide a local service yet get the benefits of group-wide solutions and lower costs.

PROCESSES

The IT function is responsible for all of the IT activities in the Group. The function works closely with the businesses and with other group-level functions to assess their current needs and longer-term strategy. It then develops architectures and solutions that work for the business and for central policies. Once the solutions are agreed, the IT function builds or procures the applications and infrastructure needed. It then runs and maintains the applications and equipment. It also provides user support and assesses performance.

SUPPLIERS

Sunshine has collaborative relationships with suppliers of managed infrastructure, and with software suppliers who are specialists in this sector.

LOCATIONS

Group IT, the leaders of the IT function and IT shared services are located at the headquarters. Most of the rest of the IT staff are located with their businesses.

ORGANIZATION MODEL

The IT function is structured into six delivery units – one for each business division and one for headquarters. These delivery units provide all the IT services needed by their division within constraints and policies - IT strategy, architecture, governance, security and compliance – set from the center.

INFORMATION

The function has typical IT4IT applications, such as applications for user access management, help desk management, and requirements management.

MANAGEMENT SYSTEM

An important part of the management system are The Design Authority and IT Council are important parts of the management system. These bodies help ensure that different parts of the Group use group-wide solutions when appropriate.

...the IT function of a financial services group

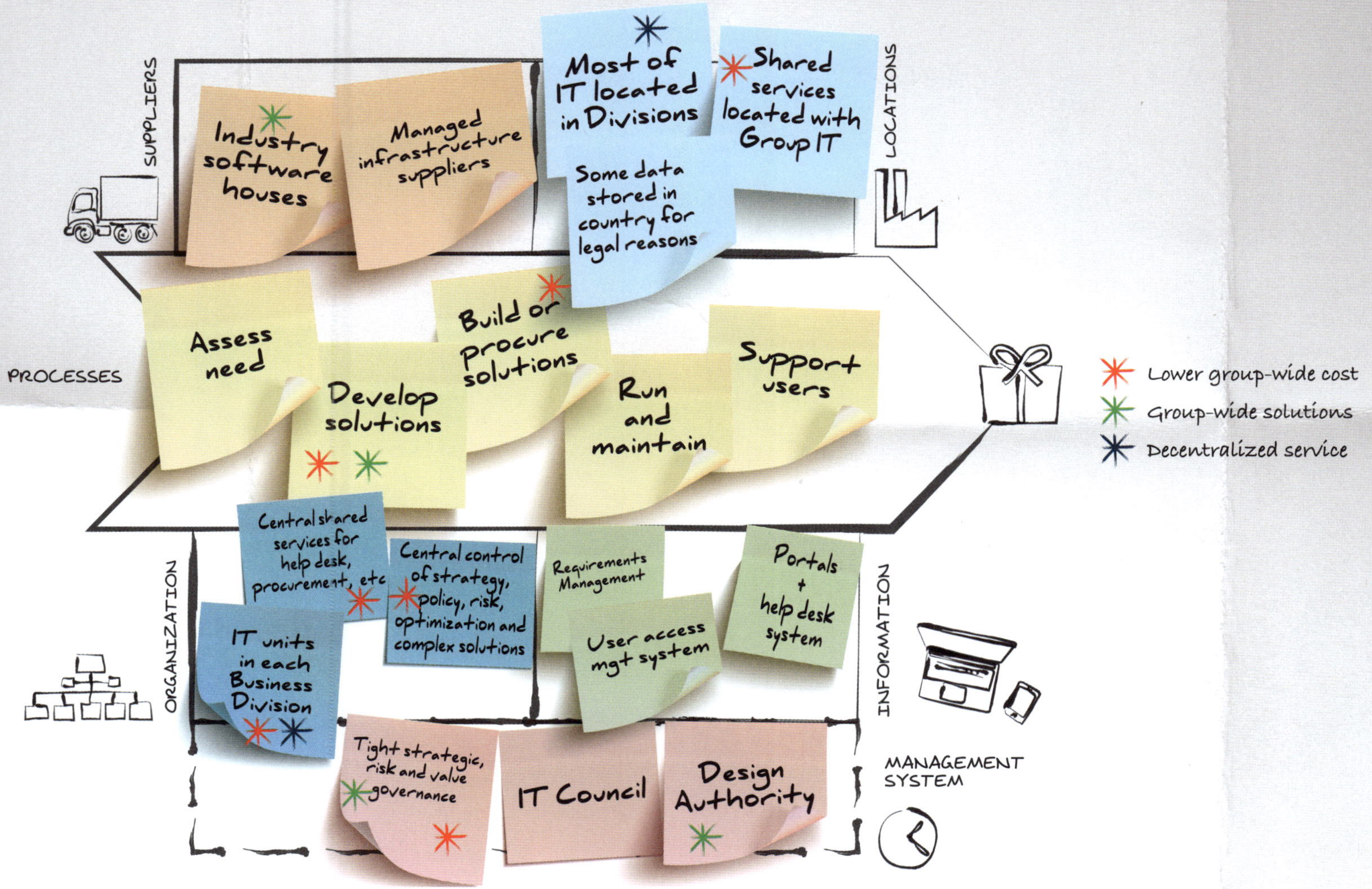

The Operating Model Canvas for the IT function of a financial services group

The Operating Model Canvas for...

CH2

The company is an online retailer of fashion items, with three different online brands. Each brand is run as a separate division with limited sharing. There is some sharing of office space and of logistics and warehousing. But, websites, marketing, photography, packaging and customer service are all run separately for each brand.

The objective is to have an integrated global HR function. Hence, all of the HR personnel in the company report to Group HR, so that HR managers working in the business divisions or in corporate functions are 'business partners'.

PROCESSES

The HR function provides four services to the organization, in addition to business partners: compensation and benefits, talent acquisition and development, organization development, and HR consulting on bigger projects that cannot be handled by the business partners. Supporting these four services and the business partners is an HR analytics group providing statistics.

SUPPLIERS

Recruitment is mainly done by external suppliers. The HR consulting unit often hires in additional support from external consultants. The IT function is an important supplier of systems.

LOCATIONS

The company operates out of four countries. Hence there are HR Business Partners and local suppliers in each country.

ORGANIZATION

The four service heads and the head of HR analytics report to the Group HR Director. Business partners operate in a matrix, reporting both to a lead business partner for the country and a lead business partner for a business division or corporate services. HR business partners act as integrators of the HR services: each service is expected to work through the relevant business partner rather than directly with a business division. Most significant decisions are taken with the Group HR Director.

INFORMATION

The function has good HR systems both for understanding what is happening in the organization and for measuring the performance of HR.

MANAGEMENT SYSTEM

There is a formal HR executive meeting every month, but the function is run quite informally with frequent ad hoc meetings and decisions by the Group HR Director. Performance is measured formally against an elaborate scorecard.

... the HR function of an online retailer

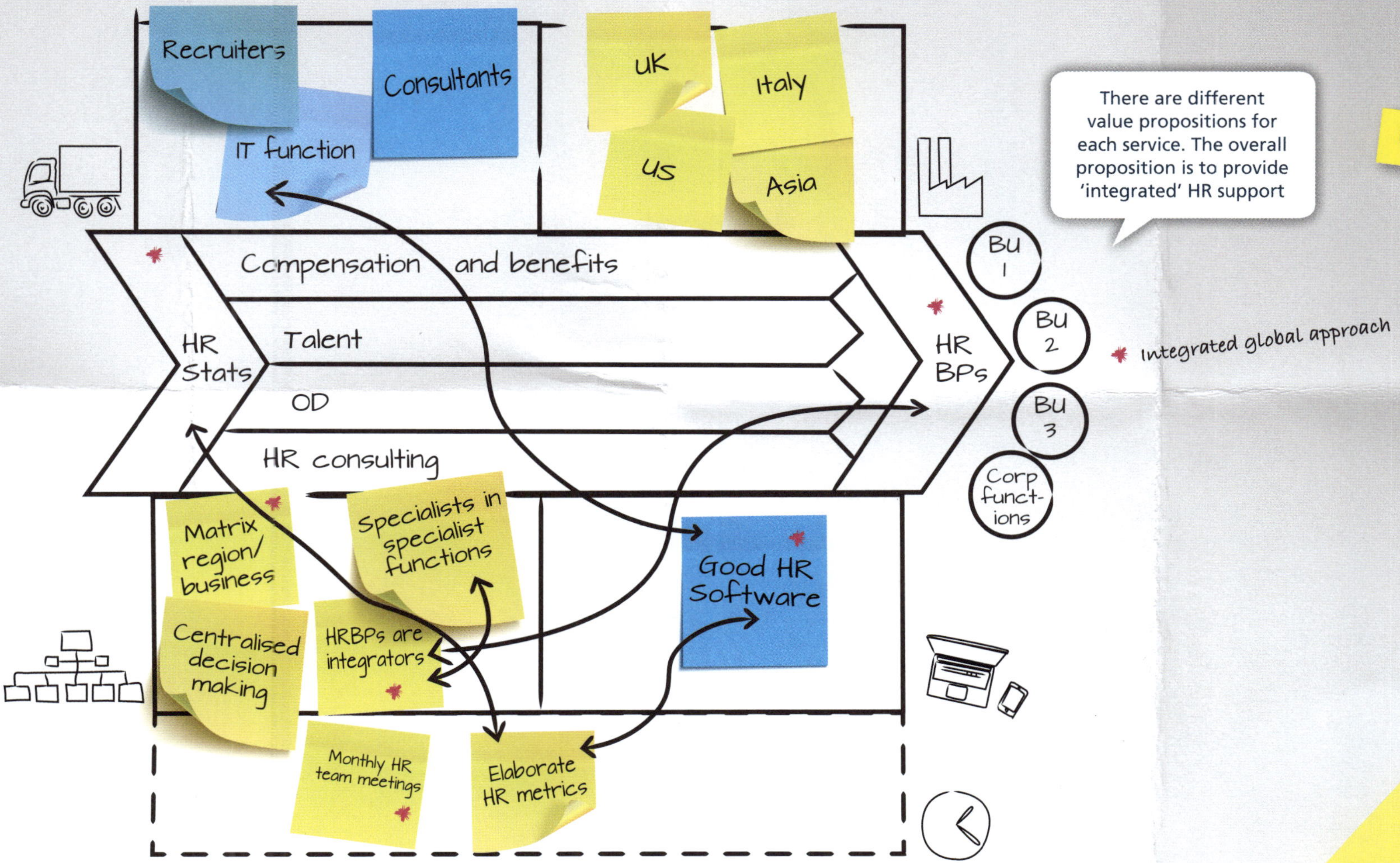

CH2

CH2

Multi-business examples

The Operating Model Canvas can be used to understand the operations of a multi-business organization either looking at the whole organization or just the corporate headquarters.

The following examples are descriptions of the current situation showing the differences between different organizations and between a model for the whole company versus one just for corporate headquarters.

The Operating Model Canvas for...

CH2

Shell

Shell is a huge global oil company, centered in The Hague and London.

Its success has come from strong relationships with governments in the countries where it operates, and from a commitment to technology and engineering excellence.

An operating model for a large multi-business company must focus either on the whole company or only on the corporate headquarters.

Later in this section we will give an example focused on corporate headquarters. This example is for the whole company.

PROCESSES

Shell is involved in three main business areas – upstream exploration and development, downstream refining and retailing, and gas and power. However these business areas share technology development and management of major projects.

ORGANIZATION

Shell has been structured as a line of business and functional matrix. The central functions – Finance, HR and Legal - have control over their functional activities within the businesses. Shell is primarily an engineering culture driven by a belief in technology as the solution to most problems and by its code of business principles 'The Shell Principles'.

MANAGEMENT SYSTEM

Shell has been strategically driven by its leaders, historically a committee of managing directors. Despite the drive to make Shell more centralized and profit driven, the bias towards strategic thinking and distributed power has continued.

LOCATIONS

Shell operates in most countries in the world. Its core assets, oil fields, are often licensed from local governments. Hence relationships with these governments have been critical to success.
Headquarters is shared between The Hague and London.

INFORMATION

Shell has different ERP systems in its different divisions. But has global applications for those functions that have been 'centralized'.

SUPPLIERS

Shell has many suppliers, but the most important are contractors who work on major projects and joint venture partners. As BP found out in the Gulf of Mexico, these relationships are critical to success.

...... Shell

When developing an operating model for a multi-divisional organization, the high-level value propositions are the products/services of the divisions.

CH2

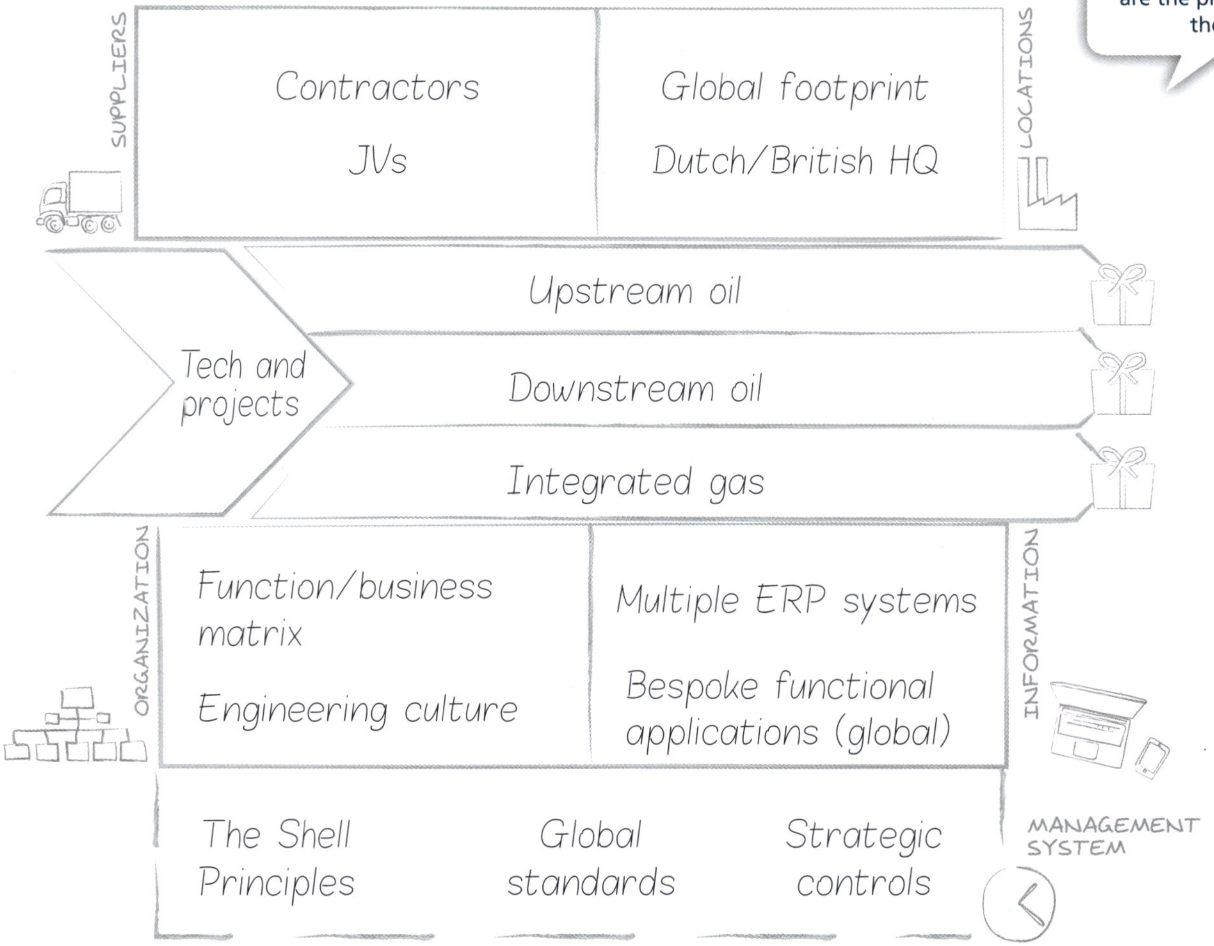

The Operating Model Canvas for...

ASHRIDGE EXECUTIVE EDUCATION HULT

CH2

Ashridge Executive Education is a part of Hult International Business School. Ashridge's main business is providing courses for executives, both open to any company and tailored for a specific company.

Ashridge also does research, uses its dramatic buildings for conferences and for weddings, and runs some qualifications programs. It does not offer MBA programs, these are provided by Hult.

Ashridge is partly a single business and partly a multi-business organization. It is a highly integrated multi-business organization or a complex single business.

There have been changes to this operating model since this page was created

PROCESSES

Each product line has some similar processes and some separate processes. 'Client' covers tailored courses and consulting work. 'Open' covers open courses. There is considerable sharing of elements like faculty, teaching rooms, and back- office activities.

One peculiarity is an operation in Dubai covering the Middle East. This unit acts as a separate profit center.

ORGANIZATION

The separate lines of business are profit or performance accountable with considerable decision rights, but they all share the same core resource – the teaching faculty – which provides the prime people model.

Course administration, sales and marketing are shared across product lines to different degrees. 'House' provides conference and hotel services to the other lines of business.

LOCATIONS

Ashridge House is a unique building with beautiful grounds, and is one of the organization's core assets. International offices (excluding Dubai) are provided by Hult.

INFORMATION

The website, database and applications to support teaching and take bookings are important information resources.

SUPPLIERS

Hult is a supplier of some back-office support, such as IT, as well as some international sales support. Associate faculty is an important teaching resource.

MANAGEMENT SYSTEM

Planning is done on an annual basis. Monthly meetings are sufficient for coordination and performance management, alongside clear business KPIs and a faculty scorecard for ensuring that each member of faculty is delivering value to Ashridge.

.. Ashridge Executive Education

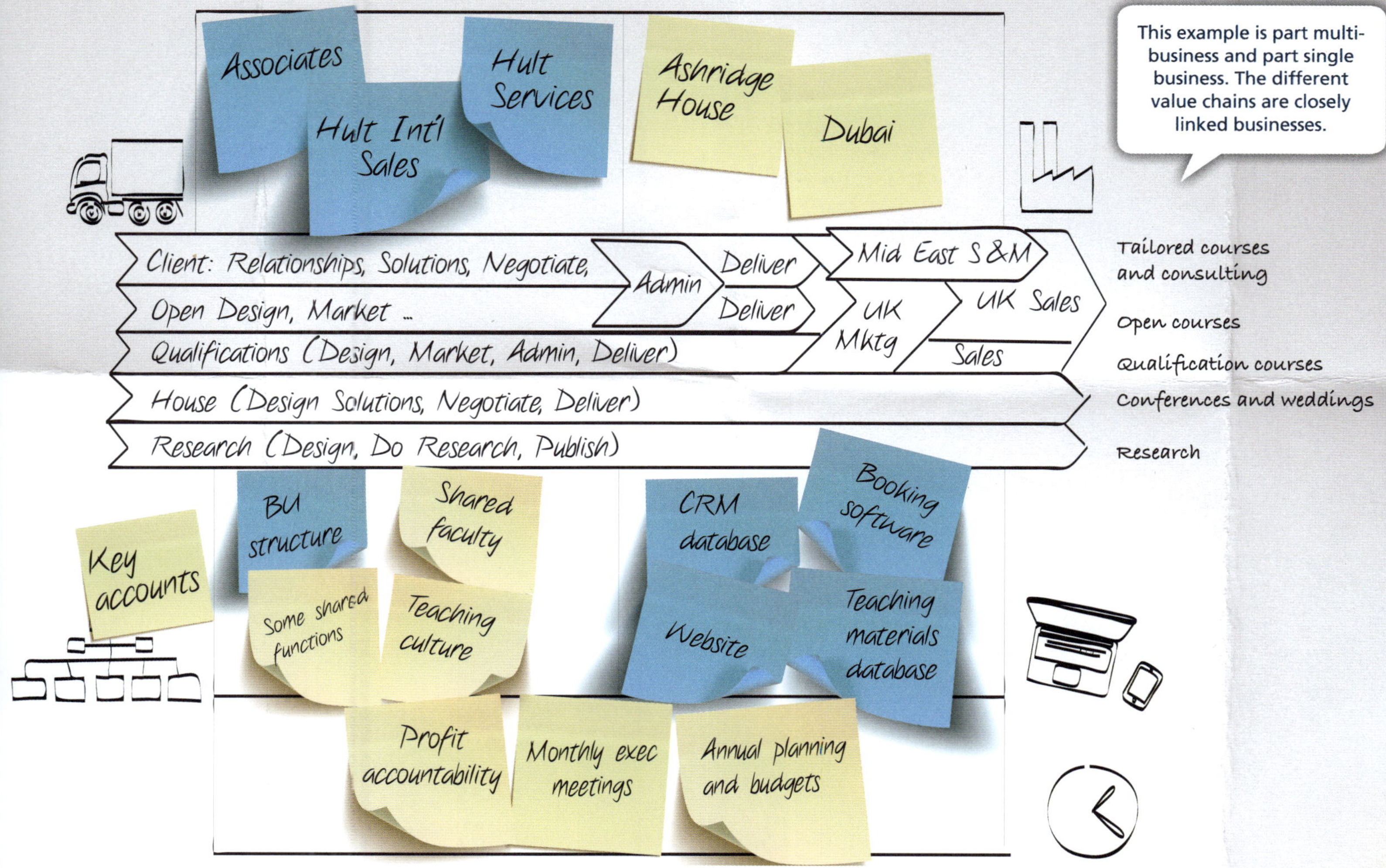

This example is part multi-business and part single business. The different value chains are closely linked businesses.

CH2

The Operating Model Canvas for Ashridge Executive Education

The Operating Model Canvas for...

This is a disguised example of a European company (AIBS) whose main business divisions are in mining, oil and shipping.

These are all asset-intensive businesses in cyclical industries. The problem in these businesses is that, when markets are good and prices are rising, managers are keen to expand capacity and make new investments. Also, at these times, profits are easy, so managers become more concerned with adding capacity than with controlling costs.

When the down-cycle comes managers find that their operating costs are too high and they have too much expensive capacity.

PROCESSES

The corporate offices are involved in governance activities such as supporting the Board, paying taxes and checking that the businesses are operating within the law. The Board is the main beneficiary of these activities. But the core activity of the corporate office is to add value. AIBS has decided to add value to its business divisions in three ways:

- By helping them make better capital investment decisions, particularly at the top of the cycle.
- By helping them keep control of operating costs, particularly in good times.
- By helping them find and retain the best talent.

INFORMATION

There is a corporate ERP system and separate software applications for assessing the stage of the industry cycle and for talent management.

ORGANIZATION

The corporate office is structured by function – Finance, HR, Legal, etc. Each function incorporates a different people model and has decision rights over functional policies. Coordination is achieved through the HQ Committee and through cross-functional teams for each of the three ways of adding value.

LOCATIONS

AIBS has one headquarters building in Amsterdam. All functions are on one site to encourage collaboration around the three sources of added value.

SUPPLIERS

The main suppliers are banks, who provide capital for investment and whose support is often needed in the down-cycle. The providers of the ERP system and other applications are also important.

MANAGEMENT SYSTEM

The monthly executive committee links corporate functions to the businesses. Formal feedback on the corporate functions is collected from the business divisions.

... the corporate office of a diversified company

CH2

The value propositions of this organization align with the four value chains – for the board, better governance; for the divisions, wiser investments, lower costs and better people

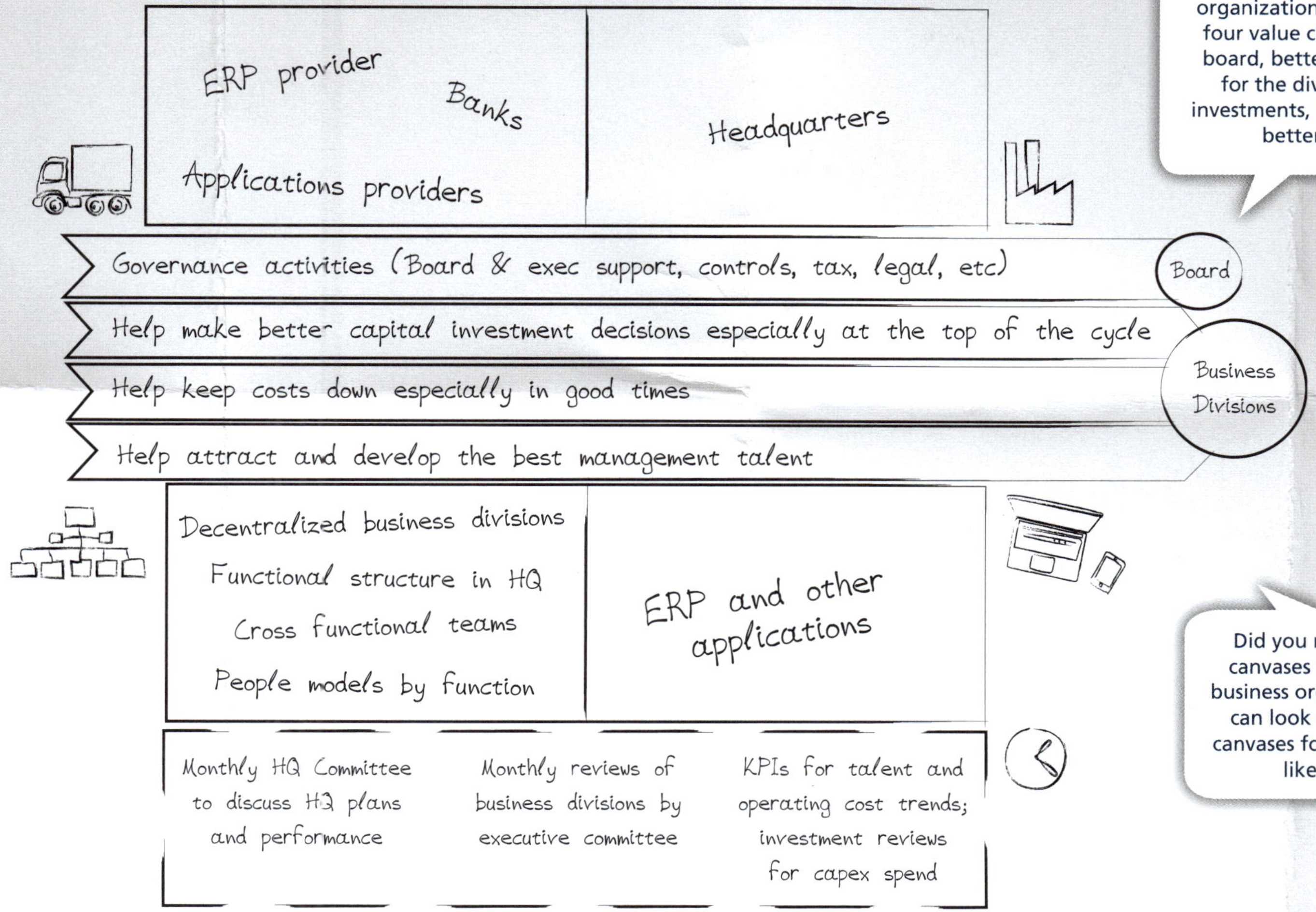

Did you note that canvases for multi-business organizations can look similar to canvases for functions like HR

A company involved in motorsport ...

Creative use of the Canvas format can help communication

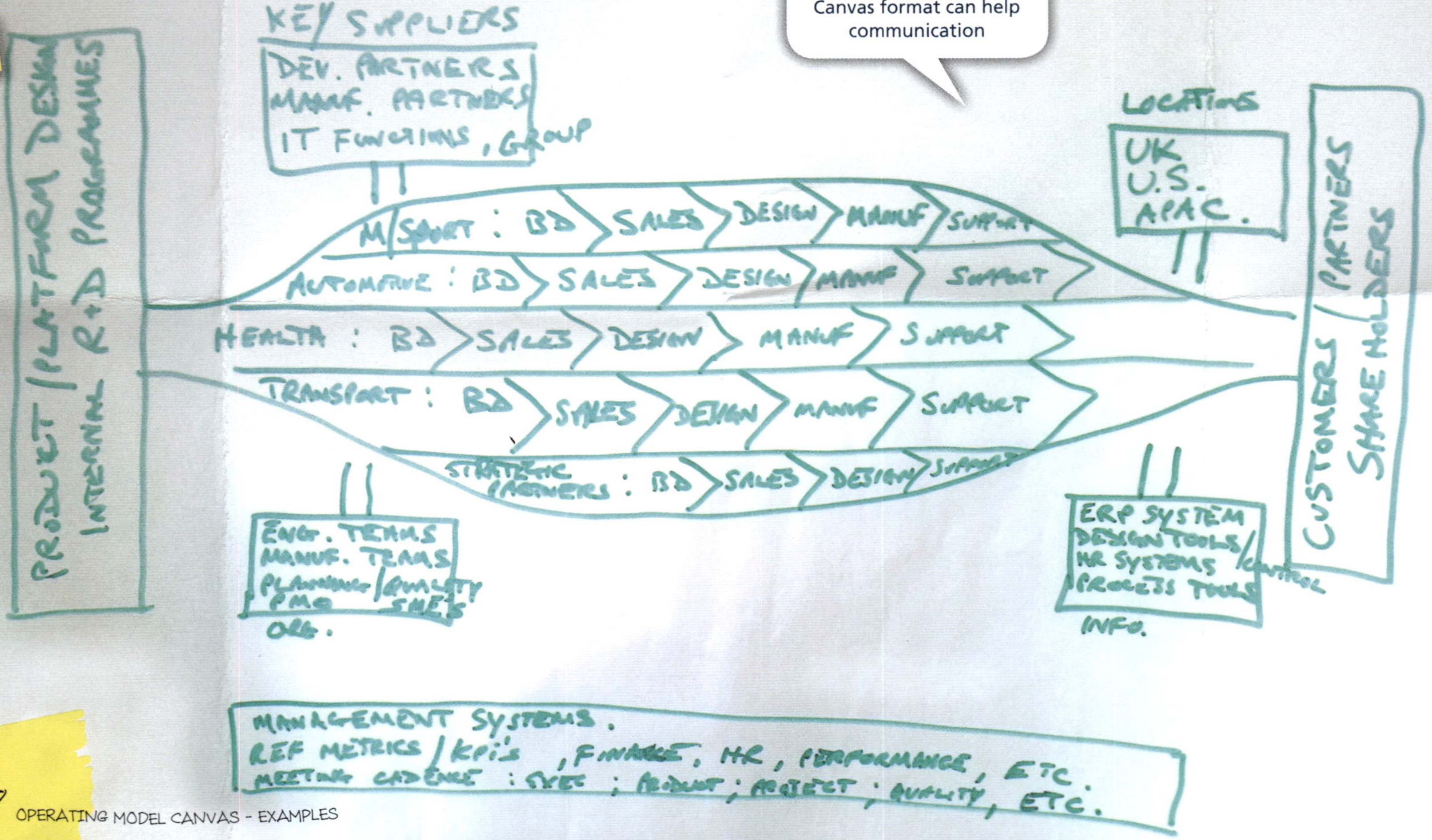

Consulting company (flip chart example)

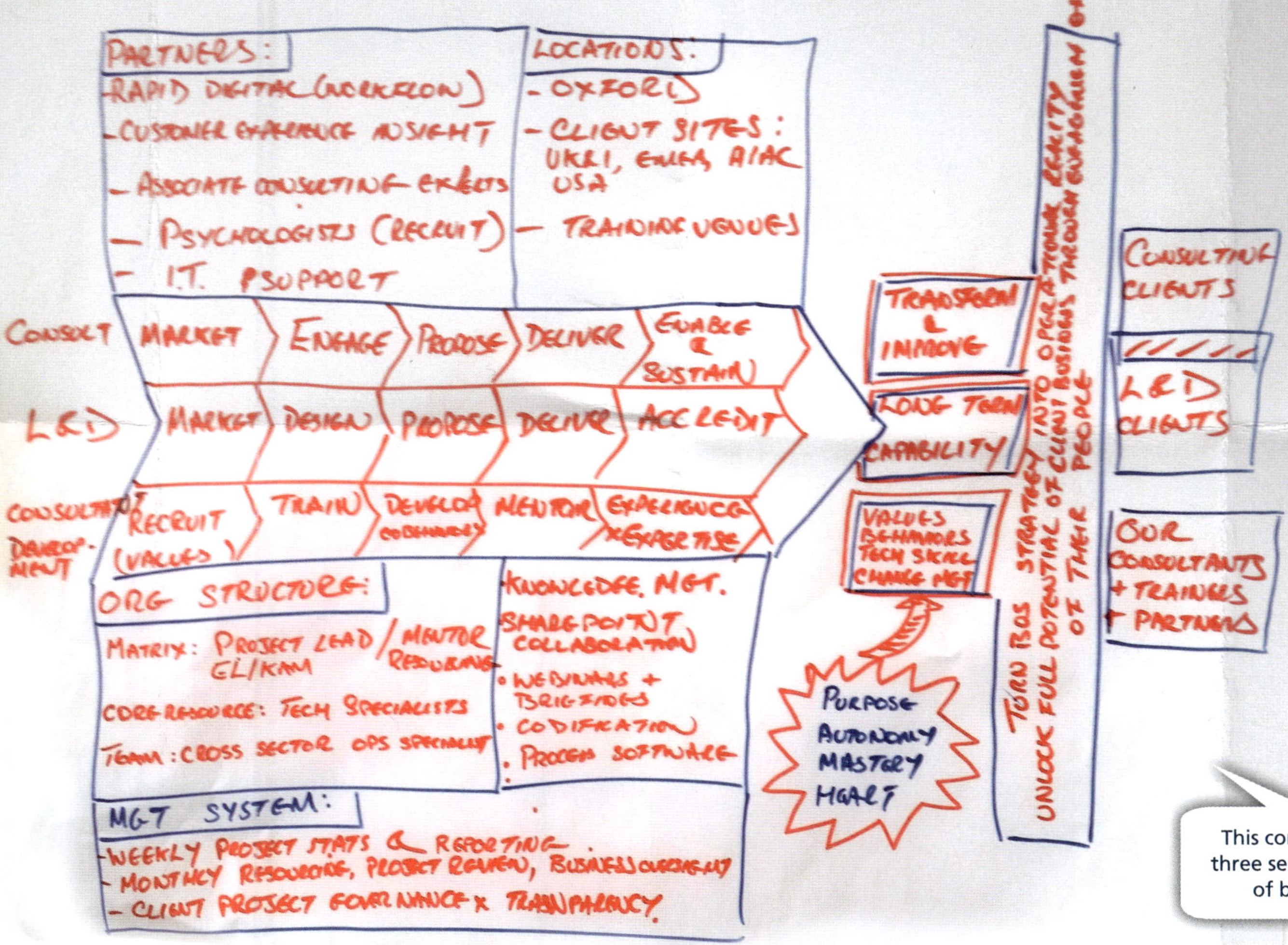

This company has three separate lines of business

CH2

Public sector examples

The Operating Model Canvas can be used to understand the operations of public sector organizations. These organizations also create value for beneficiaries and have value delivery processes, just like commercial organizations

The following examples are descriptions of the current situation showing the differences between different organizations.

CH2

The Operating Model Canvas for

CH2

This is a disguised example of a qualifications regulator. In this country, the government decides the curriculum to be taught in schools, the qualifications that can be offered, and the accountability framework by which schools are evaluated. It also determines the vocational qualifications that can be taught in schools and colleges and used in apprenticeships.

The qualifications regulator makes sure that qualifications are of the right standard and that the qualification system works well, so that those who take, or rely on, qualifications can have confidence in them.

The organization regulates two market segments: educational qualifications and vocational qualifications.

PROCESSES

The value chains for both segments are similar: set strategy and policy for the qualifications, develop standards and guidance for providers, authorize providers, supervise providers, moderate the awarding of key qualifications and enforce sanctions. Vocational qualifications involve less 'moderation' of qualifications and less 'enforcement'.

SUPPLIERS

It is not entirely obvious which stakeholders are suppliers and which are customers – the relationships are complex. The operating model has been developed assuming the main beneficiaries are students, schools and universities, and businesses and organizations. This, in turn, assumes the qualification providers and providers of apprenticeships are suppliers.

LOCATIONS

The regulator has one main office, and some regional offices that facilitate supervising local providers.

ORGANIZATION

The bulk of the work of the organization had historically been structured into three departments – an authorization department, a supervision department, and an enforcement department. The operating model has been developed so that there would be one operations team, a single strategy team, and dedicated teams focusing on policy and standards for each market segment.

INFORMATION

The regulator has bespoke applications for helping manage its unique operations.

MANAGEMENT SYSTEM

The executive committee, plans most activity on an annual cycle, but regulatory strategy is on a three year cycle and issues are handled on an ad hoc basis. There are extensive KPIs.

... a qualifications regulator

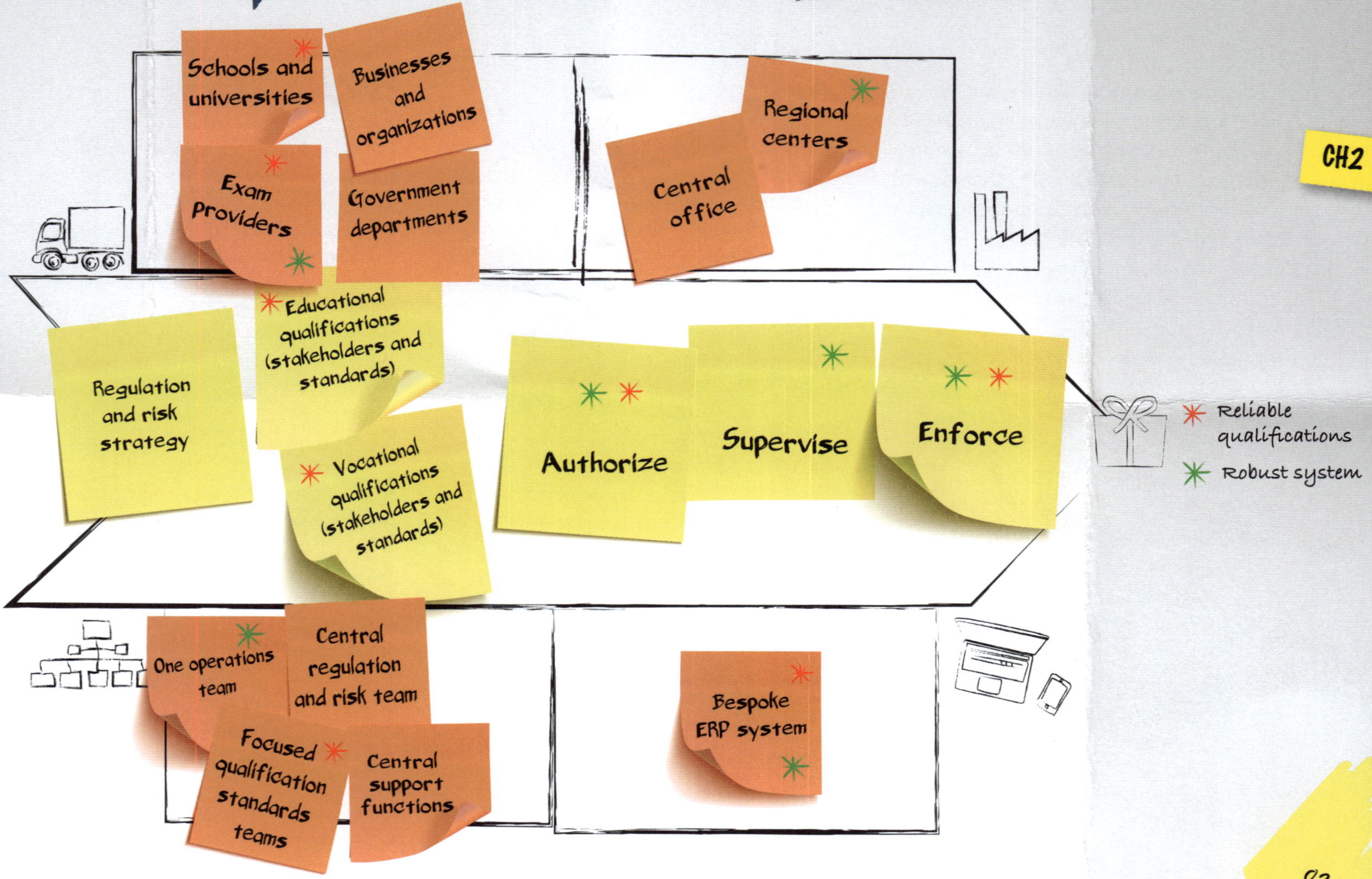

The Operating Model Canvas for..

This Operating Model Canvas is for a government department that administers payments for housing benefits, unemployment benefits and other benefits such as single parent benefits.

CH2

PROCESSES

Those seeking benefit make a claim, typically through a website. The claim is then processed by a benefits team to assess its validity. The benefits team then pass the claim to a local office where the claimant is interviewed and additional information is collected. The claim is then returned to the benefits team for final approval, which is subsequently passed to the payments team who instruct the bank to make payments.

SUPPLIERS

The National Tax Office is an important supplier of information about claimants. Other important suppliers include organizations who help unemployed people into jobs, so reducing claimants. The organization gets its HR, finance and IT support from another government department.

MANAGEMENT SYSTEM

A clear scorecard of KPIs is monitored through monthly performance reviews by the whole team.

ORGANIZATION

The organization is a simple value chain structure. The benefit centers deal with all types of benefit claimants. This helps create a single decision-making team reporting to a CEO with a focus on cost, accuracy and on-time payment. Most support activities come from outside this organization, except for an operational efficiency team. There are important differences in the people models along the value chain, recognizing the different skills in benefits assessment and benefit centers.

INFORMATION

Applications are maintained and managed in-house to ensure good integration of systems as the organization upgrades its IT support.

LOCATIONS

The organization has offices in all significant towns and cities, enabling claimants to visit a benefits center and ensuring some local knowledge. Major processing tasks are done in lower cost locations.

… a benefits department

CH2

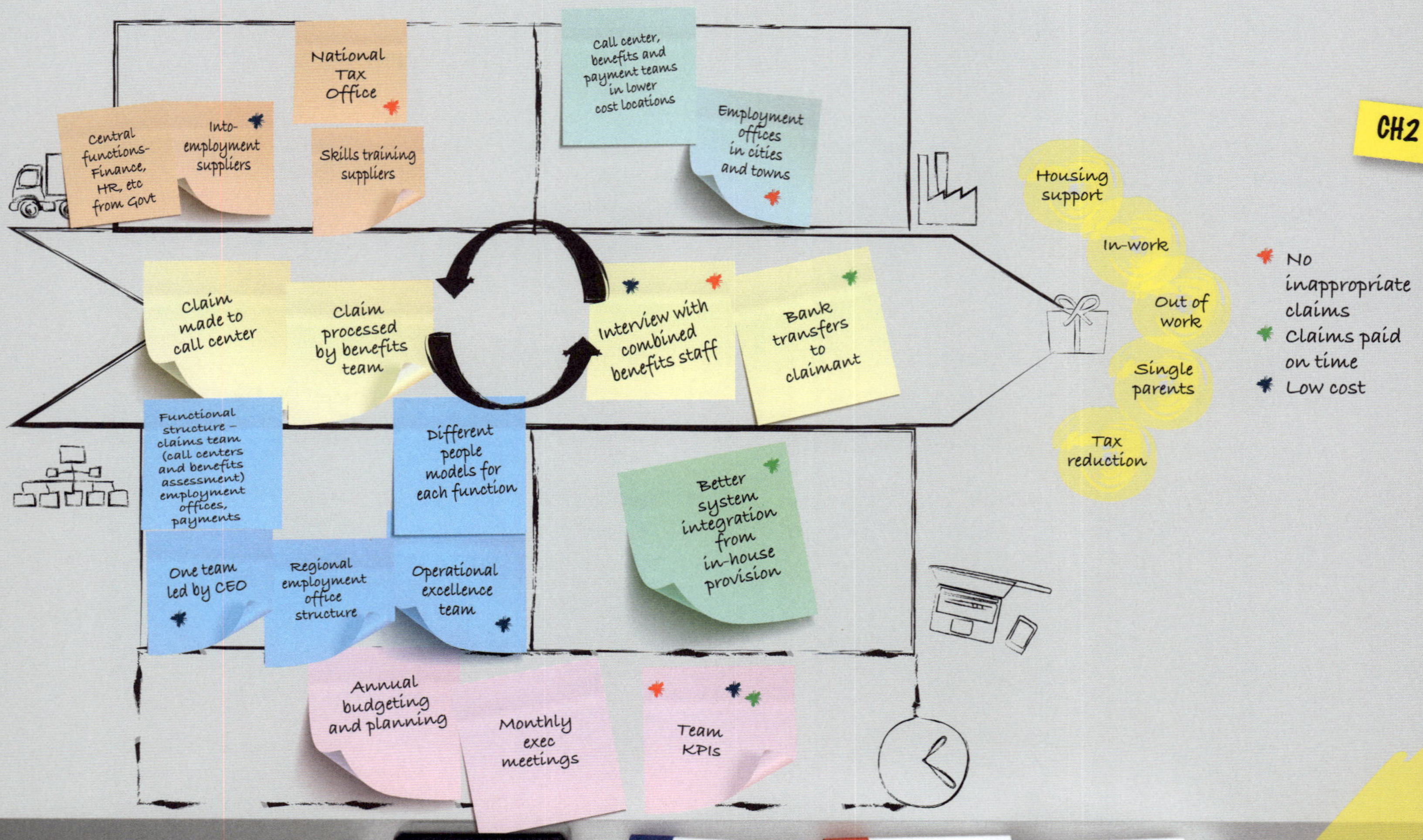

CH2

Other examples

The Operating Model Canvas is also helpful for understanding any organization from a pop-up group of volunteers to a charity.

Crescent

The Operating Model Canvas for...

CH2

DEF CON is the Las Vegas conference for computer hackers. There are only two paid staff who run the DEF CON offices all year. The rest of the organization, over 100 volunteers, 'forms' for the conference each year and then disbands.

Quartermaster Stores is one of the 13 departments run by volunteers. It issues and administers the equipment needed by other departments at the conference from flip charts to computers and from guitar stands to TV screens. Historically most equipment was provided by the venue. But it proved cheaper and better to buy equipment and store it between conferences.

LOCATIONS

The store rooms need to be near the loading dock and near the conference rooms. Ideally there is a counter that goons can come to – if not, one is 'built'. The equipment is the main asset.

PROCESSES

The equipment is stored in a warehouse. The team arrives two days before the conference. First task is to get a removal service to deliver the pallets of equipment. At the same time the 'office' is being set up with the help of NOC (Network Operations Center) another department. Each item is scanned and moved to one of two 'stores'. Then the bar code inventory system is set up and Quartermaster is ready to issue equipment to 'Goons' (volunteer organizers).

ORGANIZATION

The organization is staffed by volunteers who come together for the event. There is a Quarter Master (the boss), a Load Master (responsible for issuing equipment), three loaders, three internal runners (helping and chasing goons) and one external runner (buying equipment). The Load Master is a coffee connoisseur and trainer of baristas, so the coffee is good. High levels of initiative are expected from all team members.

SUPPLIERS

NOC supplies networks. Production buys major equipment that is needed. Dispatch eases communications with other departments, some of which also share external runners.

INFORMATION

Quartermaster developed its own inventory system based on bar codes. Every conference room, every goon and every piece of equipment has a bar code.

MANAGEMENT SYSTEM

DEF CON is run as an holocracy. Issues are posted on Basecamp for discussion. Each department has the final say in its area unless there is an intervention from DEF CON boss Jeff Moss.

Any equipment not returned on time is chased at the end of each day

All departments plan together six months before the conference. There are no other 'meetings'. Less communication between departments and more autonomy proved more efficient.

... Quartermaster Stores at DEF CON

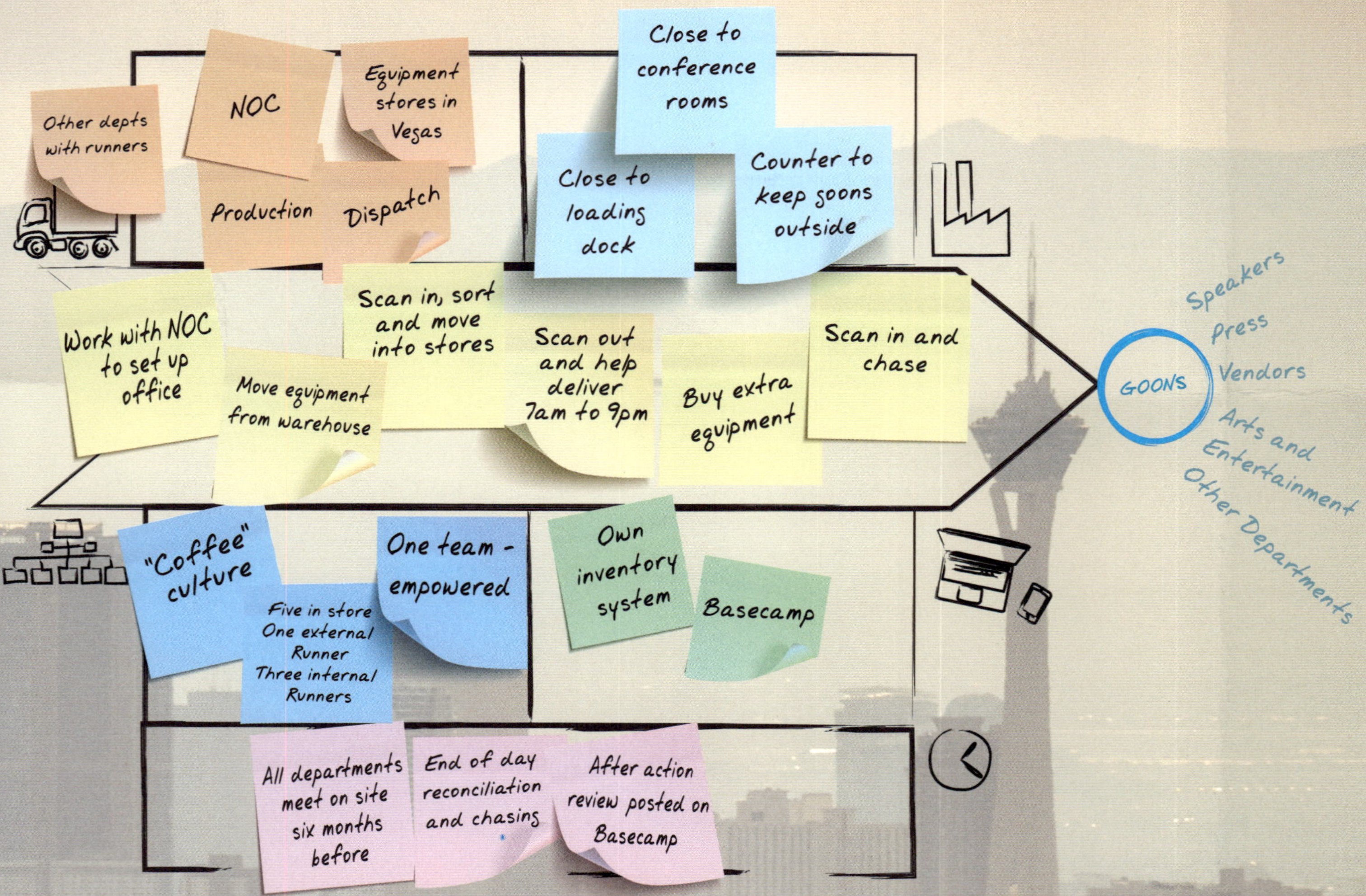

CH2

The Operating Model Canvas for...

CH2

cardboard citizens 25 YEARS

Cardboard Citizens is a charity that has been making life-changing theater with and for homeless people for 25 years. It has great expertise in improvisational 'forum theater'. Based in London, the charity "tells stories that help their tellers get a handle on their lives." Theater is performed in the street, in hostels, homeless centers, prisons and even on traditional stages.

Through participation as an actor or as part of the audience, homeless people are inspired and supported to seek help, get qualifications, take work and gain confidence about their worth in society.

PROCESSES

There are three broad value chains – performing plays, events and workshops; giving advice and guidance; training actors and theater supporters. While some of these activities raise money directly, the organization also raises money in other ways.

SUPPLIERS

Cardboard Citizens relies on a large number of suppliers including funders, volunteers, organizations that run hostels, prisons and theaters as well as donors. There are also professional actors and big names such as Kate Winslet and Kate Tempest who support the charity.

LOCATIONS

The main offices are in Whitechapel. But most of the charity's work is done on location, in towns and cities around the country: on streets, in homeless centres and even in prisons.

ORGANIZATION

The organization is a simple structure reporting to a CEO who, in turn, reports to a board of trustees. There is a development department that raises money, a projects team who organize performances, a training team who deliver theater training for homeless people, for vulnerable young people, and as development for organizations, and an advice team who provide guidance on housing, the benefits system, and on employment/training opportunities.

INFORMATION

There are no special applications. The organization is about face-to-face contact.

MANAGEMENT PROCESSES

Success is measured through stories as well as KPIs such as audience size, workshop engagement, people accessing advice and training, and financial soundness. The board of trustees meetings provide a rhythm around which the management processes revolve. With only 13 employees, internal meetings are typically 'all hands'.

...Cardboard Citizens

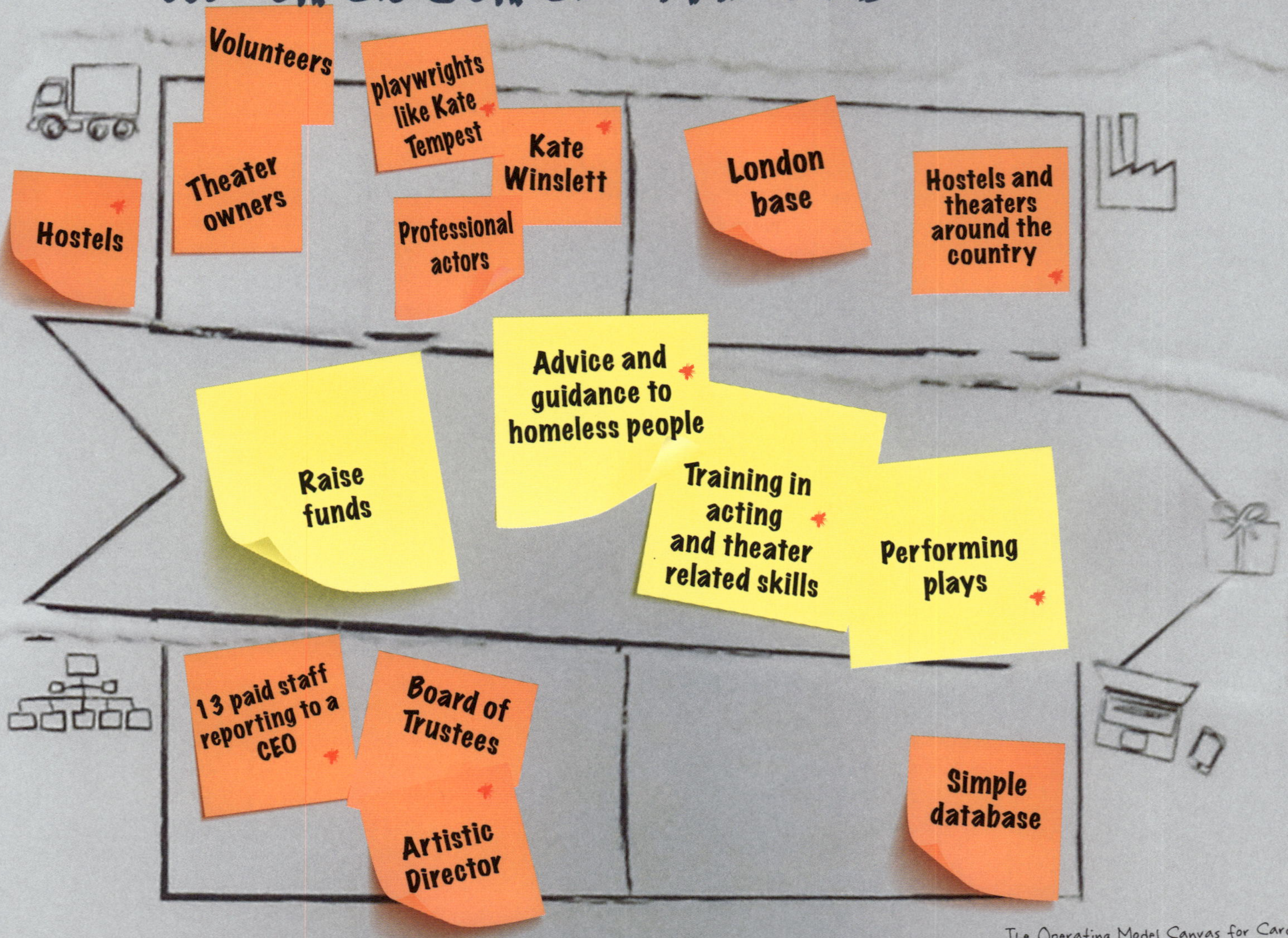

* Life changing theater

The Operating Model Canvas for

CH2

The Strategic Management Centre does research on business strategy with a view to improving theory and helping businesses perform better.

Based in London, the Centre's Directors, all ex McKinsey or BCG consultants, lead research projects, teach executive courses and interact with a group of member companies.

The value propositions are 'better and more practical theory' for the research, 'high quality' for the courses, 'capability building' for the member companies.

Revenues come from member companies and course participants.

PROCESSES

There are three value chains. The research chain involves identifying a management problem, designing research, completing research, publishing the results and teaching the conclusions. The teaching value chain involves identifying a need, designing a course, administering the course, delivering the course and follow up. The member companies value chain involves attracting companies, providing seminars, running networking events and responding to requests.

INFORMATION

Simple office systems such as Microsoft Office are all that is needed.

LOCATIONS

The Centre is located in London for easy access to executives in leading companies who are often based in London or pass through London.

ORGANIZATION

Each Director is responsible for leading or supporting a research project, for leading or teaching on an executive course and for looking after one or more member companies. There is a small administrative staff.

SUPPLIERS

Suppliers include associates who teach on courses or support research projects, a business school that provides the venue and some of the marketing for the executive courses, publishers who publish the Centre's books and magazine and journal editors who publish articles.

MANAGEMENT PROCESSES

There is a Directors Meeting focused on performance and administrative matters; and a Research Meeting that reviews and challenges progress on research projects.

...The Strategic Management Centre

CH2

CHAPTER 3

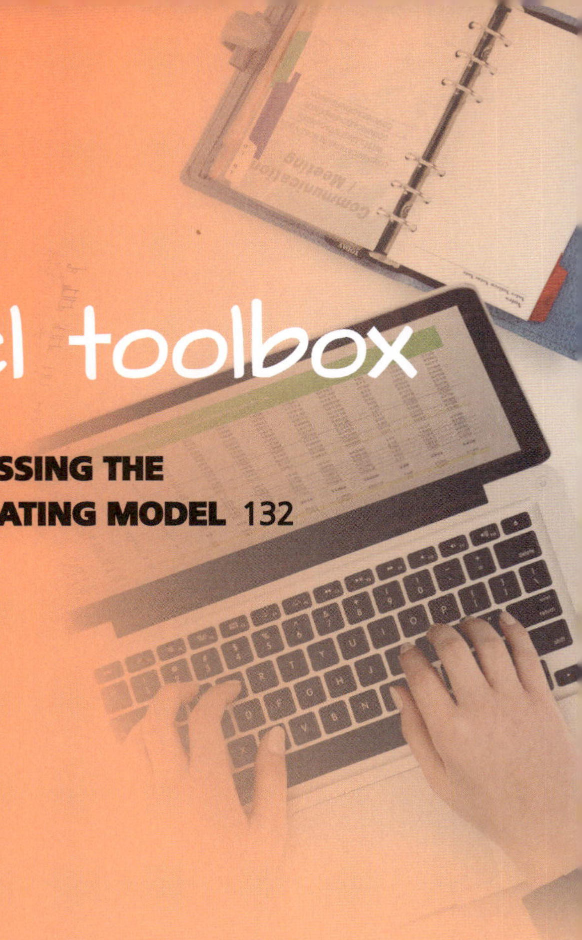

The operating model toolbox

The maps, models, tables, diagrams and charts that help describe, analyse and design an operating model.

Five core tools

The following maps and charts are tools that we have found useful in our work, both for analyzing the situation and communicating the solution. We are not trying to be dogmatic or comprehensive with this list: we are trying to be helpful! We have divided the maps and charts into 'core tools' and 'additional tools'. We are confident that the core maps and charts are easy to use, and they communicate well with a wide audience, especially senior managers and executives running operations. Some of the additional tools are less executive-friendly, but still useful.

The 'core tools' match with the five core parts of the Operating Model Canvas.

The 'additional tools' are additional maps and charts that we or others have found useful.

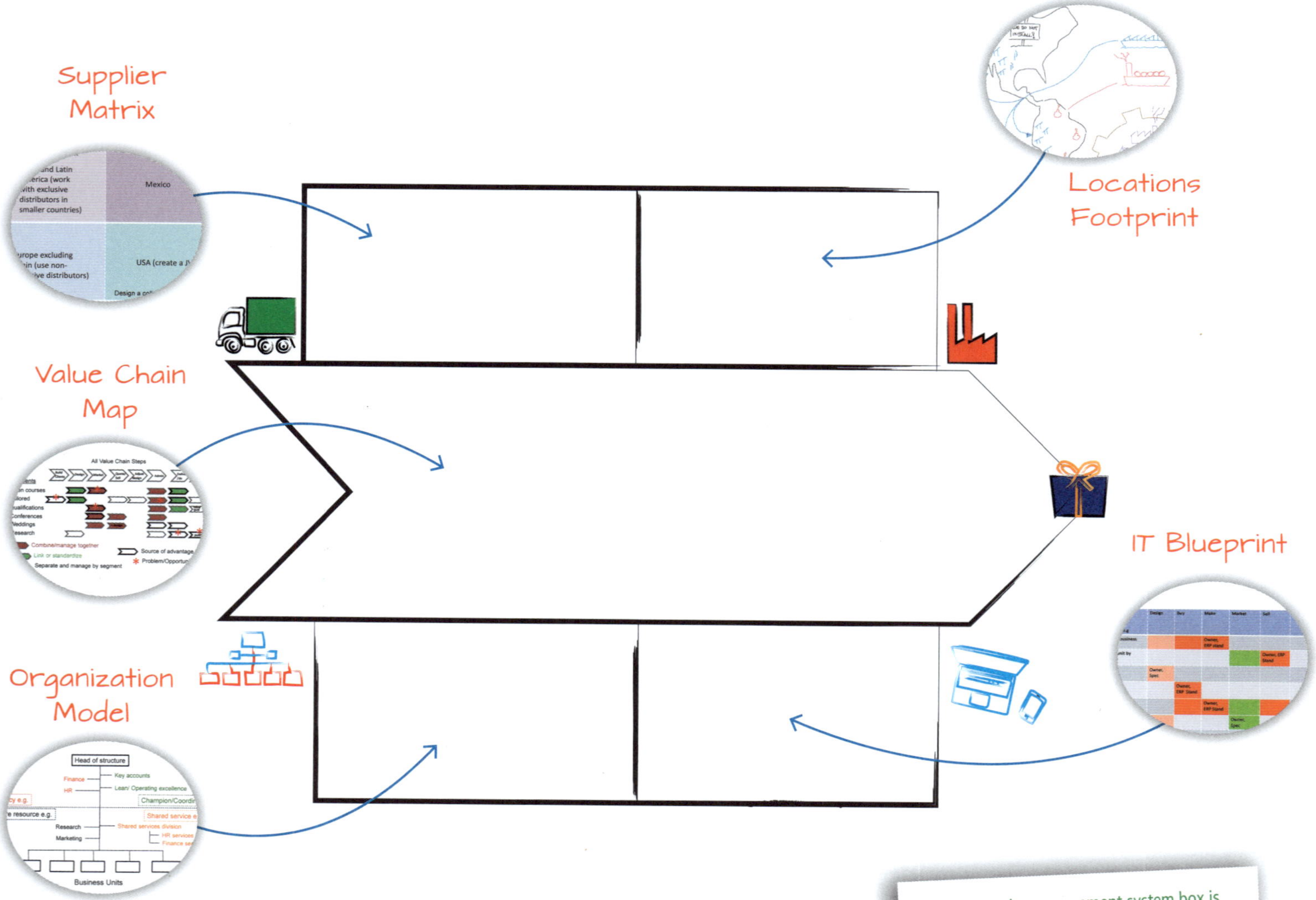

Note that the management system box is missing from this 'Canvas'. This is because it is not a 'core' part of the Canvas.
It reappears on page 118.

Value chain map

The value chain map displays the operating processes that create and deliver value. It represents the heart of the operating model – the middle arrow in the Canvas.

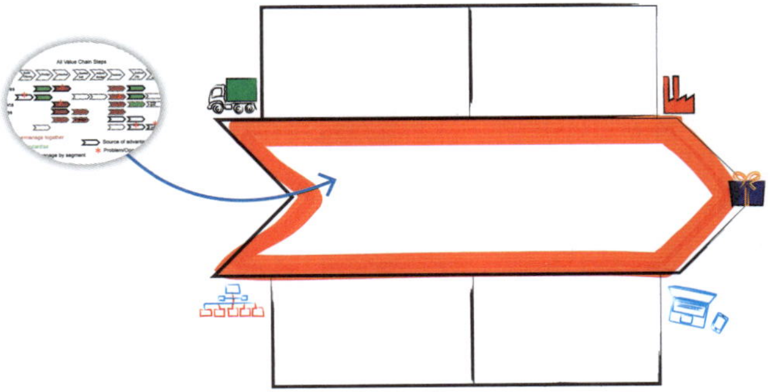

Ashridge Executive Education

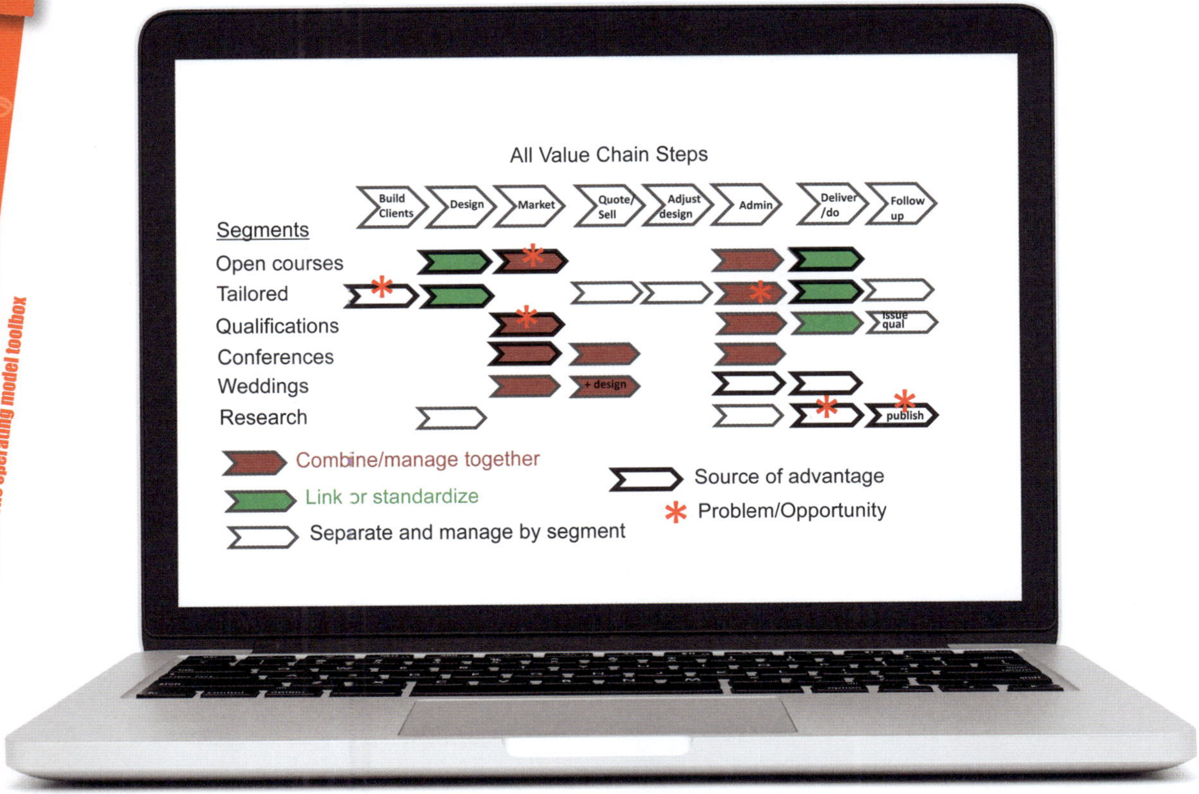

Go to www.operatingmodelcanvas.com for more on value chain maps

Creating a good value chain map is not always easy:

- ➜ It can be hard to find the best way of segmenting the organization's customers/offers;
- ➜ It can be hard to identify the best way of defining the different process steps; and
- ➜ It can be complex.

But, in our experience, a good value chain map is a powerful analytical and communication tool.

There are many ways to segment the value chains. It is often helpful to try more than one way and more than one level of detail to test alternatives. Typical ways of segmenting are:

- ➜ By customer type;
- ➜ By customer need;
- ➜ By geography;
- ➜ By product or service;
- ➜ By technology.

A value chain map for a regulator of two types of qualifications

Once customer segments have been defined, the chain of work for delivering value to each segment is summarized in four to eight process steps. Where process steps are similar, they are positioned in columns. This makes it possible to look at each column and ask three questions:

- ➜ Are the needs of the segment sufficiently different that the steps in the column should be kept separate to allow for solutions and skills that are tailored to the segment?
- ➜ Are there significant economies of scale or other reasons that suggest the steps in the column should be combined into a single unit?
- ➜ Are there opportunities to save cost or improve the offer for customers by linking the steps in the column?

These judgements inform later decisions on the organization and other parts of the operating model.

CH3

Organization Model

Organization charts are common. They provide a helpful visual guide to the organization. But they do not give as much information about how the organization operates as they could. An 'organisation model' is a way of distinguishing between the 'operating work' and the 'support work', and clarifying the relationship between the support functions and operating units. In this way, an organization model shows how the people reporting to the same boss work together.

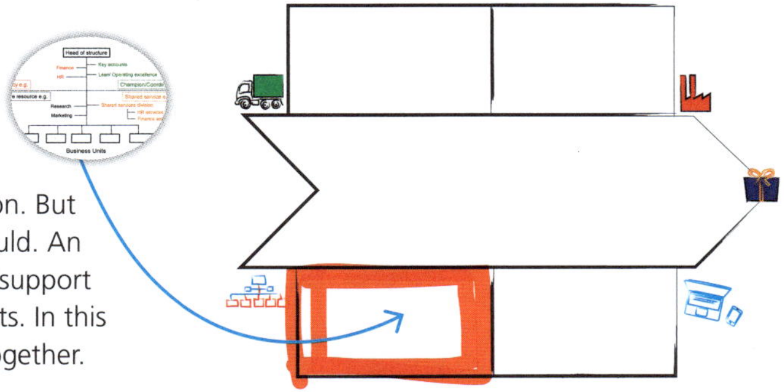

Typical large company structured into business units

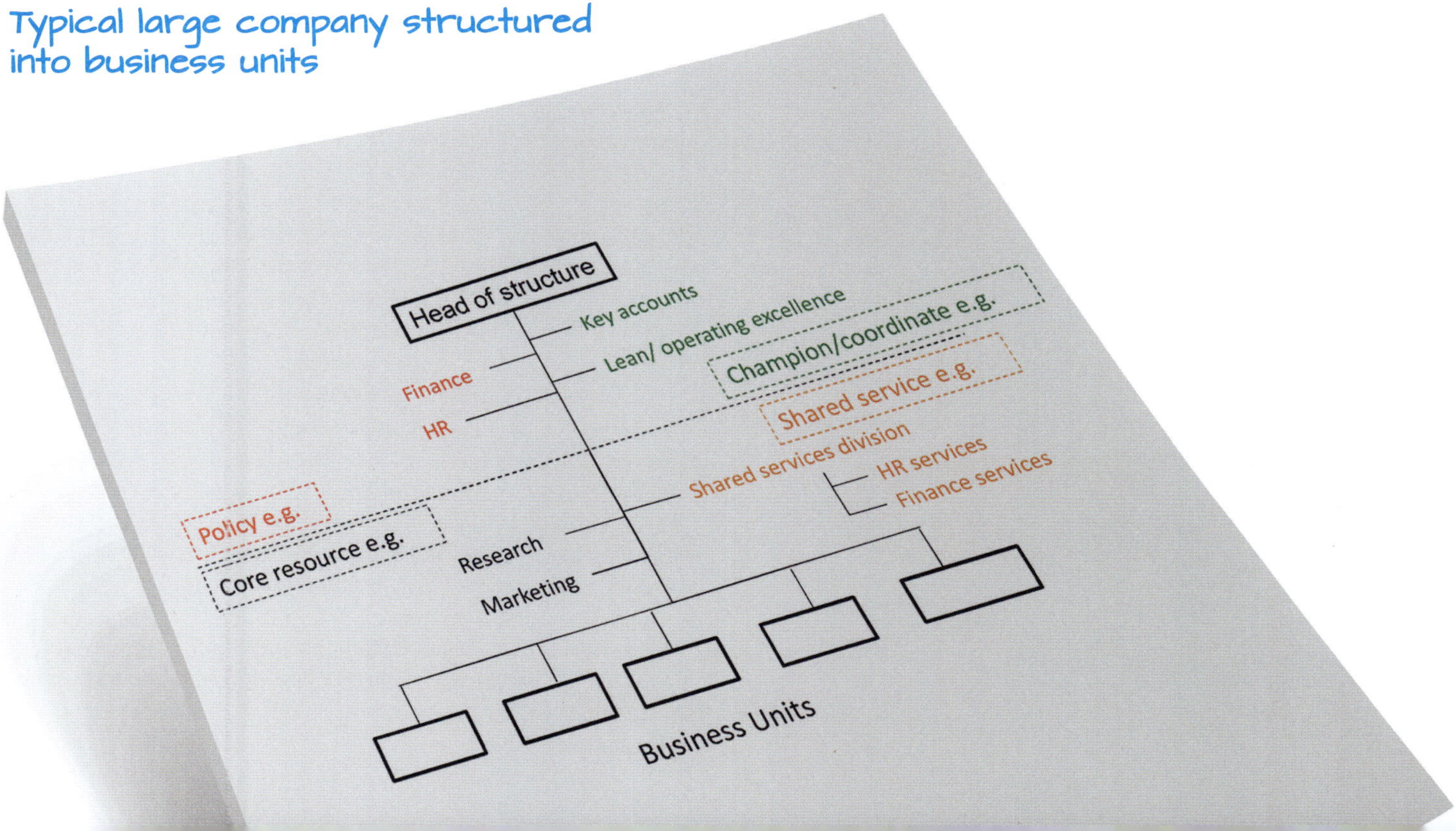

Go to www.operatingmodelcanvas.com for more on organization models

Four types of support work

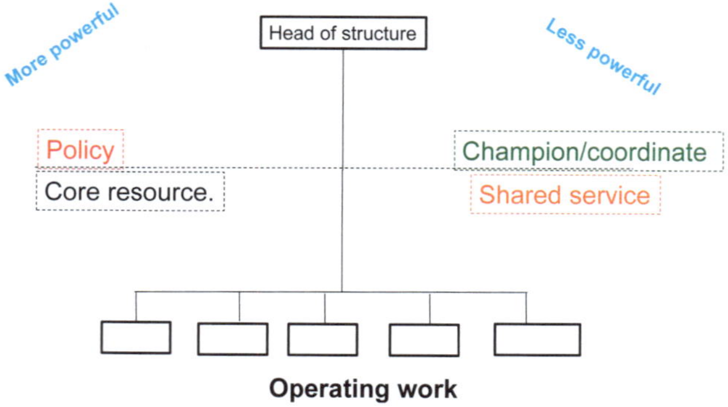

Three ways to structure the operating work

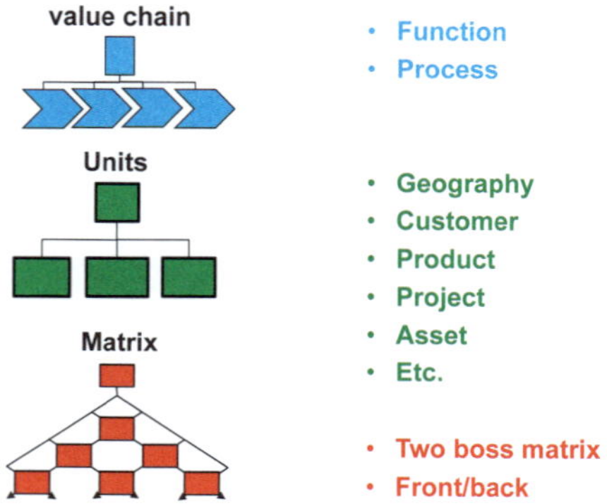

An organization model can be created for every level in the structure. It is a team model: the model of all the people who report to the same person. The roles in the model are divided between operating work (the work that needs to be done to deliver value to customers or beneficiaries of the team) and support work (the work that is done to support those people doing the operating work).

Operating work can be structured in three ways (see exhibit):

- → As a value chain of functions, where the functions need to work closely together to deliver the value;
- → As simple units (as in a typical large company), where each unit delivers a different kind of value or delivers to different customer segments; or
- → As a matrix of units, where each unit can only be successful if it works closely with other units.

The support work can be one of four types: policy, champion, shared service or core-resource. Each type has a different relationship with the operating units. Policy sets rules and polices them. Champion sells ideas and better ways of working, but has no power. Shared service provides services in a customer/supplier relationship. Core-resource provides resources and inputs as a partner to the operating units.

Locations footprint

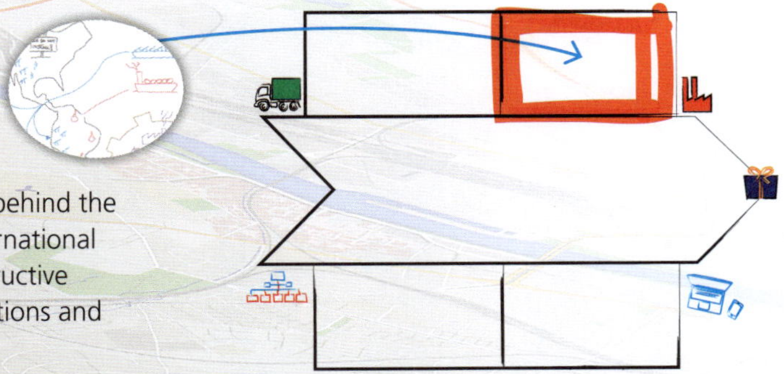

Many organizations have a map of their locations on their website, or on the wall behind the reception desk, or in the office of a senior manager. These typically show how international or widely spread the organization is. But these maps can be used for a more constructive purpose: to communicate the role of each location, some of the important connections and where important assets are located and why.

Global supplier of galvanized steel

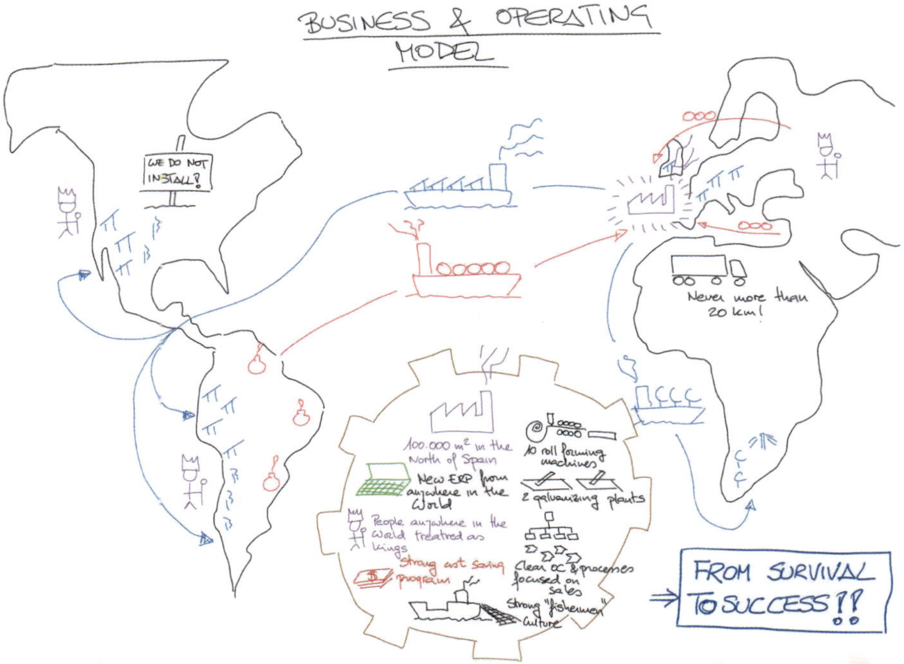

Go to www.operatingmodelcanvas.com for more on locations footprint

Stakeholder framework for thinking about location

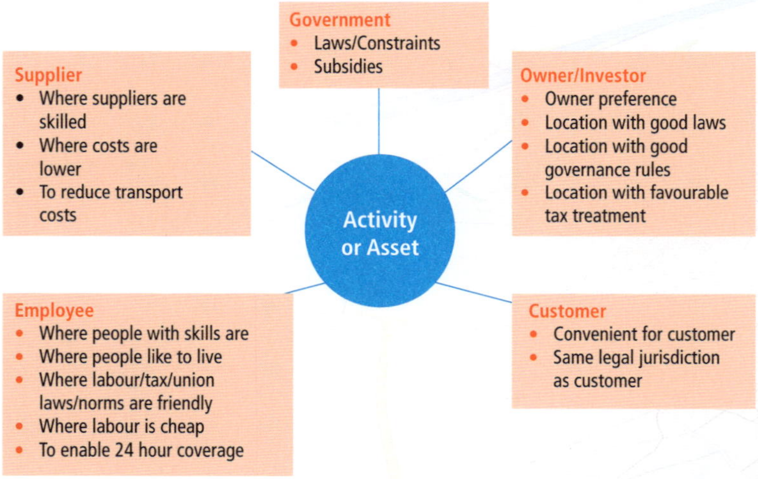

High-level factory floor plans

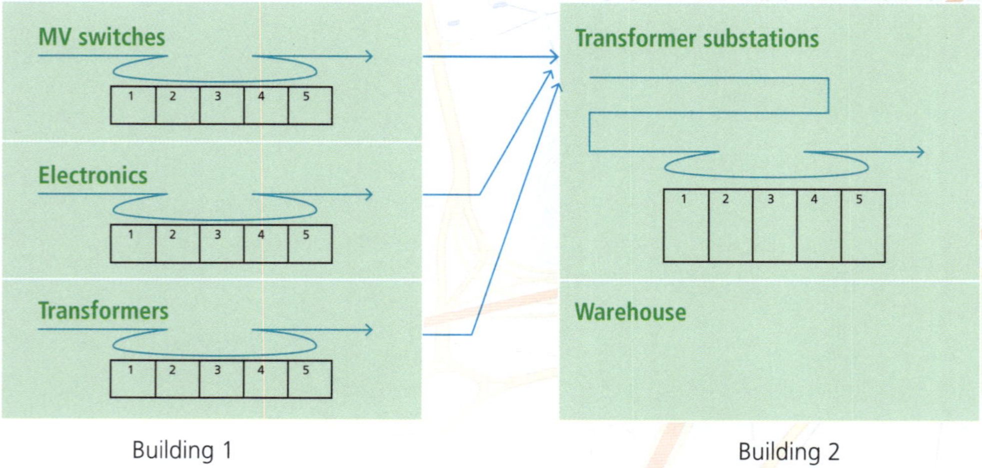

What should be included in a locations footprint? There are no set rules. So be prepared to try three or four ways of using this visualization before you find one that captures useful information and is easy to understand. Beware of adding too much information on a locations footprint. But any of the following could be included:

- → Locations of all plants, offices, warehouses, databases, intellectual property, etc.
- → Transport roots for main suppliers and to main customers and between main parts of the operations
- → Territories covered by legal entities or business units
- → If the operation is just one location, then consider floor layouts showing the different parts of the operation and how they connect

Remember that building layouts and which activity you put on which floor of an office building are location decisions.

IT blueprint

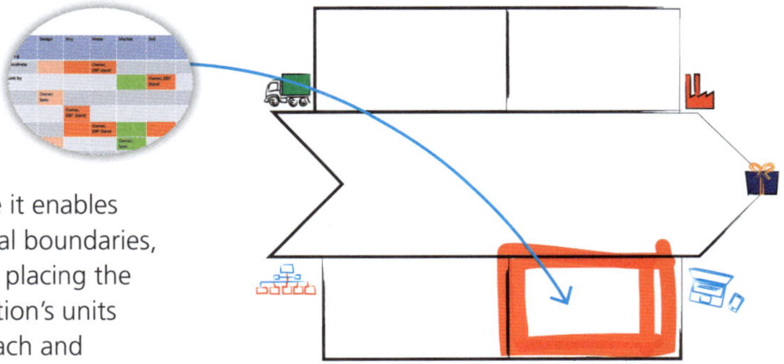

Information technology is a crucial part of nearly all modern organizations because it enables information sharing and communication across the normal functional and locational boundaries, and because it can help automate processes. A high-level IT blueprint is created by placing the process steps from the value chain map along the top of a table, and the organization's units down the side. The table shows the IT applications that are needed, who 'owns' each and which need to be integrated into an enterprise system.

Manufacturer

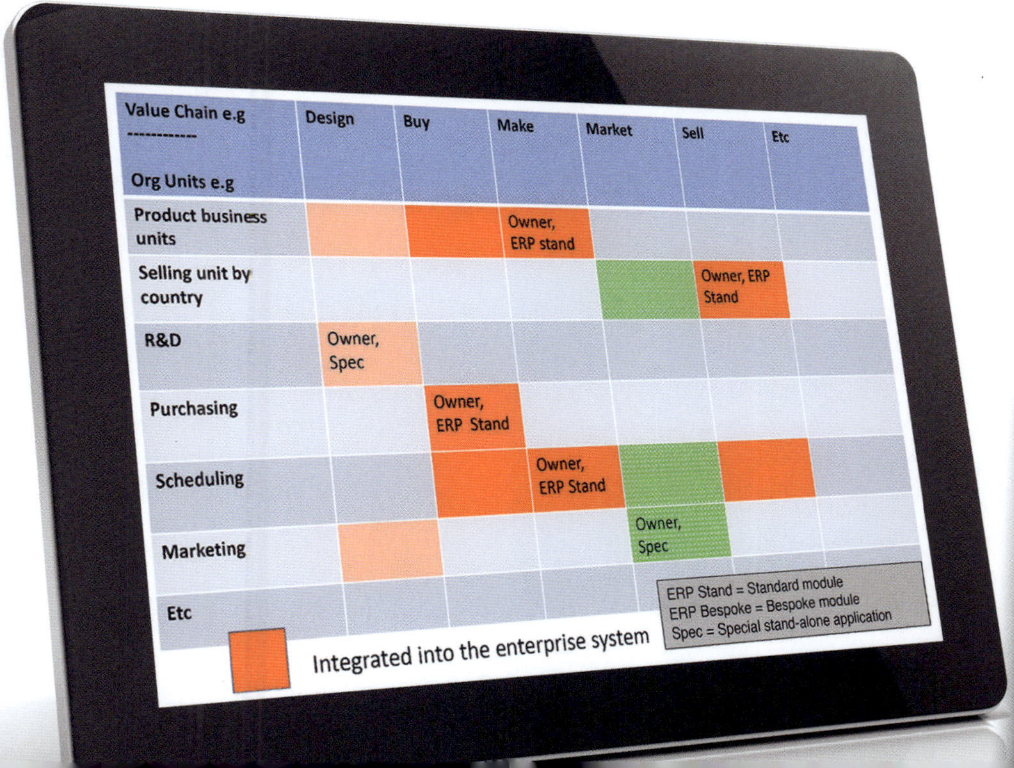

Value Chain e.g ----------- Org Units e.g	Design	Buy	Make	Market	Sell	Etc
Product business units			Owner, ERP stand			
Selling unit by country					Owner, ERP Stand	
R&D	Owner, Spec					
Purchasing		Owner, ERP Stand				
Scheduling			Owner, ERP Stand			
Marketing				Owner, Spec		
Etc						

Integrated into the enterprise system

ERP Stand = Standard module
ERP Bespoke = Bespoke module
Spec = Special stand-alone application

What is an IT blueprint? The phrase IT blueprint has been used widely in a range of contexts. The analogy is with a building blueprint. IT blueprints typically show the architecture of the IT applications, hardware and communication pipes. The use of the term here is very high-level. In fact it is little more than a visual way of representing the principles for designing the IT systems. However it is a vital step and benefits from being kept at this high-level.

Create the table by placing the process steps along the top and the organization units down the side. Then show which organization units are involved in which processes.
Then for each process, identify the software applications used in the process, whether they need to be 'integrated' into the enterprise system (show with a change in color) and which organization unit is the 'business owner'. This is likely to be the same unit that 'owns' the process (see Process Owner Grid on page 116)
Where the application does not need to be integrated, the business owner can decide what to do: a standard package or bespoke. Where integration is required, a decision needs to be made about whether to use the standard module from a reputable supplier or 'adapt' the module to fit the company's special needs. Cloud-based, 'as-a-service' systems have made it easier to work with bespoke applications and to connect applications from different suppliers. But the decision choice is still the same: 'standard' or 'adapt'. A helpful rule of thumb here is to presume that bespoke applications will only be allowed if the process is a source of excellence or competitive advantage for the organization.

Go to www.operatingmodelcanvas.com for more on IT blueprints

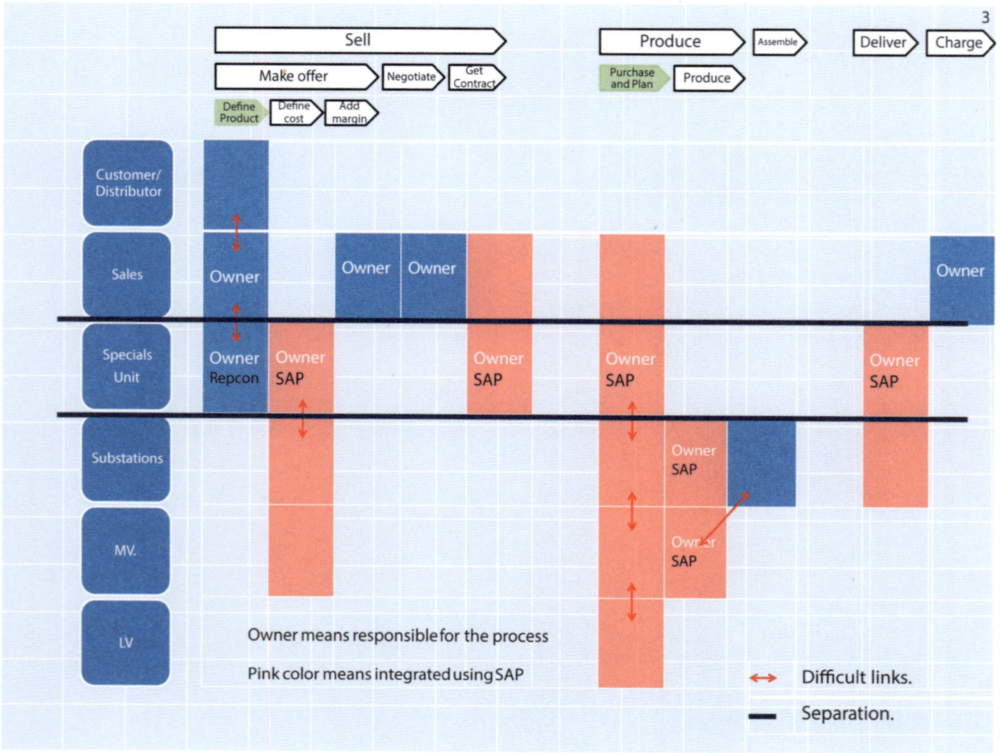

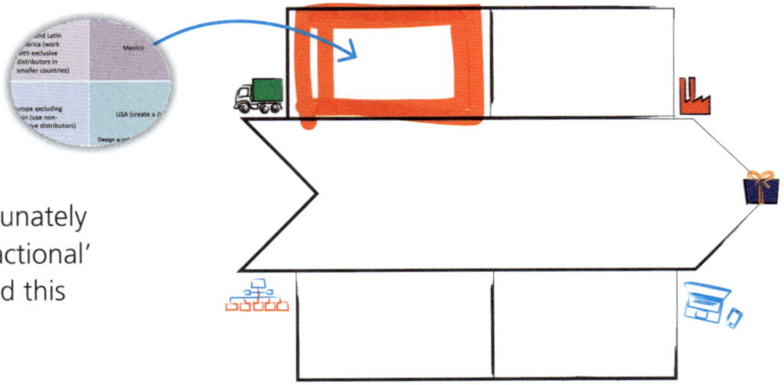

Supplier matrix

Most organizations depend on suppliers for raw materials and many other inputs. Fortunately established markets exist for many of these supplies, making it possible to have 'transactional' relationships with most suppliers. But some relationships need to be 'collaborative', and this matrix helps identify them.

The sales function of an equipment manufacturer

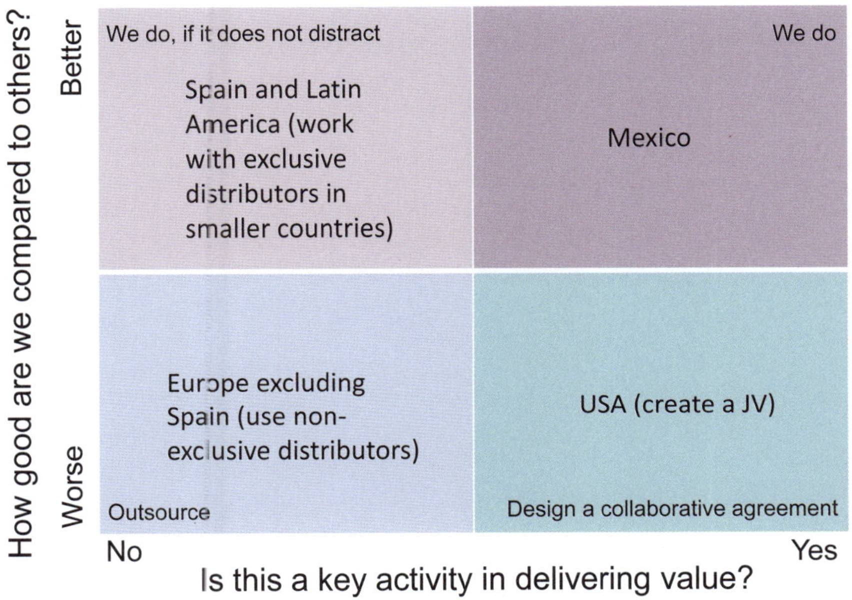

Go to www.operatingmodelcanvas.com for more on supplier matrix

A supplier matrix shows why some activities are 'outsourced' while others are done in house. It also shows which external suppliers need to be treated as business partners and which can be transactional relationships. These are high-level judgements that will guide the work at the next level of detail.

The supplier matrix can be used to think through the supplier relationships for a whole organization; or for a function, such as the sales function displayed on the previous page; or for a particular transaction, such as those on this page.

For example, a company wanting some bespoke software to help it configure special products decided that the software would be a source of advantage and did not want the developers to create the same solution for the company's competitors. As a result it created a collaborative agreement which restricted the developer from serving competitors while involving the developer in the success of the initiative.

The other example concerns a company looking for help with its branding strategy. Should the relationship be a collaboration with restraints and benefits or just a simple payment for services?

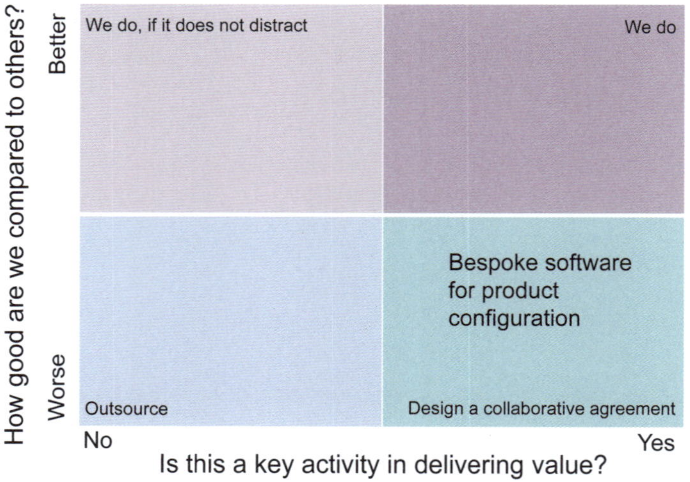

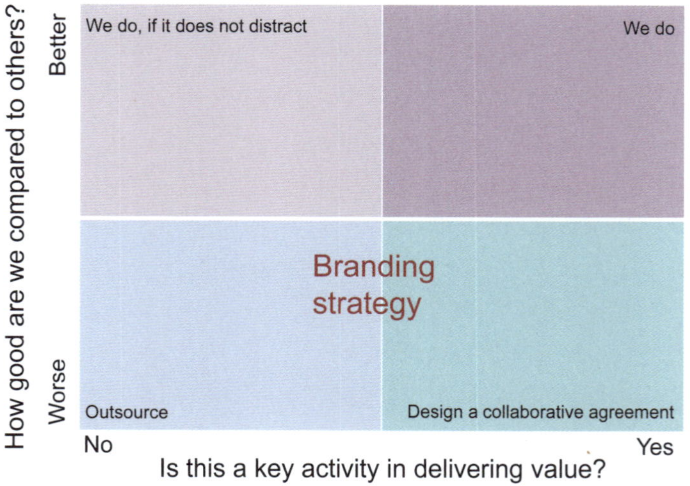

Thirteen additional tools

The following thirteen maps and charts are useful in many operating model projects.

- **A stakeholder map** helps define the boundaries of the organization that is being designed. It also helps in creating a transformation plan
- **A capability map** is a way of framing what an organization does, often used by enterprise and business architects
- **A people model** helps to put people issues on the table, particularly helpful when creating new capabilities
- **A decision grid** clarifies how the important decisions will be made
- **A process owner grid** shows how the core processes in the organization are governed
- **A management calendar** shows the rhythm of management meetings and processes needed to keep the organization on track
- **A scorecard** is the tool managers use to assess whether they are on track
- **A logic diagram** shows the logic of the business
- **An activity system** shows the connections between the main activities of the organization
- **A customer journey** shows what the customer does to acquire and consume the product or service
- **SIPOC** is a tool for understanding the larger system around a process
- **The Ross model** is a way of classifying organizations using integration and standardization
- **The globalisation grid** classifies organizations using integration and local adaption

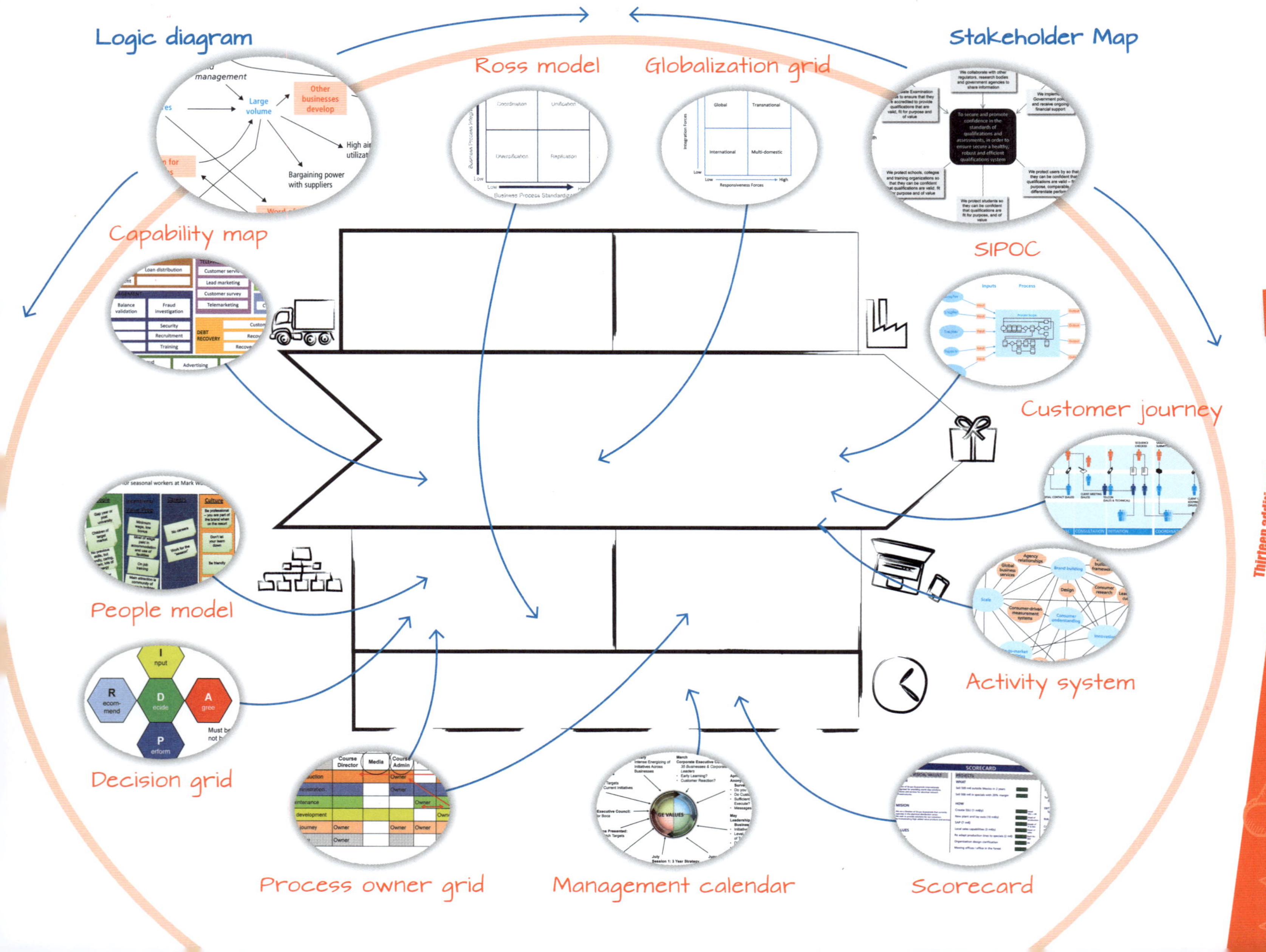
Logic diagram
Ross model
Globalization grid
Stakeholder Map
Capability map
SIPOC
Customer journey
People model
Activity system
Decision grid
Process owner grid
Management calendar
Scorecard

Stakeholder map

The stakeholder map helps define the organization for which we are developing an operating model: it helps clarify what is 'inside' the operation that is being designed and what is 'outside'. It also helps define those groups other than the organization itself that are likely to be involved in, and affected by, any changes.

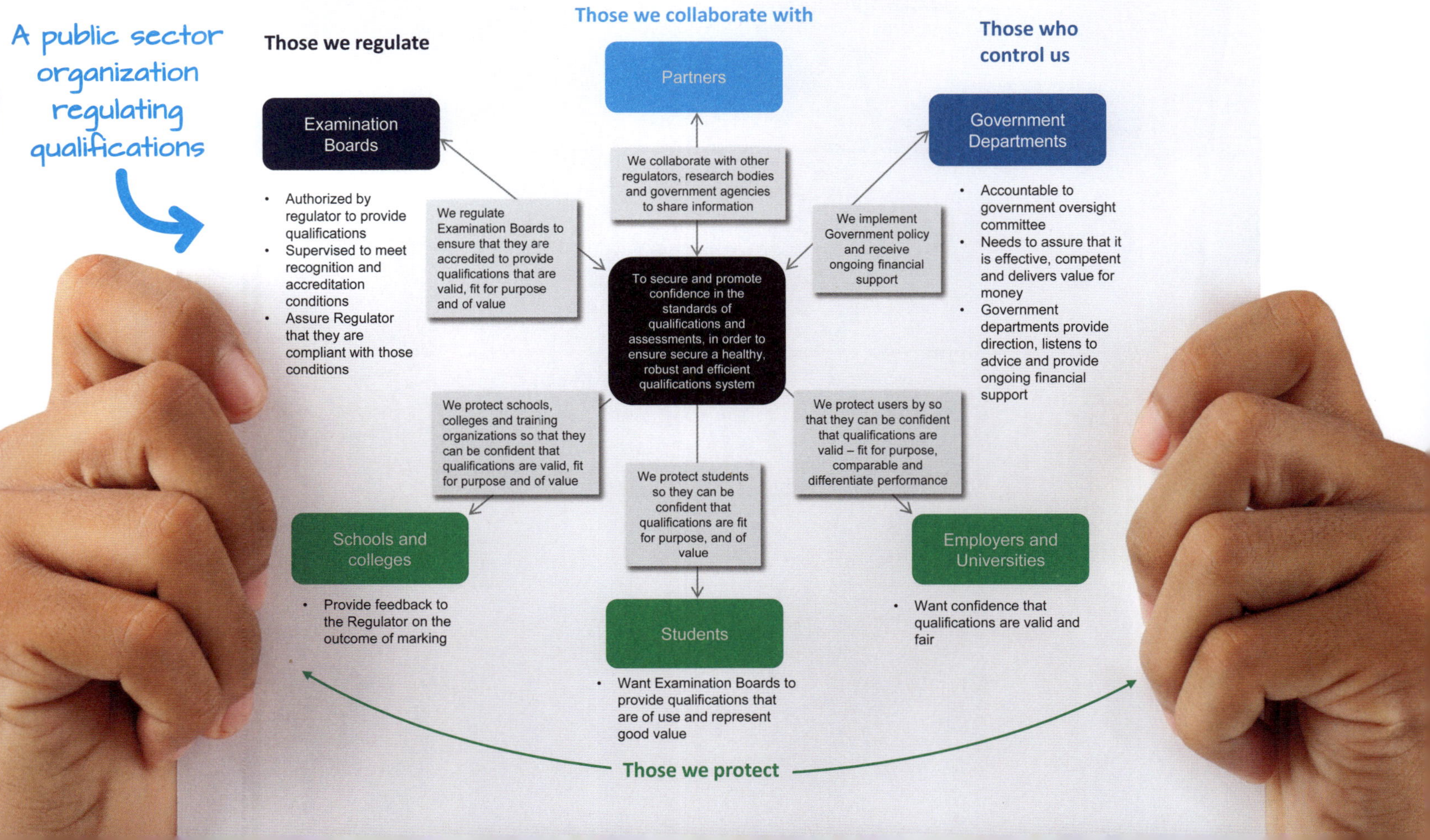

IT function in an online retailer

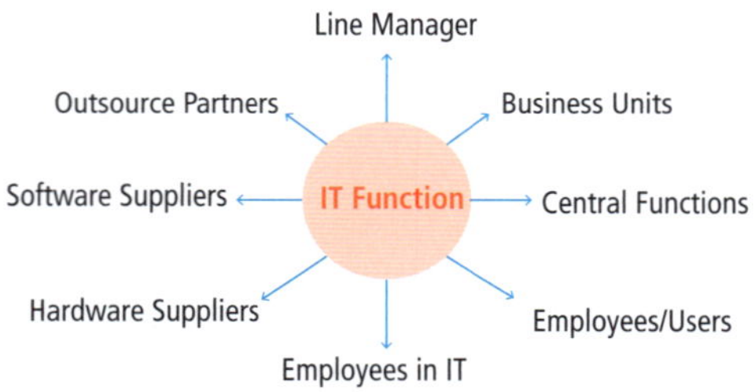

The operating model work will focus on everything that is 'inside' the central box/circle. It will also focus on the agreements and relationships with each of the stakeholders. But it will not address how the stakeholders operate. Of course changes to the operating model may well require stakeholders to change the way they operate in order to interact appropriately with the organization being redesigned. For example moving to self-service requires the customer to change his or her behaviour.

When designing an operating model for a department or unit within an organization, a good stakeholder map is a vital part of defining the scope of the project.

Go to www.operatingmodelcanvas.com for more on stakeholder map

Provider of own label products to supermarkets

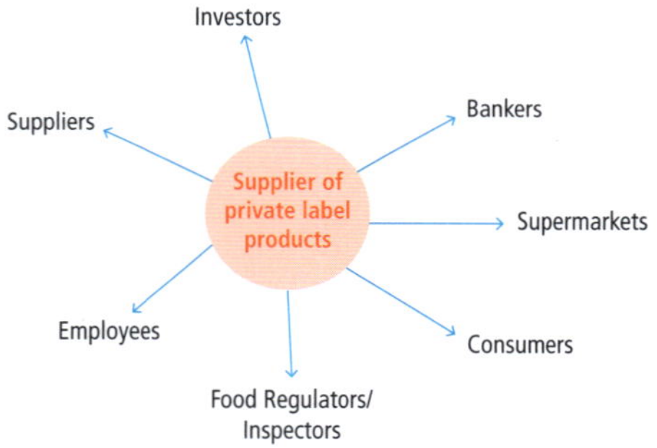

There are no special rules for generating stakeholder maps.

It is normally helpful to start by identifying the most important stakeholders and those most likely to be affected by the operating model work.

Simple questions help to identify all the relevant stakeholders:

1. Who are the customers or beneficiaries?
2. Who provides supplies or inputs?
3. Who works in/for the organization?
4. Who owns or controls the organization?
5. Who has an interest in the success of the organization?

For each stakeholder group, it is helpful to consider the value the stakeholder is getting from the organization and the value the stakeholder is contributing.

People model

The people model describes, for each important skill group, the type of people needed, the incentives needed to attract and motivate these people, the career paths or recruitment strategies needed to ensure there is a flow of people available and, the culture needed to attract and guide these people.

Seasonal workers at Mark Warner

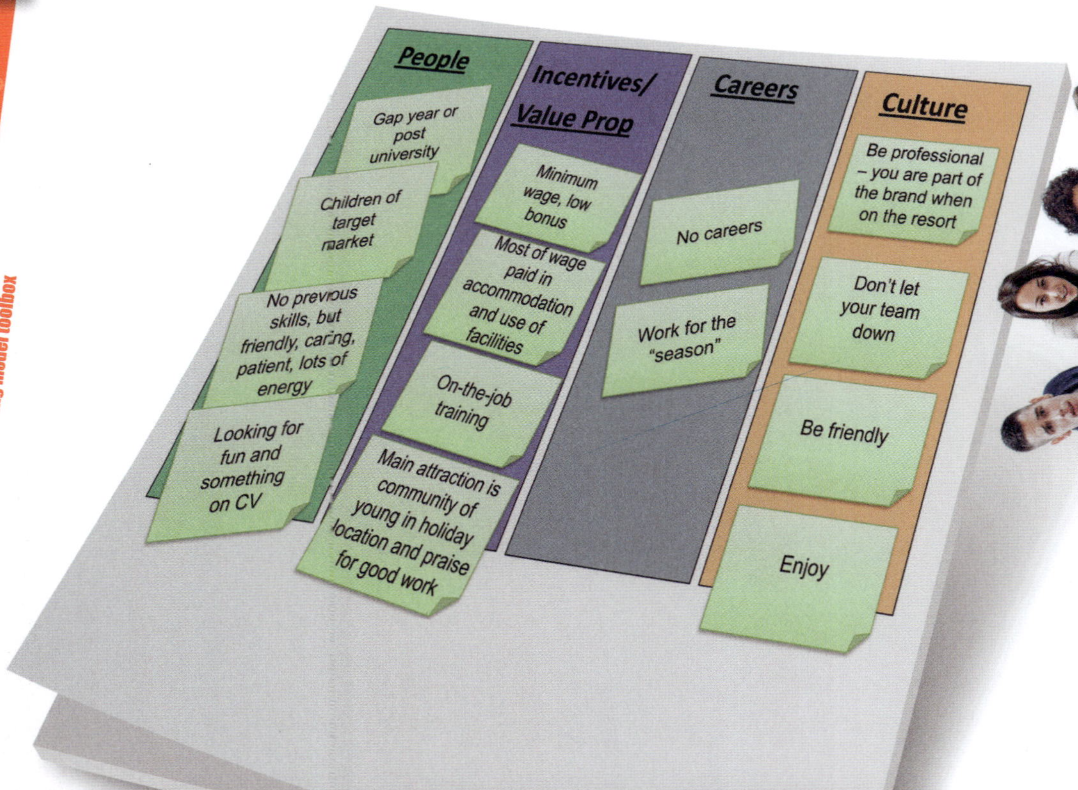

The Mark Warner people model is interesting because it is unusual. Mark Warner is a holiday company aimed at middle class families. The company runs ski chalets and summer camps in Europe.

The people model shown on the previous page is for their seasonal staff. The company recruits young people often with no previous service experience. These young people, particularly in Britain, take a gap year before or after university. The company pays a small amount of weekly cash (little more than pocket money), and, to meet minimum wage laws, the rest is paid in accommodation, food and use of facilities. Employees are contracted for a season, and get free flights out to the resort and back (unless they do not complete their contract).

Training is on-the-job. There is no career opportunity because most employees are going back into education.

The main attraction is the holiday location, the opportunity to use facilities during breaks and on days off, and the community of young people of similar ages.

Go to www.operatingmodelcanvas.com for more on people model

People model: categories to consider

People	Incentives/ Value Prop	Careers	Culture
Contract	Mission	Pre-role	Behavior standards
Location	Freedom	....	....
Education	Training	....	....
Skill	Career	In-role	....
Career	Pay	....	
Stage	Bonus	....	
Personality	Benefits	Post-role	
Motivation	....	....	
....		....	

Each people model is likely to be unique, as the Mark Warner example shows. The chart above lists some categories to consider when designing or analysing a people model. The chart below shows the analysis of Mark Warner's people model

People model for seasonal workers at Mark Warner

People	Incentives/ Value Prop	Careers	Culture
Contract: *Short term*	Mission: *No*	Pre-role: *In education*	Behavior standards
Location: *Anywhere*	Freedom: *Low*	In-role: *None*	*Don't let the team down*
Education: *University potential*	Training: *On job*	Post-role: *In education or career*	*Be friendly*
Skill: *None*	Career: *No*		*Enjoy*
Career: *No*	Pay: *Low*		
Stage: *Gap year*	Bonus: *Low*		
Personality: *Friendly*	Benefits: *Use of facilities, other young people*		
Motivation: *Fun*	....		
....			

Decision grid

A decision grid is a way of showing the role of each senior position with regard to the important decisions. A list of decisions is placed on the vertical axis and the organizational positions (from the organization chart) along the horizontal axis. The boxes where the vertical and horizontal axes meet are populated with letters, symbolizing the role played by that position with regard to a particular decision.

Consumer goods company with business units

Decisions	CEO	HR	Mkg	Finance	BU MD	BU Sales
Sales targets					D	R/P
Pricing for new customer			D		A	R/P
Marketing budget			R/P	D	A	I
Product features			D			I
Salary structure		D/P		A		
BU team appointments	A	I		I	D/P	
Stock levels in warehouse			I	A	A	I
etc						

Go to www.operatingmodelcanvas.com for more on decision grids

Our preferred choice of letters is **RAPID**, standing for **Recommend, Agree, Perform, Input and Decide**. What is important is that the '**D**' is clear, and ideally not shared: just one person should hold the '**D**' for each decision. It is also helpful if there are few '**A**'s; and, when used, '**A**' is only for legal or governance controls. '**P**' is for those who will have to do something as a result of the decision. '**R**' is for those who are expected to have a point of view, but do not have the power to decide.

RAPID

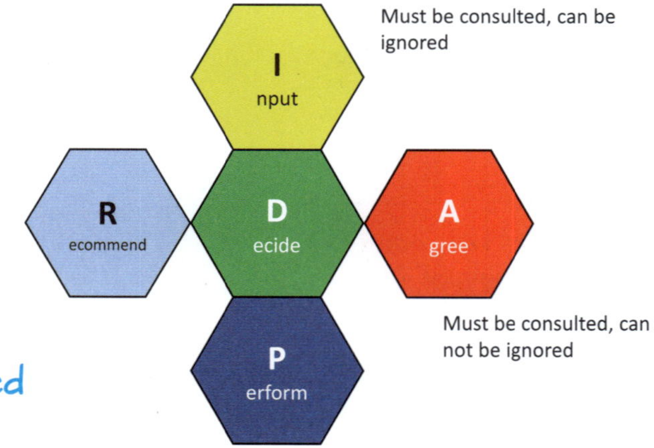

RAPID and RASCI - compared

	RAPID	RASCI
Recommends	**R**	**-**
Decides/accountable	D	A
Authorizes	**A?**	**A?**
Inputs with veto	A	A?
Inputs with no veto	**I**	**C**
Performs/executes	**P**	**R**
Support execution	**-**	**S**
Must be informed	-	I

There are other systems of lettering. **RACI** is widely used: standing for **Responsible, Accountable, Consult and Inform**. **RACSI** adds a **Support** role. It is also possible to invent your own lettering. Rupert Morrison, author of Data Driven Organization Design ('Data Driven Organization Design', Kogan Page, 2015), uses **RAS**: standing for Responsible, Approve and Support.

Process owner grid

A process owner grid is a form of decision grid. The focus is on the core operating processes. Place the main processes (from the value chain map) down the left hand side of the grid. List the organizational units, from the organization chart, along the top. For each process, use a color to show which organization units are involved. Then identify the process 'owner' or 'owners'.

Electrical equipment manufacturer

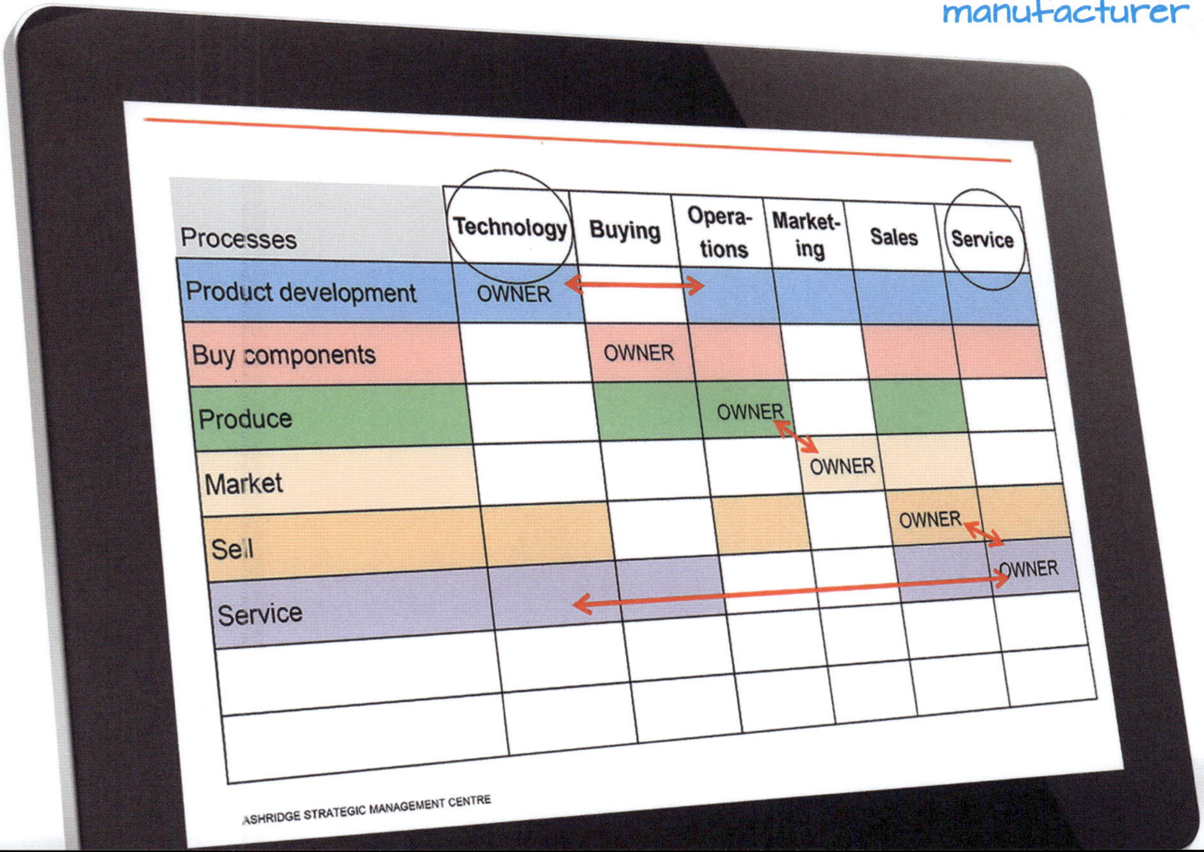

Processes	Technology	Buying	Opera-tions	Market-ing	Sales	Service
Product development	OWNER					
Buy components		OWNER				
Produce			OWNER			
Market				OWNER		
Sell					OWNER	
Service						OWNER

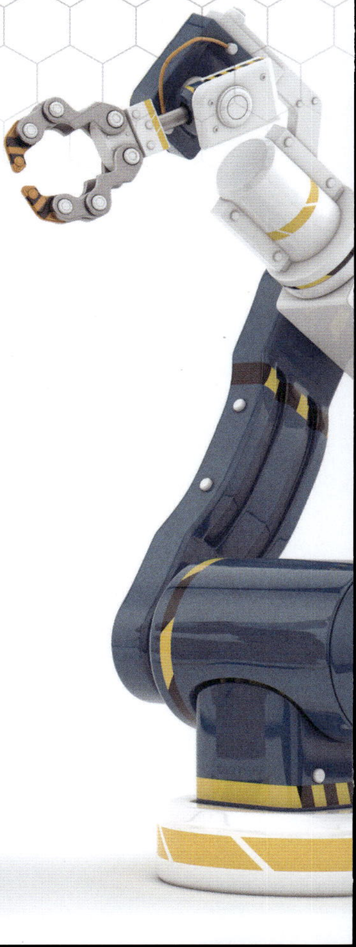

What needs to be made clear in a high-level design is who is responsible for making decisions about the the main cross-organizational processes. In other words, who is responsible for ensuring the process is fit for purpose and for initiating changes when needed. This person, or persons, will also be responsible for doing more detailed design work for this process. So the process owner grid defines responsibility for the next level of design for those processes that cross organization unit boundaries.

Processes for running courses

Processes	Course Director	Media	Course Admin	House	Faculty
Workbook production			Owner		
Course administration			Owner		
Room maintenance				Owner	
Materials development					Owner
Participant journey	Owner		Owner	Owner	
Course delivery	Owner				

Once the grid has been colored to show which organizational units are involved in each process, there are two options regarding process ownership:

1. The process is either 'owned' by one of the units involved or;
2. The process is broken down into sub-processes with different units owning each sub-process.

The second option is the easiest from a political point of view; each unit can be responsible for the part of the process that it is involved in. But this is only the best choice if the sub-processes can be connected by 'simple' hand-offs. A 'simple' hand-off is one where the 'receiving' unit can specify what it needs from the 'delivering' unit, and measure whether it gets what it needs. This is rare. Normally hand-offs are complex requiring interaction between units to achieve the best result.

There are two further uses of this grid: to highlight 'difficult links' and to highlight 'specialist cultures'.

Difficult links exist where two or more units involved in a process will find it difficult to work well together. This happens when the units have conflicting objectives, like manufacturing looking to achieve low cost and marketing aiming for tailored solutions. Difficult links can also happen for other reasons, such as when the managers do not get on. Mark the chart with a **red arrow**, for each 'difficult link'.

Specialist cultures often need to exist to support specialist skills. If a unit needs to have a culture different from other units involved in the process, circle the unit to show that it needs some 'protection' from other units.

Go to www.operatingmodelcanvas.com for more on process owner grids

Management calendar

The management calendar is the annual or periodic set of meetings, planning processes, targets and performance reviews that are used to set direction, make decisions and monitor progress. The calendar will include the processes for defining priorities and following through on their delivery – as for GE below. It may also include the processes of continuous improvement.

A management calendar focusing on corporate initiatives

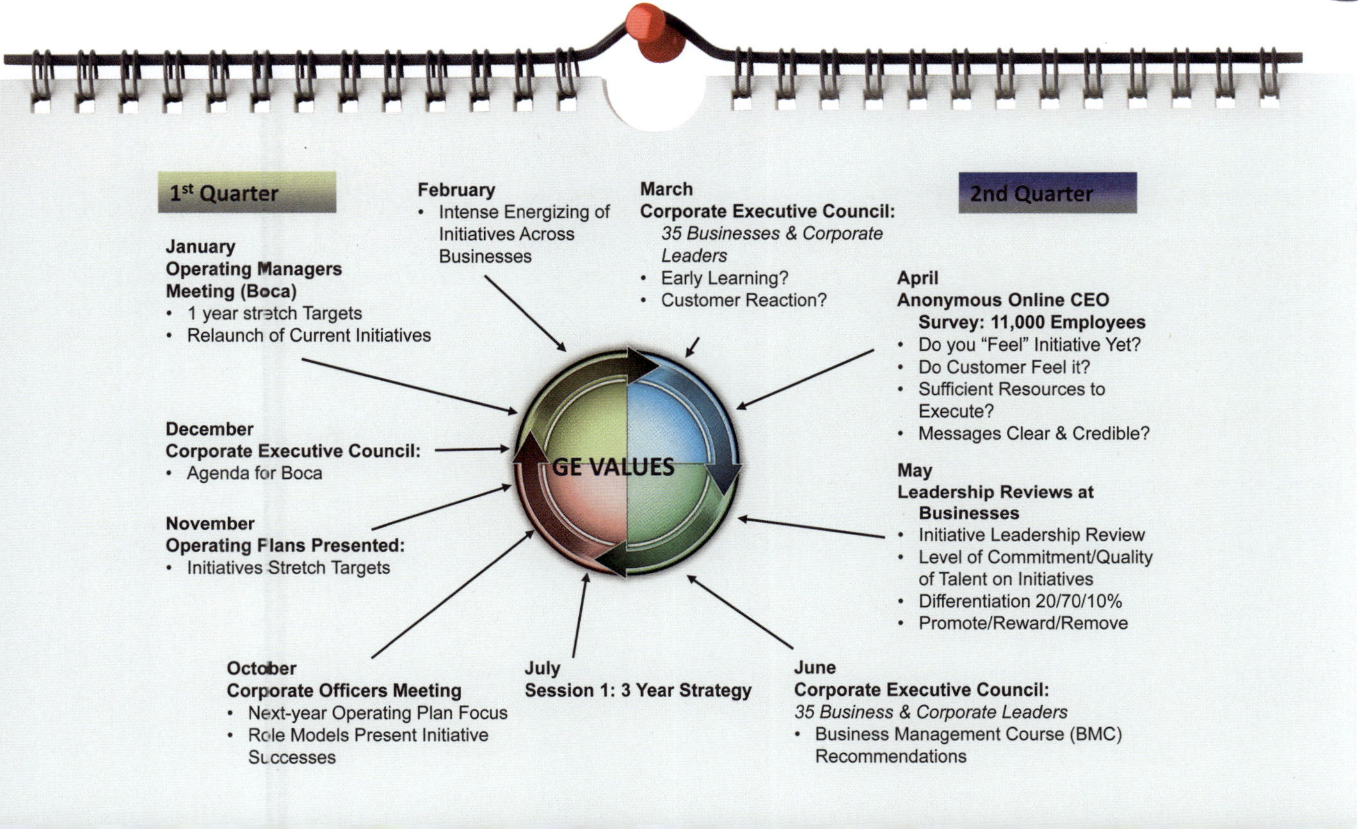

CH3

Go to www.operatingmodelcanvas.com for more on management calendar

There is no set format for visualising the management calendar.

Often the visual is a calendar presented in the form of a clock or circle. But it can also be presented as a table – looking more like a project plan (as below).

Management System	Jan	Feb	Mar	Apr	May	Jun	Jul	Aug	Sep	Oct	Nov	Dec
Board and Executive Committee	EC	EC B	EC	EC B	EC	EC B	EC		EC B	EC B	EC	EC B
Strategic Planning		—	*	—	—	—	*					
Budgets and Target Setting							*	—	—	—	*	
Performance Monitoring	P	P	P	P	P	P	P	P	P	P	P	P
People Review			—	*								
Major Project Reviews	MP	MP	MP	MP	MP	MP	MP	MP	MP	MP	MP	MP
Continuous Improvement	—	—	—	—	—	—	—	—	—	—	—	

What should be included in the management calendar?

1. The annual timetable of key meetings, such as the board and/or executive committee meetings
2. The strategy processes, both reviewing performance against strategy and developing new strategy
3. The budgeting and target-setting process, usually an annual process
4. The performance monitoring and operational guidance process, typically monthly meetings
5. The operational decision-making and alignment process, typically a monthly or weekly executive meeting
6. The continuous improvement processes, typically a central team who review operational processes
7. The people review process that assesses people, their development needs and their career paths

Scorecard

The scorecard is a part of performance management. However it is more than that. It is a summarized statement of strategy in the form of objectives. It is a tool for managing change. It is the glue that ensures all parts of the organization are working together.
The scorecard typically contains some statements of strategy, a list of the main projects and the most important KPIs.

Manufacturer of transformers

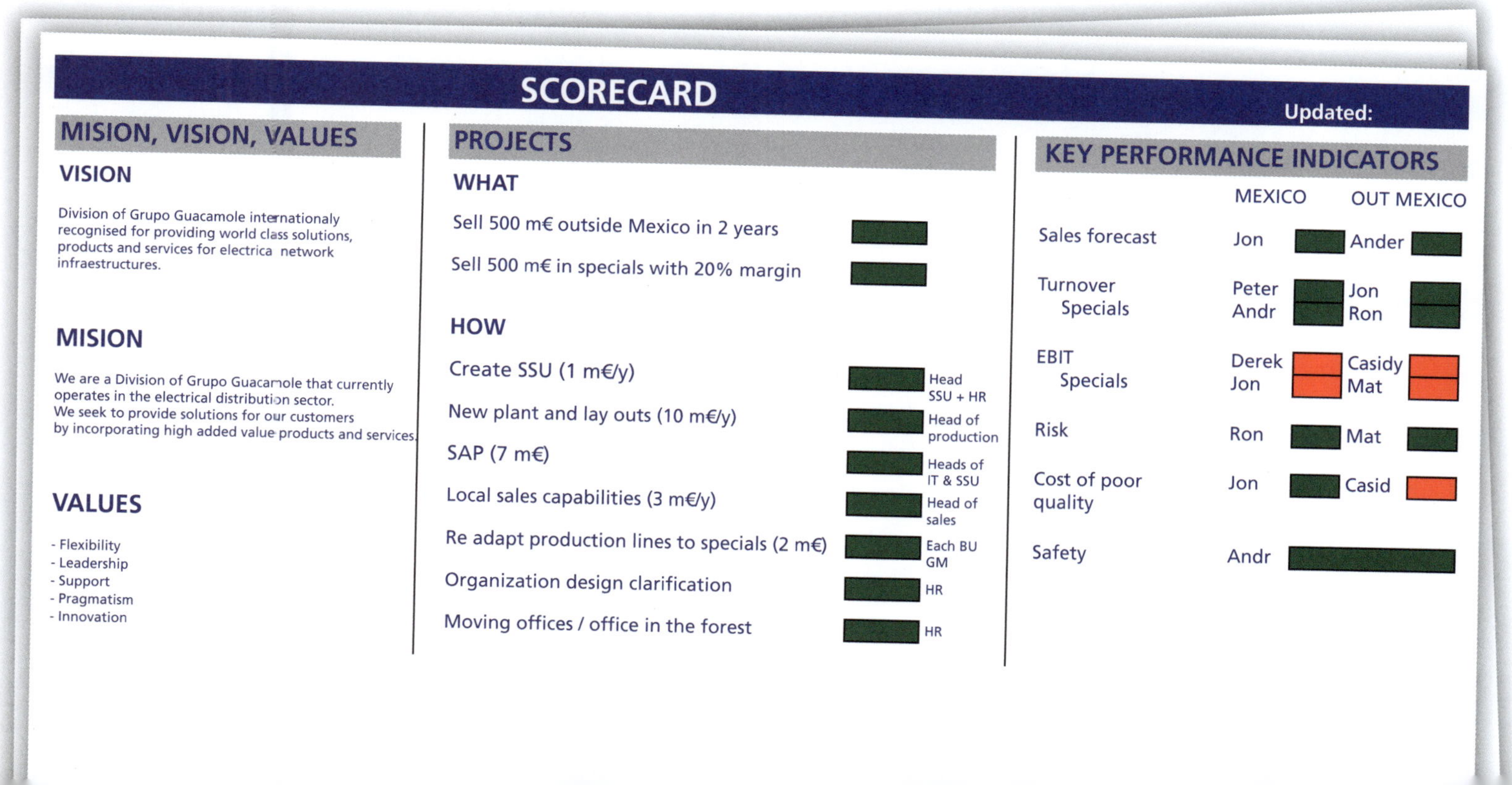

A list of the main projects or experiments. Projects transform the organization from its current state to a desired future state. Experiments confirm or challenge the strategy. Projects and experiments may be short (three months) or long (three years). The color codes can be based on quantitative as well as qualitative data.

The main KPIs that assess whether the organization is succeeding or not. Ideally KPIs should exist for each major unit in the organization, so there is some connection between KPIs and the organization model. The color codes need to be backed up by graphs of the measures.

Statements that summarize the strategy.

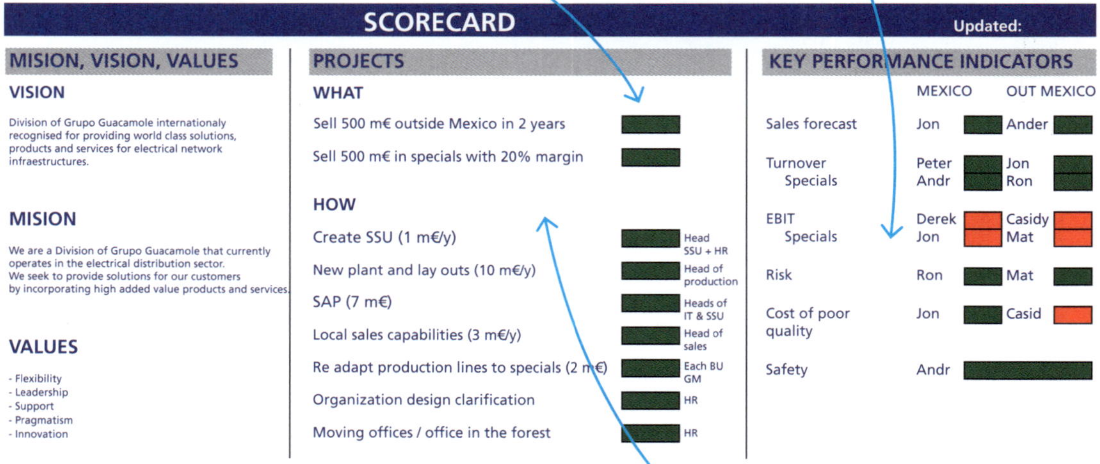

Projects separated between "What" linking to strategic objectives and "How" driven by the operating model

The balanced scorecard
Originated by Robert Kaplan and David Norton as a performance framework that added strategic non-financial performance measures to traditional financial metrics to give managers and executives a more 'balanced' view of organizational performance. While the term *balanced scorecard* was coined in the early 1990s, the roots go back to the pioneering work of General Electric in the 1950s and the work of French process engineers (who created the *Tableau de Bord* – literally, a "dashboard") in the early part of the 20th century.

More about scorecards can be found at www.operatingmodelcanvas.com

Capability map

A capability map is a common visual in the IT world. It is taught to business architects and enterprise architects (see page 130). The map represents the organization as a series of boxes, each defined in terms of the output or 'capability' of the box. There is often a distinction between support activities and the core work of the organization.

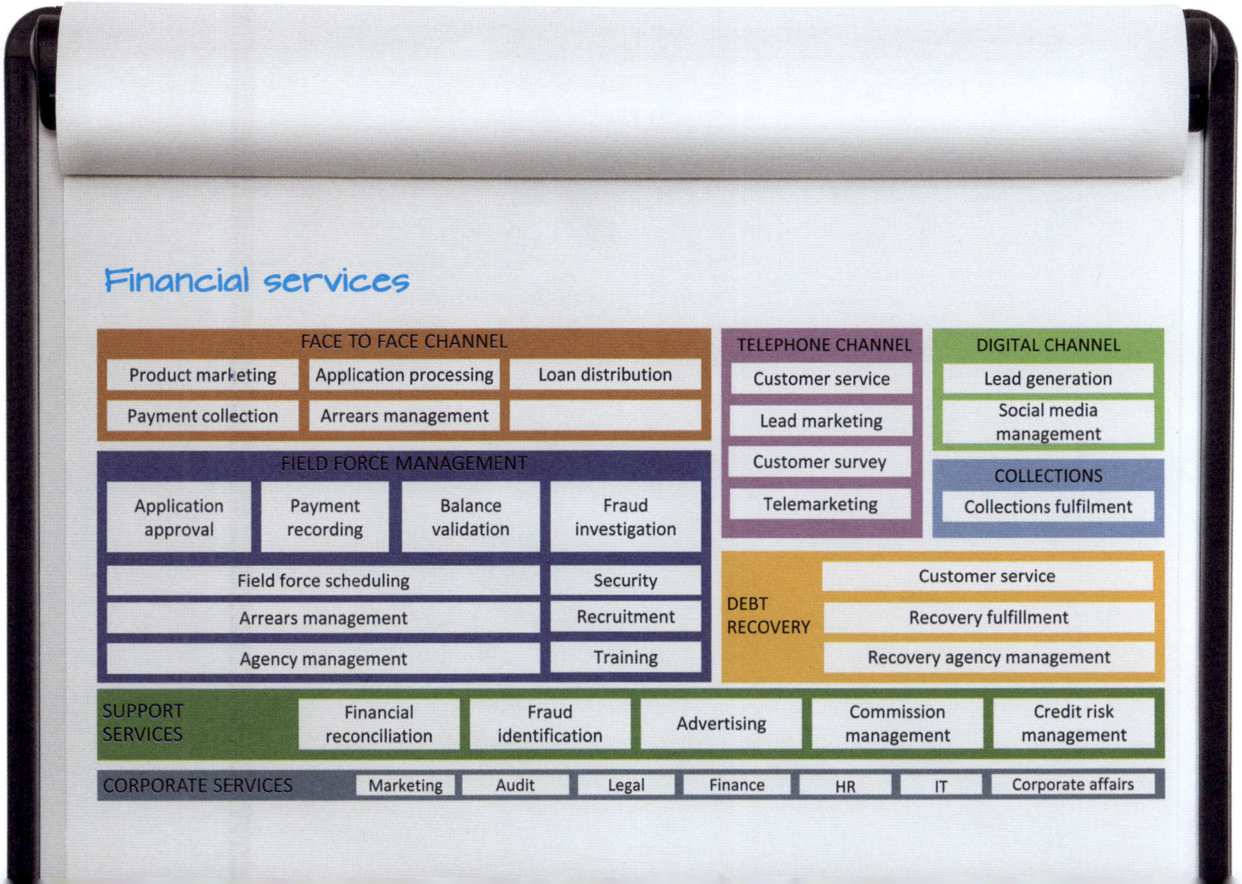

CH3

For more on capability maps versus value chain maps go to www.operatingmodelcanvas.com

Strengths

1. Capability maps include all of the activities of an organization on one page. Value chain maps focus on the core work of the organization.

2. Capability maps are structurally agnostic, making it easier to imagine combining activities in different ways.

3. Capability maps can be easily used in multiple ways:
   - → As 'heat maps' of 'maturity' or expertise/ competence
   - → As a background for understanding the IT systems that support the organization (see chart)
   - → As a background for identifying the main areas of cost or where the most people are employed

Capability map with FTE overlay

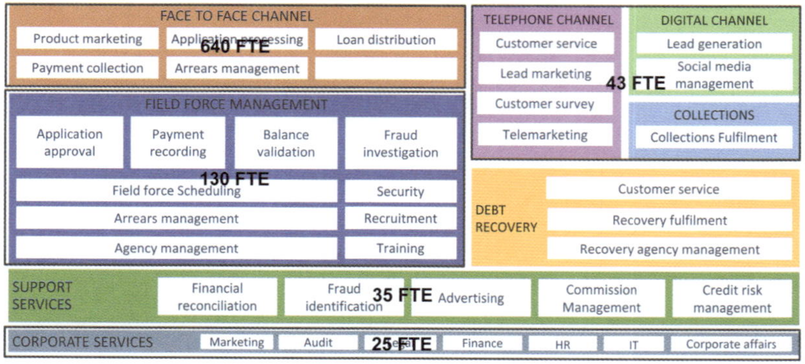

Capability map with IT overlay

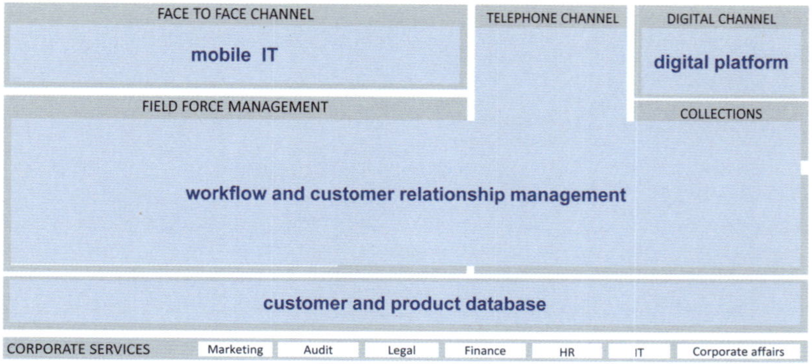

Weaknesses

1. Capability maps can distract attention from a focus on the core work of the organization because they can visually suggest that the 'governance work' and 'support work' are equally, if not more important.

2. Capability maps do not provide any guidance on the organization structure. Whereas value chain maps have direct implications for the structure.

3. Capability maps encourage decision-making about IT and other support functions without consideration of the organization structure. The sequence of a value chain map followed by the organization structure ensures that the structure of the core work is clear before any decisions about IT and other support are made.

Logic diagram

A logic diagram links the choices made in an operating model to the value proposition and to the financial model. The example below shows how the operating model of the low cost airline, Ryanair, delivers low fares through low fixed costs (FC) and low variable costs (VC).

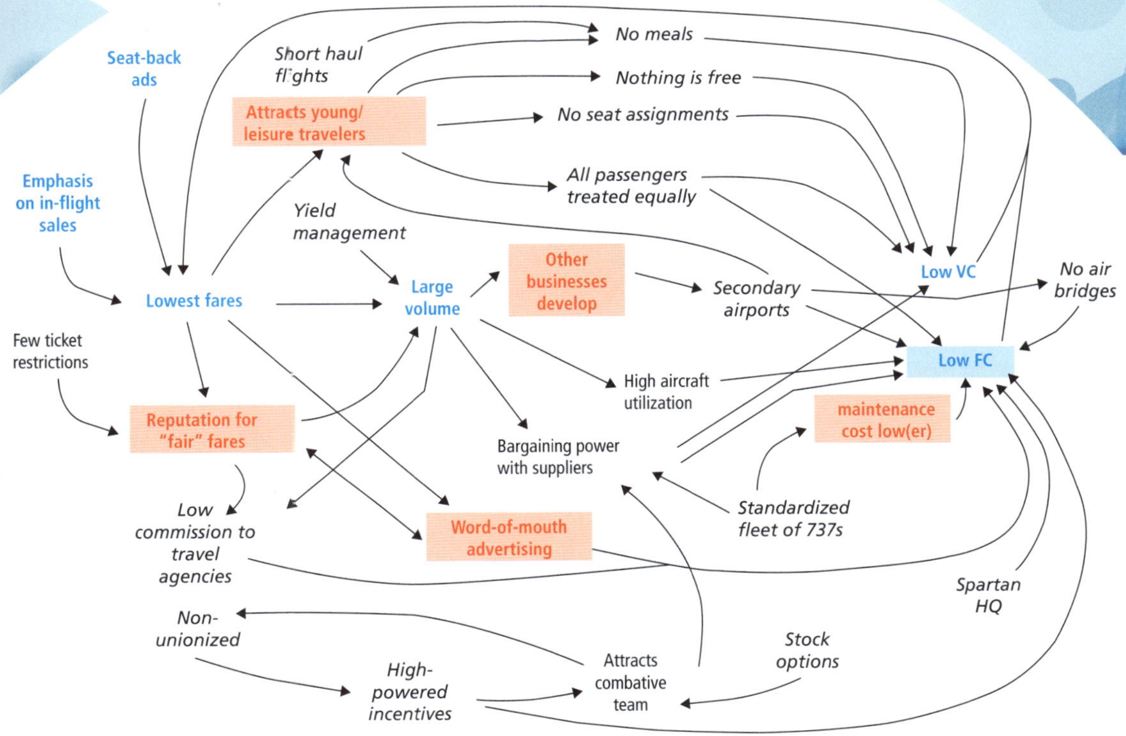

Activity System

An activity system shows how the main activities in the operating model work together to achieve objectives, such as consumer understanding or innovation. The example below shows the activity system map for Procter & Gamble. The activity 'design' connects to the objectives 'brand', 'consumer understanding' and "innovation".

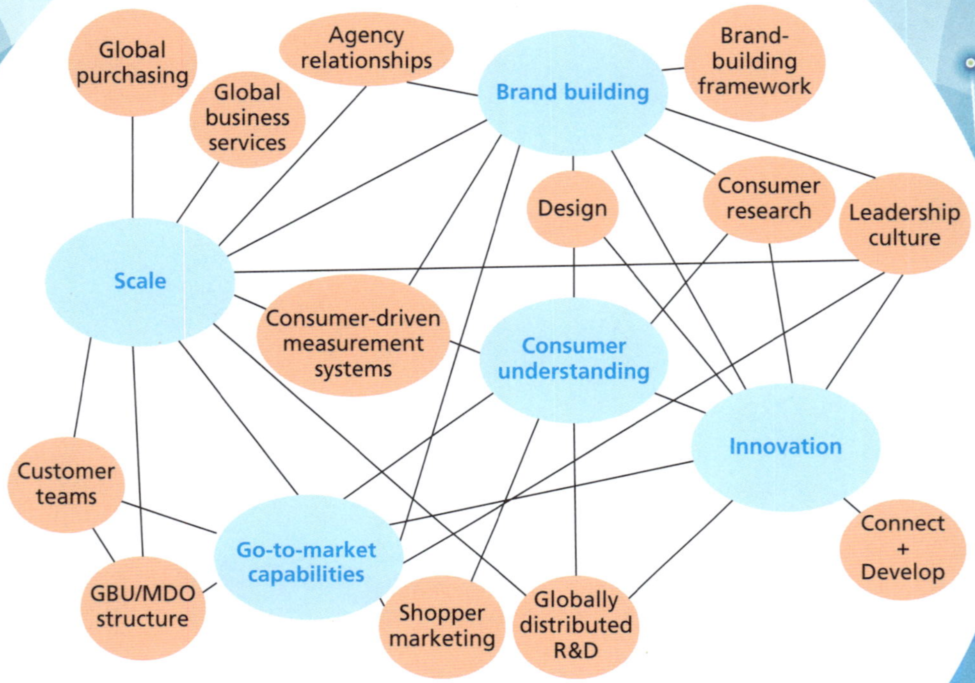

Customer journey map

A customer journey records all of the activities a customer executes in order to 'consume' something. It may start well before interacting with the supplier and continue well after the product or service has been acquired. However, the main value for operating model work is that part of the journey where the customer 'touches' the supplier.

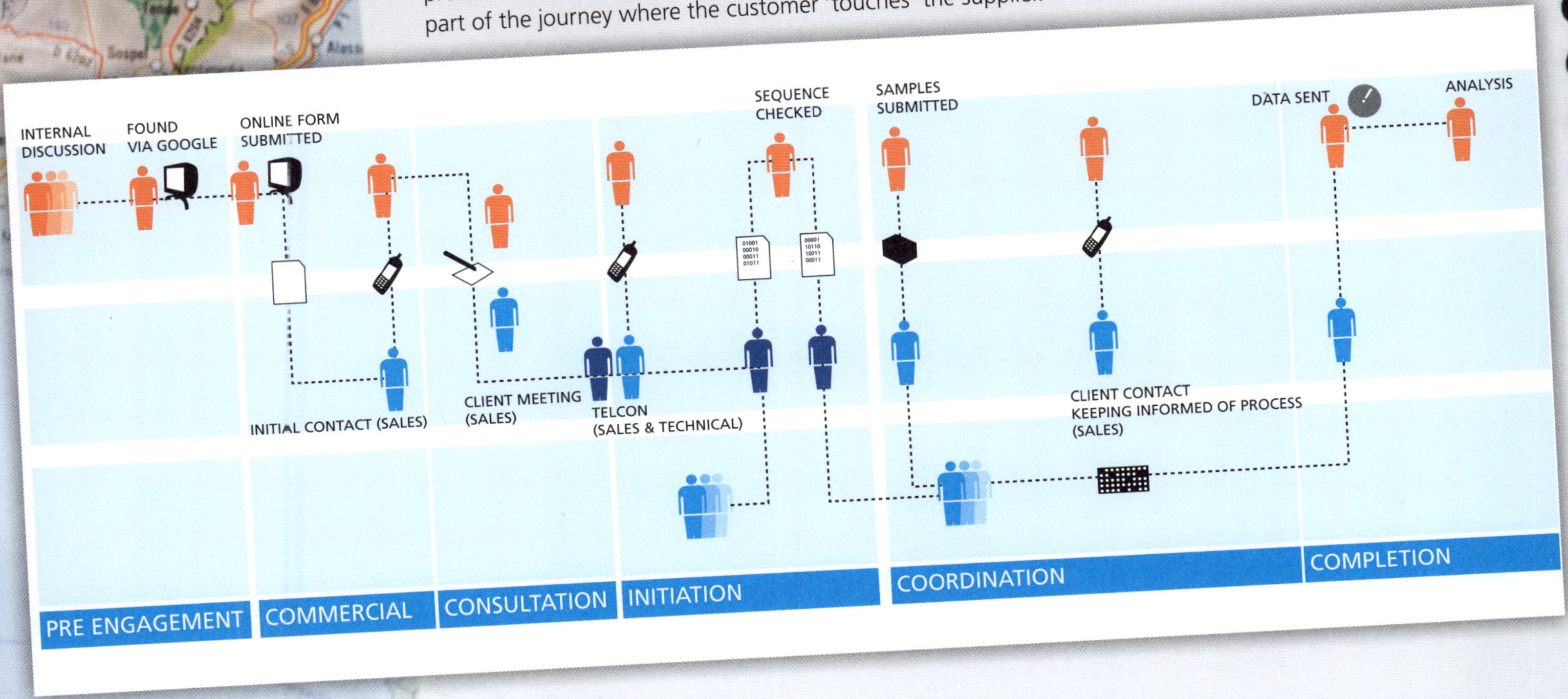

SIPOC

SIPOC is a tool for examining a productive system. It recognizes a system has inputs and that these are processed into outputs. The inputs are provided by suppliers and the outputs are consumed by, or required by, customers. A SIPOC analysis is often done prior to analyzing a process in order to understand the system that the process is part of.

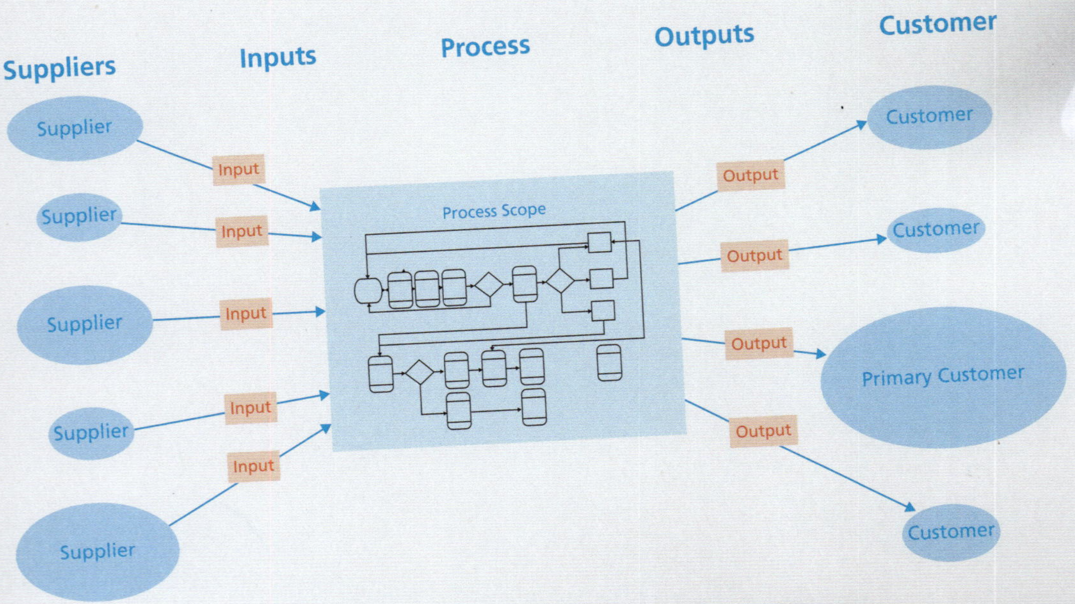

Ross model

The Ross model classifies organizations by assessing the degree of process integration and process standardization. 'Integration' means the degree to which processes in d fferent parts of the organization need to be connected to enable the easy flow of work and information from one to the next. 'Standardization' means the degree to which processes in different parts of the organization are standardized.

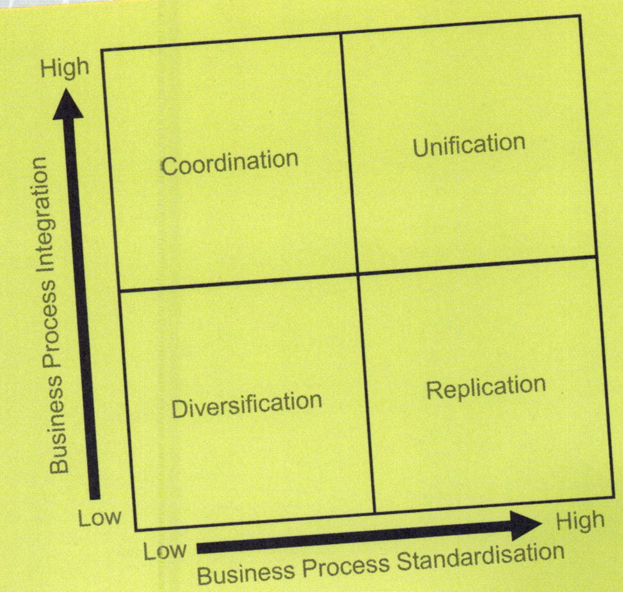

From 'Enterprise Architecture as Strategy' by Ross, Weill and, Robertson

Globalization grid

The globalization grid is a way of classifying activities and organizations by understanding the economic forces at work. How big are the forces for 'integration' meaning globalization, such as economies of scale or demand for standardization. How big are the forces for 'responsiveness' meaning local adaptation to fit with local customers or local needs? Based on these answers, judgements are then made about the degree of globalization required.

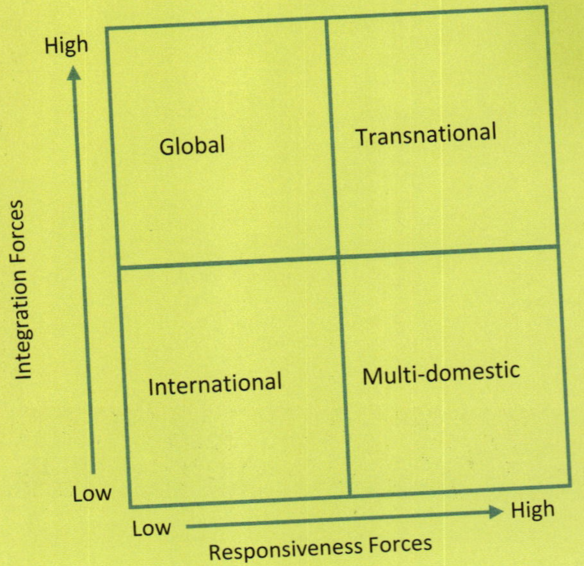

From Professor Sharm Manwani, Henley Business School, adapted from "Managing Across Borders", Bartlett & Ghoshal (1989), and "The Multinational Mission" Prahalad & Doz (1987).

Business architecture

Business architecture is a formal discipline that enables organizations to turn business strategies into effective, operational solutions. Business architecture can help to interpret, and make actionable, design ideas developed using the Operating Model Canvas. The chart below represents the architecture framework of the Business Architecture Guild®. The blue text shows selected connections between this framework and the Operating Model Canvas. For more information go to http://www.businessarchitectureguild.org.

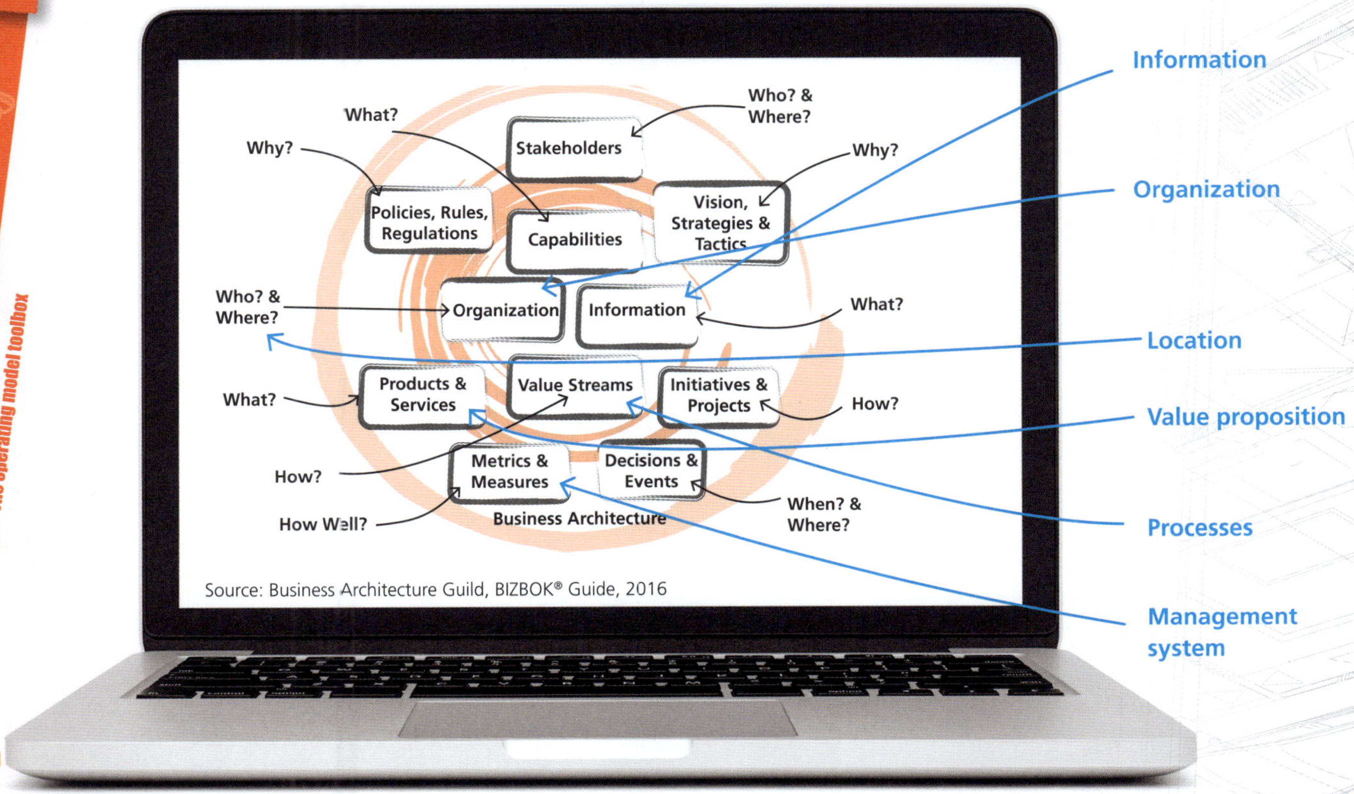

History of business architecture

Business architecture has its origins in the 1980s. It arose from IT professionals seeking to understand business requirements and business people, and consultancies working on business improvement, processes, quality and strategy execution.

Technical influences came from bodies such as IEEE Computer Society, ISACA, The Open Group and the Object Management Group. Authors of note are Marc Lankhorst, who devised the enterprise modelling language ArchiMate, Whittle and Myrick, and Ross, Weill and Robertson who worked on enterprise architecture. Other influences came from quality standards published by ISO and EPQM, and from publications on business process management, lean six sigma and soft systems thinking. Authors of note are: Peter Checkland, Womack and Jones, and Pande, Neuman and Cavanagh.

By the early 2000s the discipline began to be recognized as a specialist role and organizations started to appoint business architects to help design and document the way their businesses operated.

In 2010 the Business Architecture Guild was formed in the US and it assembled a body of knowledge - BIZBOK® - which is updated regularly and provides a valuable resource for practitioners.

Object Management Group

The Object Management Group (OMG) is a body dedicated to developing standards for the modelling of businesses. The OMG emerged to fill gaps in design methods not fully addressed previously in enterprise architecture. The OMG has developed standards for Unified Modelling Language (UML), Model Driven Architecture (MDA), Business Model Motivation (BMM), Semantics of Business Vocabulary and Rules (SBVR) and the Business Process Modelling Notation (BPMN). These help analysts to record and design processes and systems. The OMG has also developed Value Delivery Modelling Language (VDML), a standard modelling language for analysis and design of the operation of an enterprise with particular focus on the creation and exchange of value.

The Open Group and enterprise architecture

The Open Group is a consortium of companies and individuals developing standards to help the information technology community. The Open Group Architecture Framework (TOGAF) is widely used by enterprise architects to guide their design of the information and systems architecture of the organization. Enterprise architects typically work for the chief information officer (CIO). Another framework commonly used by enterprise architects is Zachman. This framework has six interrogative categories (columns): What, How, Where, Who, When, Why, and six perspectives (rows): Executive, Business Management, Architect, Engineer, Technician, and Functioning Enterprise. The perspectives represent increased levels of detail and physicality to assist different stakeholders in 'seeing' the business.

Business Architecture is just one of a range of disciplines that have toolkits that are relevant to operating model work. Other disciplines include Business Strategy, Organization Design, Organization Behavior, Operations Strategy, Lean6Sigma, and Change Management.

Assessing the operating model

Stakeholders and Processes

	YES	IN PART	NO
1. Do you have a list of stakeholders, and clarity about which are 'customers/beneficiaries' of the operating model?	○	○	○
2. Do you have an agreed 'customer' segmentation and an understanding of the 'value proposition' you are offering to each customer type?	○	○	○
3. Do you know which operating processes are most important for creating value for each customer type, and does each process have an 'owner'?	○	○	○
4. Are the most important processes advantaged/excellent?	○	○	○
5. Are the most important processes flexible enough to respond to likely changes in the environment?	○	○	○

Organization Model

	YES	IN PART	NO
6. Is the structure of operating units (value chain, units or matrix) helping deliver value to customer segments?	○	○	○
7. Do the support functions add value to the operating units with few tensions?	○	○	○
8. Does each layer in the organization structure have an added value role?	○	○	○
9. Do you have a list of the most important integration challenges in your organization (places where processes or people need to work together but are unlikely to do so without help), and have you designed solutions for these integration challenges?	○	○	○
10. Do you have a list of critical roles and critical skill groups? Do you have 'capable', 'appropriately resourced' and 'accountable' people in each role?	○	○	○
11. Do the incentives motivate the key people to give their best to the organization?	○	○	○
12. Do you have career paths or recruitment strategies that enable you to replace key people when needed?	○	○	○
13. Have you identified the values that are important to your operating model, and do you have behavior norms that symbolise each value?	○	○	○
14. Do you have a list of the most important decisions in your organization, and are the decision processes, information requirements and controls clear for each type of decision?	○	○	○

Locations, Buildings and Assets

YES IN PART NO

15. Do you have your operations in the locations and properties that are most appropriate for your strategy?
16. Do you have a list of other assets (brands, IP, key relationships, equipment, etc) that are critical to the success of your operating model; are these assets 'advantaged'; and does each asset have an asset owner?

Information and Other Links

YES IN PART NO

17. Do you have a list of the important data resources underpinning your processes and do these data resources have owners?
18. Do you have a list of the software applications used to support your important processes and does each application have an owner?
19. Do you know which applications need to be integrated into an enterprise system?

Suppliers and Business Partners

YES IN PART NO

20. Do you have a clear logic for those activities you do in-house rather than through suppliers and business partners?
21. Where you are working with business partners, do your agreements with these partners motivate them to help you succeed?

Management System: Meetings and KPIs

YES IN PART NO

22. Do you have a planning process that is designed to develop creative and practical plans and strategies?
23. Do you have a target setting process that helps managers set high ambitions?
24. Do you have a scorecard that records the most important performance dimensions?
25. Do you have a review and performance management system that has appropriate controls and motivates managers to perform and to continuously improve?
26. Do you have decision forums that make timely, well governed and well-supported decisions?

Visualisation and Communication

YES IN PART NO

27. Are all senior managers able to describe or draw the operating model?

CHAPTER

4

Creating a target ...

... or 'to be' operating model for a business

CH4

The electrical equipment industry

Transporting electricity

Our example comes from the electrical equipment industry. Electricity, at the point of domestic or normal business use, is provided at low voltages (typically 240/220/110 volts). However, for efficient distribution (i.e. low transmission losses), electricity is transported from power stations at high voltage, generally above 100,000 volts.

Linking high voltage to low voltage

To link the high voltages coming out of power stations to the low voltages going into our homes, the distribution system is operated at three different voltage levels. Bulk energy is carried long distances from power generating plants to the outskirts of industrial and residential areas at high voltage (HV). This is the **HV Transmission Network.**

Within industrial and residential areas, electricity is distributed from the outskirts to distribution points, at reduced voltages, generally 10,000, 20,000 or 30,000 volts. This is the **MV Distribution Network.**

Finally, electricity is delivered to the final users at low voltage (240/220/110 volts), via the **LV Distribution Network.**

Substations

The transitions between the three networks of the electrical system are performed in installations known as substations.
Primary substations transform the high voltage of the HV Network to the lower voltage of the MV Network
Secondary substations exist between the MV and LV Networks.

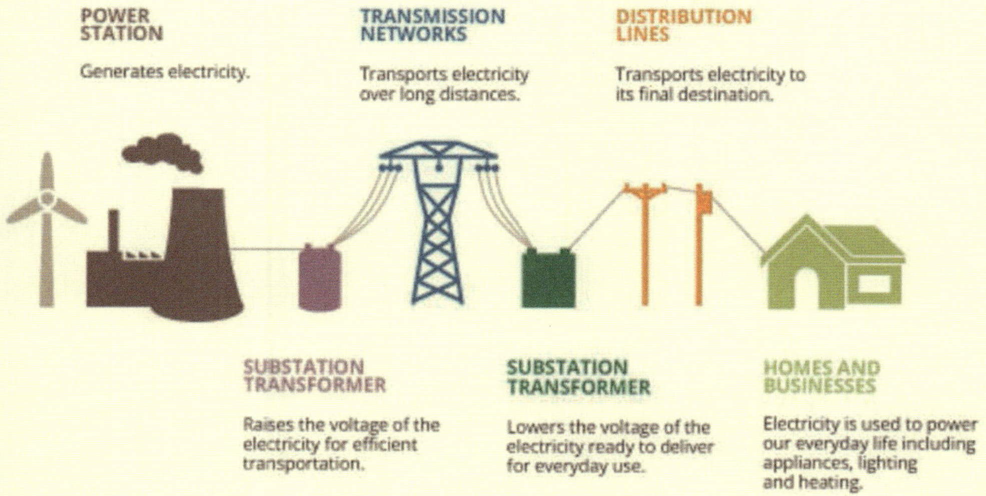

The company - Electrical Equipment International (EEI)

The main business of Electrical Equipment International (EEI) is selling **secondary substations**. The substations perform not only the basic task of transforming the voltage from MV to LV, but also the more complex task of protecting, operating and controlling the distribution system. In addition to the transformer equipment, a substation contains several types of switchgear together with some sophisticated electronics for measuring, monitoring and controlling the devices and circuits. EEI produces transformers, switchgear and electronics – most of the components that go into a substation. The company, founded in Mexico in 1942, also produces the concrete or metal buildings that house all the equipment. These buildings, with all the equipment inside, make up most of the sales. But the company also sells components, such as transformers and switchgear.

This family company has been successful because of the strength of its technology, because of its efficient manufacturing process, because it sells substations as a turn-key product and because of good relationships with its main customers in the Mexican market. In the last few years, the company has expanded in a small way into other countries. Further international expansion is planned.

The substations can be 'standard' or 'special'. **Standard substations** involve a standard building design filled with standard components.

Special substations can be standard buildings filled with a special selection of components and specially designed electronics. They can also require special buildings to suit customer needs or to house the special selection of components.

Secondary substation

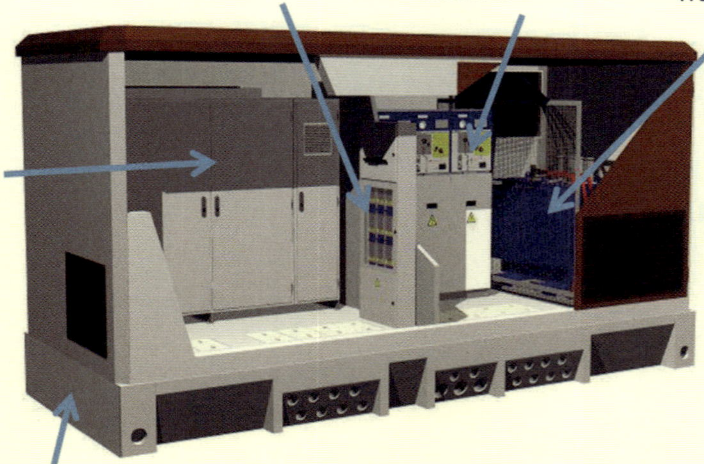

EEI strategy

Strategy Challenges

EEI had grown due to the high growth of the local market in Mexico and the company's technical advantages. However, the company now faced some challenges:

- The main location had become overloaded. So some activities had to be undertaken in other locations, which added to the complexity and transport costs.
- Competitors had begun to copy EEI's efficient production process, which was leading to reduced margins on standard products, threatening profitability.
- The margins on special products were much higher. But the production of specials was highly disruptive to the efficiency of standard production, raising costs and further reducing margins on standard products.
- Typical sales teams were capable of selling standard products but did not have enough product knowledge to convert special customer requirements into quotations for special products. Only a very few people were capable of selling and preparing quotes for special products and there was no software supporting this activity so all special quotes were done manually.
- Growth in the Mexican market was beginning to slow and there were significant growth opportunities in the US, South American and in European markets.

The strategic objectives

The company had defined three priorities:

- Maintain leadership in the Mexican market;
- Increase sales outside Mexico;
- Increase sales and profits from special products.

EEI's challenges

The CEO recognized that he needed to make some significant changes to his operations and organization to successfully execute the strategy. He identified the following issues:

Organization

While he had a growing international sales force, managers responsible for technology and production did not feel strongly motivated to support international sales. Sales in the Mexican market were still good. This meant that they were reluctant to devote time and capacity to support international sales.

There were few people in the organization with the capability to interact with customers in order to understand their need for special products, assess delivery challenges and negotiate contracts. Even the few who had some or all of these skills were spread out in different functions and locations.

There was only one profit and loss statement for the whole company, making it hard to judge accurately the profitability of different product lines, different countries, or between standard products and special products.

Selling specials

Most of the sales people could help customers choose between standard products but did not know how to respond to special requirements. They were used to selling to the customer's purchasing team. To sell special products, sales people needed to sell to the customer's engineering function.

When working on the sale of a special product, it was difficult to get cost estimates from the production units and even harder to get commitments for delivery dates. This was partly because the production department often delayed the production of specials in order to complete their standard product runs. But it was also because of the need to coordinate different special components and special buildings to be ready at the same time. International sales posed additional problems. In new countries, it was more cost effective to use distributors rather than own sales teams, at least until sale volumes reached a threshold. But many distributors did not have the skills to sell specials.

Producing specials

The first and last steps of the production process were similar for both standard products and for special products. But the central steps were different. The complexity this was creating in the factories was raising costs, even for standard products.

IT for specials

For legacy reasons, the sales function and each product line had different IT systems. This was not a problem for standard products that were built for stock. But it was a huge problem for specials. Each special component needed its own product code. But none of the systems were flexible enough to generate a separate code for each customer order. As a result, much work was being done manually. Also, the company did not have a software application, that could support the product design and specification process for specials.

Buildings

The existing buildings did not have enough space and there was an awkward combination of production, offices and technology in the same space. The offices, in particular, were over-crowded.

The technical laboratory needed some more suitable space that would help attract and retain top scientists and technicians.

EEI's design principles

Design principles are the guiding thoughts for the design effort. They set boundaries on the new design, defining what the new design must be able to achieve and what constraints it must live within.

They are derived from a number of sources:

- The strategic objectives of the organization;
- The problems/challenges the organization is trying to address;
- The strengths that the organization wants to retain;
- Constraints imposed by stakeholders.

EEI has three strategic objectives:

- Maintain leadership in Mexico;
- Sell outside Mexico;
- Sell special products.

The main problems EEI is trying to solve are:

- To build capabilities in specials;
- To reduce the disruption caused by specials in the factories;
- To increase profit accountability and empowerment.

The strengths EEI wants to retain are:

- Product development;
- Cost advantage;
- Mexican market position.

There do not seem to be any stakeholder constraints other than normal legal limits.

Based on these inputs, EEI produced these design principles:

EEI'S DESIGN PRINCIPLES

- **MAINTAIN LEADERSHIP IN MEXICO**
  - Produce specials without disturbing production of standards
- **SELL OUTSIDE MEXICO**
  - Develop an international sales force
- **SELL SPECIAL PRODUCTS**
  - Ensure the translation of customer needs into a special product
  - 'Connect' IT so that specials can be planned and produced
- **MAKING SURE THAT**
  - The management team is empowered
  - The use of design engineers is optimized

A tool for design principles

How to create good principles

It is hard to create good design principles. So here are four guiding thoughts:

1. Focus on the top five or so. These will be your guiding lights, so it is worth spending extra time on them.
2. Ask why you have this principle. How does it link with your strategic objectives?
3. Make sure each principle represents a real design dilemma: the opposite which, you have rejected, must be a realistic possibility.
4. Make sure the choice you have made has design implications. It must eliminate some options. It must have some implications for POLISM.

There is a way of laying out design principles that will help you focus on these four guiding thoughts (see chart).

Why design principles are important

- They help reduce political tensions
- They are the first step in the design journey because they help reduce the options
- They are the criteria against which you can evaluate options

Can design principles be challenged?

- Design principles evolve throughout the design journey
- The core thoughts, particularly the strategic logic for the principles, should not change
- If the principles do not change, it makes the political tensions easier to handle

Design principle *'the design must...'*	**Rationale** *'...in order to...'*	**Implications** *'...and may feature...'*
Produce specials without disturbing production of standards	Maintain leadership in Mexico with standard products	Either a separate factory or some way of eliminating disruption in the same factory
Develop an international sales capability	Sell outside Mexico	Either own sales or JVs or distributors in each target country
Make it possible to translate customer needs into special products	Sell specials	Some combination of capable people and IT support
Connect IT to help plan for and produce specials	Sell specials	Some integrated IT system probably an ERP system

For more information on design principles go to www.ashridgeonoperatingmodels.com

Organization 'as is'

The current organization

The organization was structured by function. This meant that most difficult decisions were escalated to the CEO. Fortunately all of the functions were in one location (except sales which was located by region in Mexico or by country). This co-location made it possible for the CEO to run a tightly integrated operation.

The main functions

- 'Develop' was responsible for developing the technology and all the products sold by the company;
- 'Product' was responsible for producing components and buildings; also responsible for Logistics, Quality and Purchasing;
- 'Sales' was responsible for Mexico and for expanding into other countries;
- 'Finance' defined the accounting policies, managed payments and collections, and funded the balance sheet. Finance also included IT;
- 'HR' focused mainly on administrative work supporting the other functions.

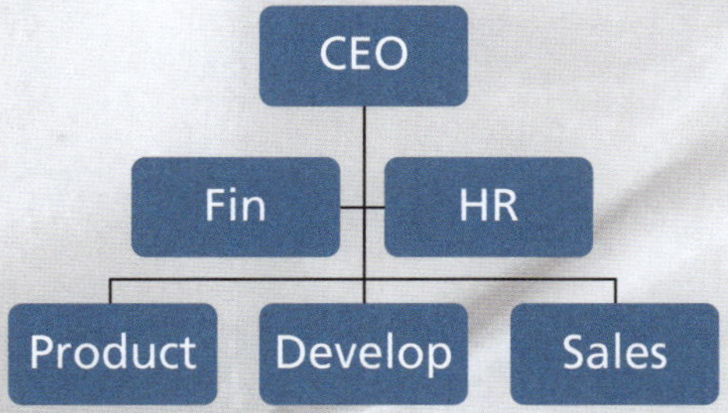

The product development function ('Develop') was historically the most important function. This had been the main focus of the founder. It had been the reason for the company's success. The next most important function was production ('Product') where the company had an important strength in efficient manufacturing. Logistics and Quality were subordinated to production. Sales had historically been the least powerful function.

The 'as is' process steps

The steps for **standard products** were: develop, produce, assemble, etc.
Problems existed in the "Produce" step because of the difficulty of mixing standards and specials. Also there were problems in the "Sell" step due to the lack of international sales staff.

The steps for **special products** were sell, produce, assemble, etc.
There was no "Develop" step for specials.
The specials had to take existing products and components, and with combinations of them or with small adjustments to the manufacturing process design a solution for the customer.

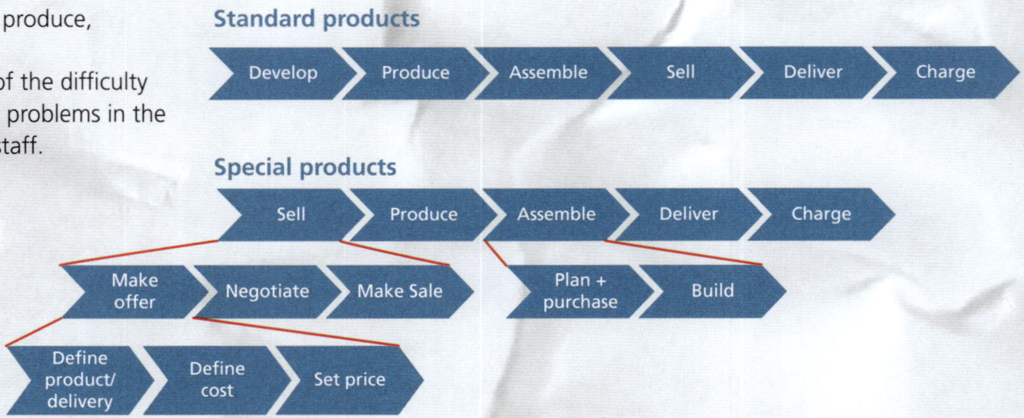

The 'Sell' step was the most difficult step because of the skills needed to define a product that would suit the customer's need, negotiate delivery dates with production and determine costs. For standard products sales people ordered from a catalog.

The source of competitive advantage for the **standard products** was in the 'Produce' step, particularly with the MV switches. It was also in the 'Assemble' step, which created fully functional substations. The company was one of very few that provided substations as a turn-key solution.

The 'Produce' and 'Assemble' steps were also difficult because of the problems caused by mixing standards and specials on the same production lines. 'Assemble' was additionally difficult because of the need to coordinate special components from different production lines. For standard assembly, components were taken from stock, but when special components were involved it was necessary to wait for them to be manufactured.

To be successful in **special products**, the company would need to develop competitive advantage in 'Define product', by being able to translate the customer need into a product; in 'Plan and purchase' by being able to send an accurate specification to all product lines, plan their plants, and track the production; in 'Produce' and 'Assemble', so that specials could take advantage of the company's low cost production without disrupting efficiency.

EEI's stakeholder map

WHEN DOING A STAKEHOLDER ANALYSIS IT IS HELPFUL TO ASSESS THE RELATIONSHIP WITH EACH STAKEHOLDER AND RECORD THE CHALLENGES WITH RESPECT TO EACH STAKEHOLDER.

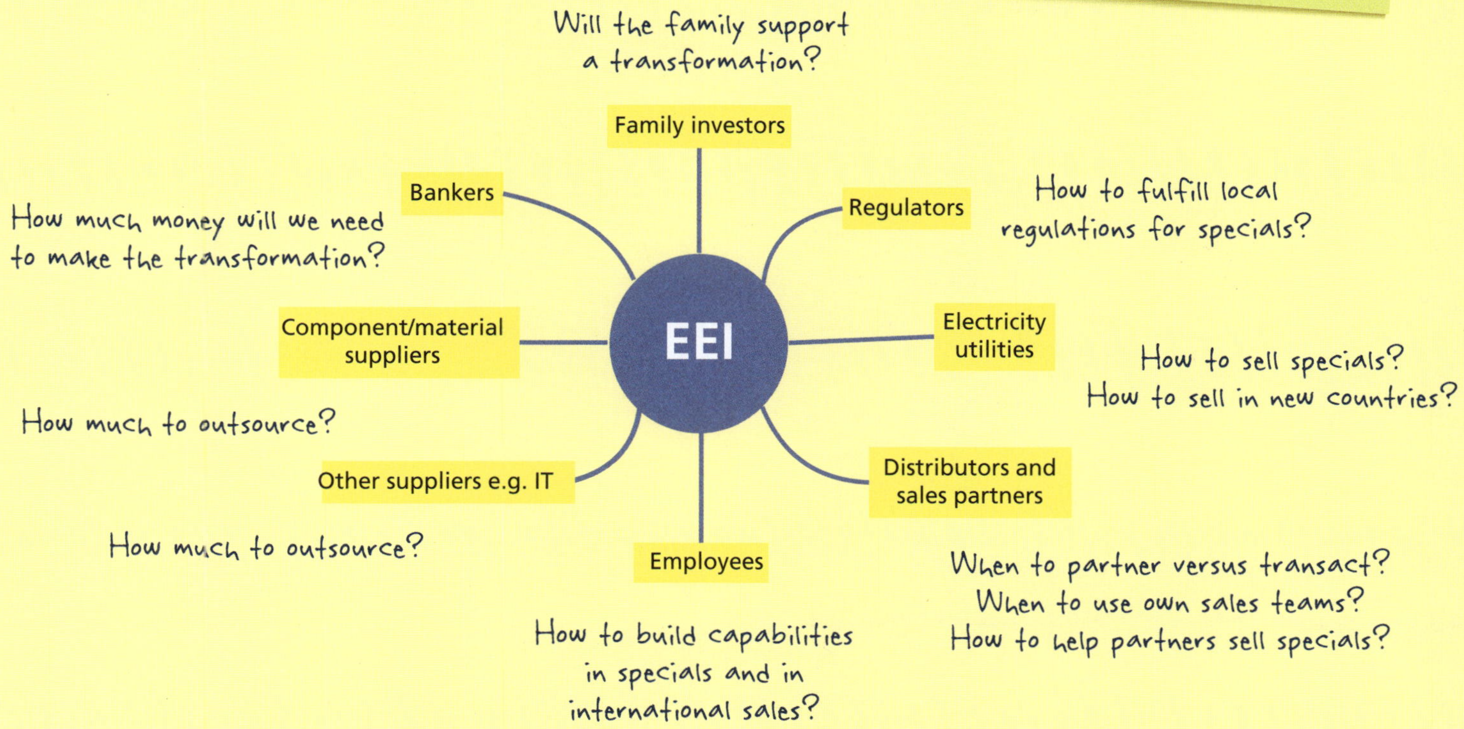

'As is' Canvas with challenges

What arrangements to have with distributors in new/growing countries? When to set up own sales team in new/growing countries?

How much to outsource?

Should there be separate business units or separate production lines in one business?

Should the structure be functional or by product or by country or a matrix?

How to utilize/develop limited skills in specials?

How to empower managers so that fewer decisions come to the CEO?

Retain one location for production?

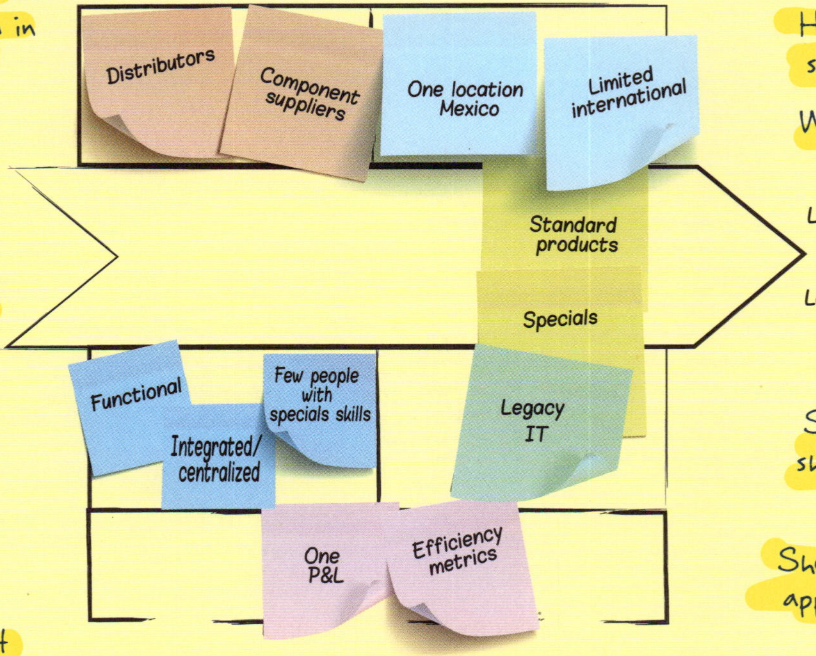

Leading technology/low cost

Leading technology/fully tailored

How to solve the space problem?

Which countries to set up in?

Should there be one shared ERP system?

Should there be a special application for specials?

How to know the profitability of specials and components?

How to balance efficiency metrics with the need to do specials?

EEI's steps for designing ...

1. Draw processes

2. Analyse processes

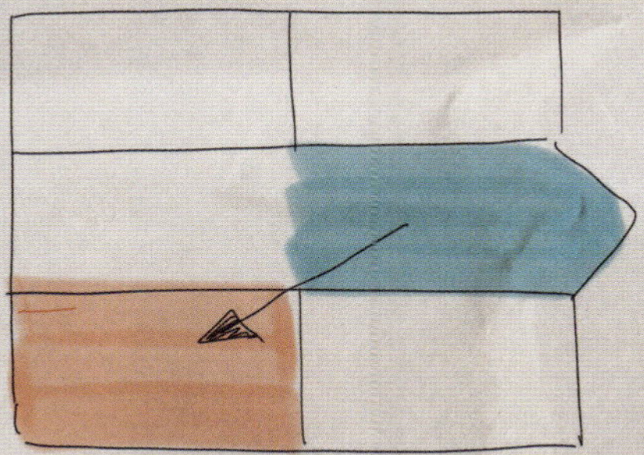

3. Organisation chart

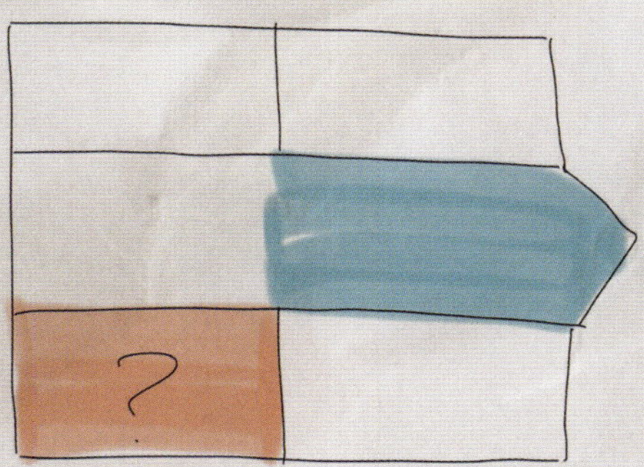

4. Org chart analysis

EEI used the Operating Model Canvas to help create a 'to be' design. The team followed these 10 steps.

Not all design projects will follow these 10 steps. Depending on the situation, there may be more or fewer steps and the steps may be in a different order. Have a look at the steps listed on page 12.

We recommend always starting with a value chain map followed by an organization model. After that, it is often helpful to follow the order of POLISM, but it is not required.

... the 'to be' operating model

IN THE PAGES THAT FOLLOW, WE WILL SHOW YOU WHAT THE EEI TEAM DID AND PROVIDE SOME COMMENTARY ON THE TOOLS USED, AS WE ALREADY HAVE ON THE TOPIC OF DESIGN PRINCIPLES.

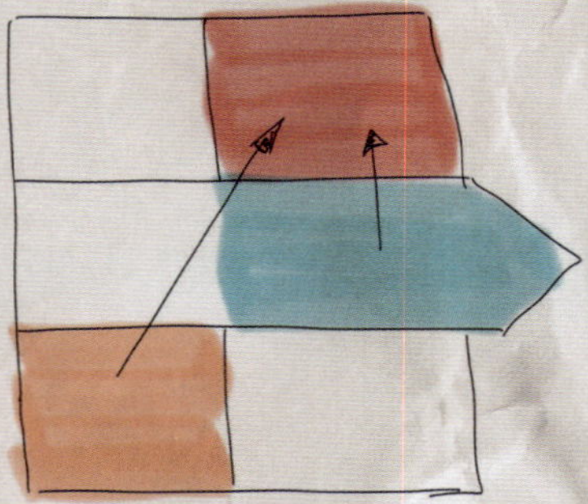

5. Locations & Assets

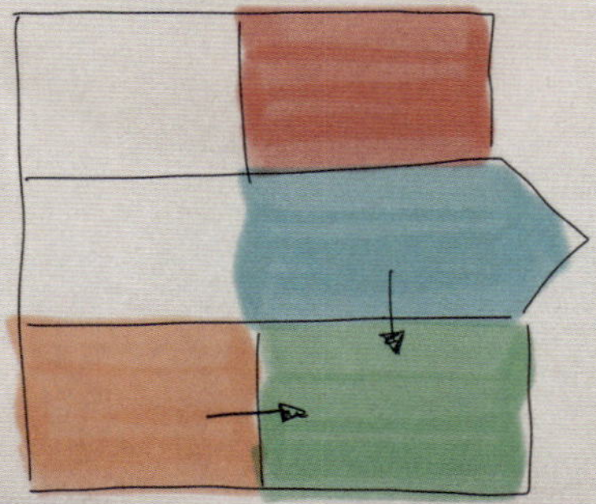

6. Decision rights

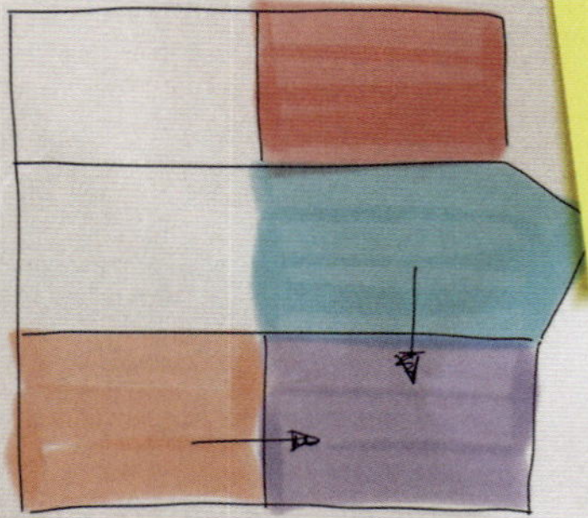

7. IT blueprint

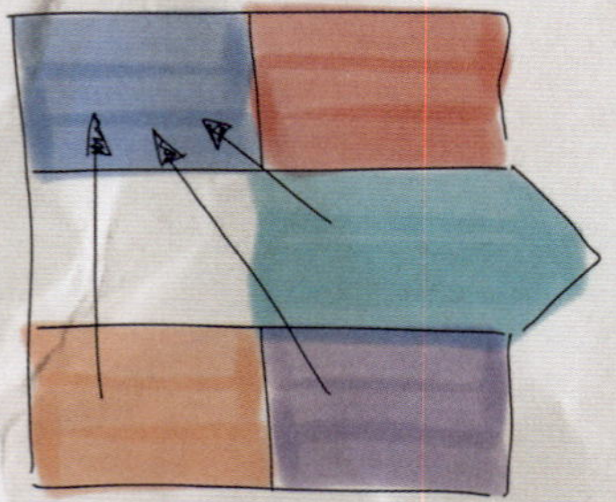

8. Suppliers

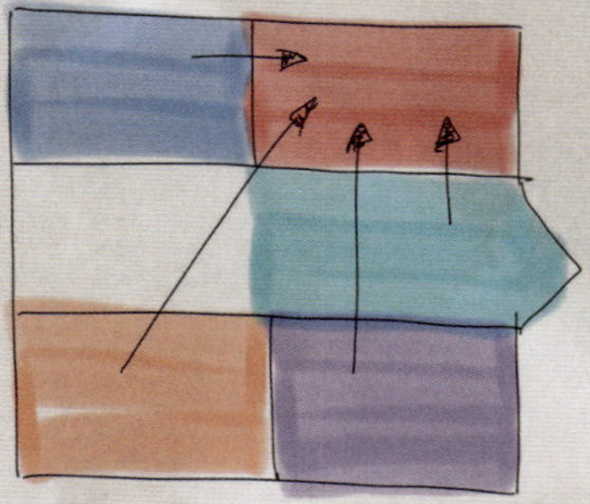

9. Re-visit locations & Assets

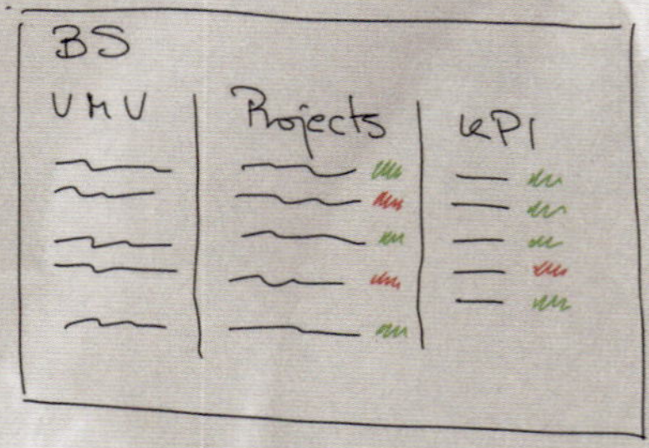

10. Management system

1. Draw processes (same as a value chain map!)

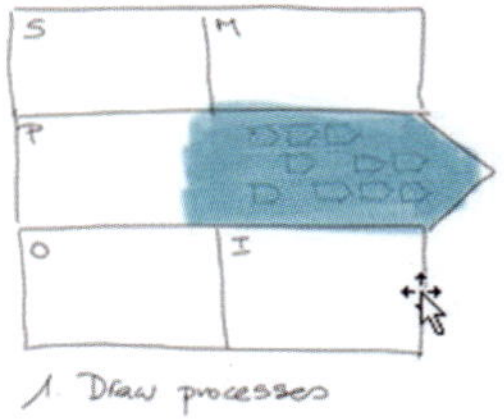

How to draw a value chain

Drawing a value chain can be complex and exhausting. The challenge is to generate enough detail without consuming too much time. We recommend a 'top down' approach. For each segment, start with a simple chain of no more than five or six steps. Where necessary break some of these steps down to the next level of detail (i.e. another chain of around five steps). Avoid creating a chain of 20 steps at any one level: the mind cannot cope with this number. Avoid breaking down every step into lower and lower levels of detail. It is rarely necessary.

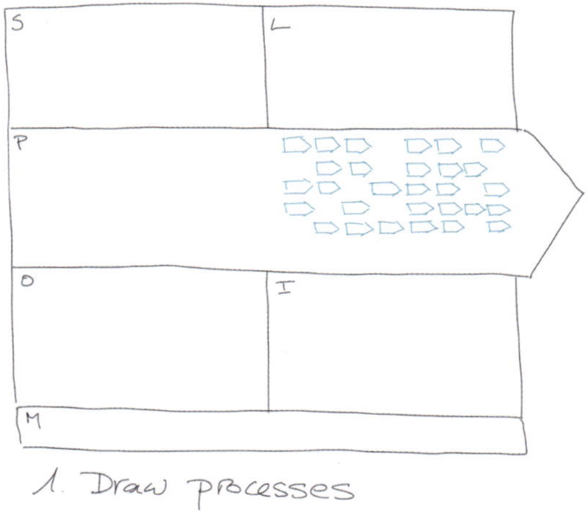

We recommend using post-it notes. Ask those involved to list the five to six steps in the chain. When you have them, ask the team to mark in red those with 'problems'. Then only expand the steps with problems. You will get something like this:

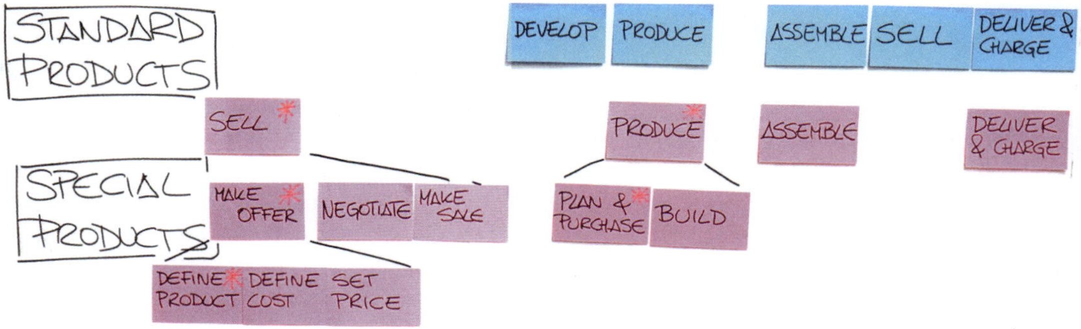

Choosing a segmentation

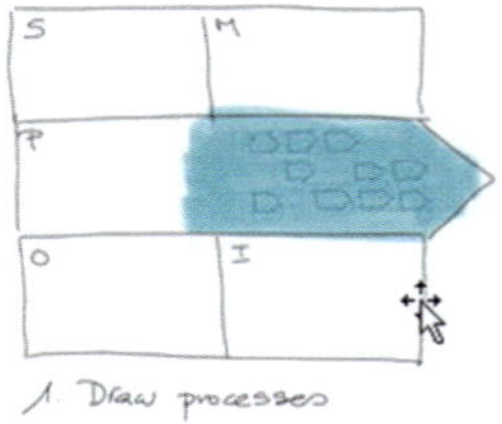

Segmentation options

Since your value chain map will have a value chain for each segment, choosing how to segment is an important step. In most situations there are alternative ways to segment. Choosing a 'good' segmentation is an important part of creating a good 'value chain map'. In the EEI Case, there were three different possible ways of segmenting:

- By type of product;
- By geography;
- By type of customer.

There was also, clearly, a need to segment by specials versus standard products: the desire to do specials had created the need for a new operating model in the first place. Hence it was necessary to split between standards and specials in all three segmentation options.

There is no simple rule to help you choose the best way of segmenting. Often you will try several ways before you are comfortable that you have found the segmentation that is most helpful to you. Typically the best segmentation is the one that reflects differences in the type of 'value proposition' being made by the organization to its beneficiaries.

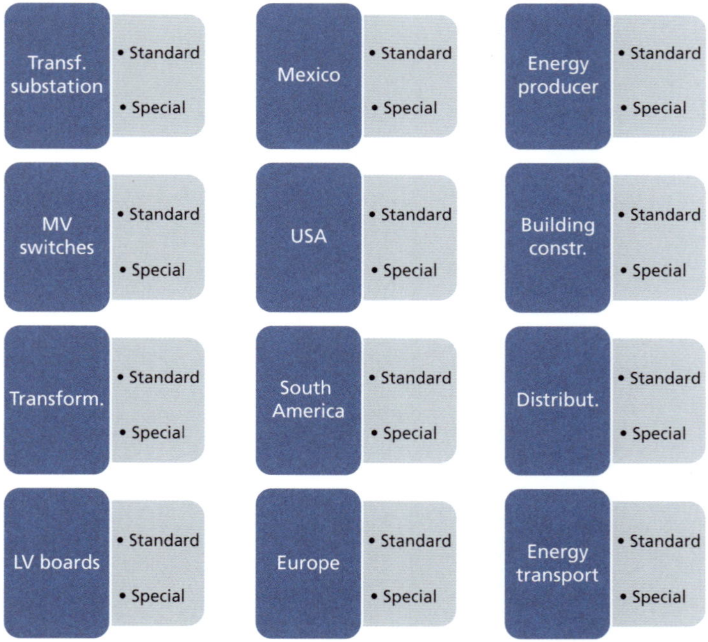

The team at EEI considered all three ways of segmenting the business. Segmenting by product proved to be most helpful.

You can see the result on the following pages.

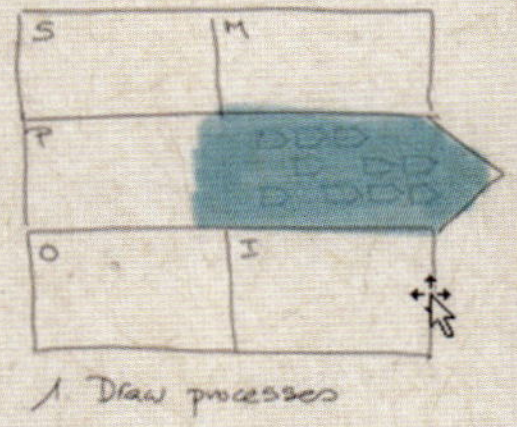

EEI's initial value chain map

This value chain map marks the 'problem' areas with red stars. Some steps are elongated because they will be expanded later. LV (Low Voltage) boards will be outsourced.

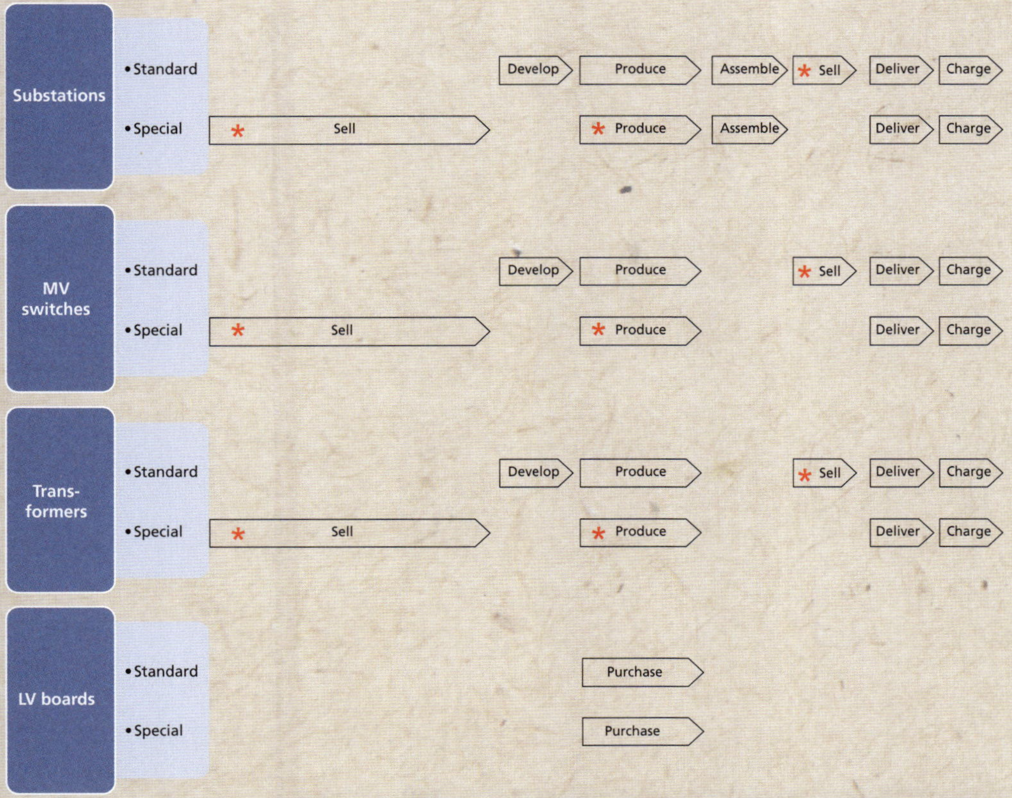

'As is' or 'to be'?

Often, as in this case, the basic process steps do not change. The 'as is' value chain is the same as the 'to be'. But when you are drawing a value chain for the first time, as it was when EEI first introduced special products, it is important to draw the 'to be' chain.

EEI's next level of detail

In this version, the problem areas are highlighted in red and numbered. They are described at the bottom right.

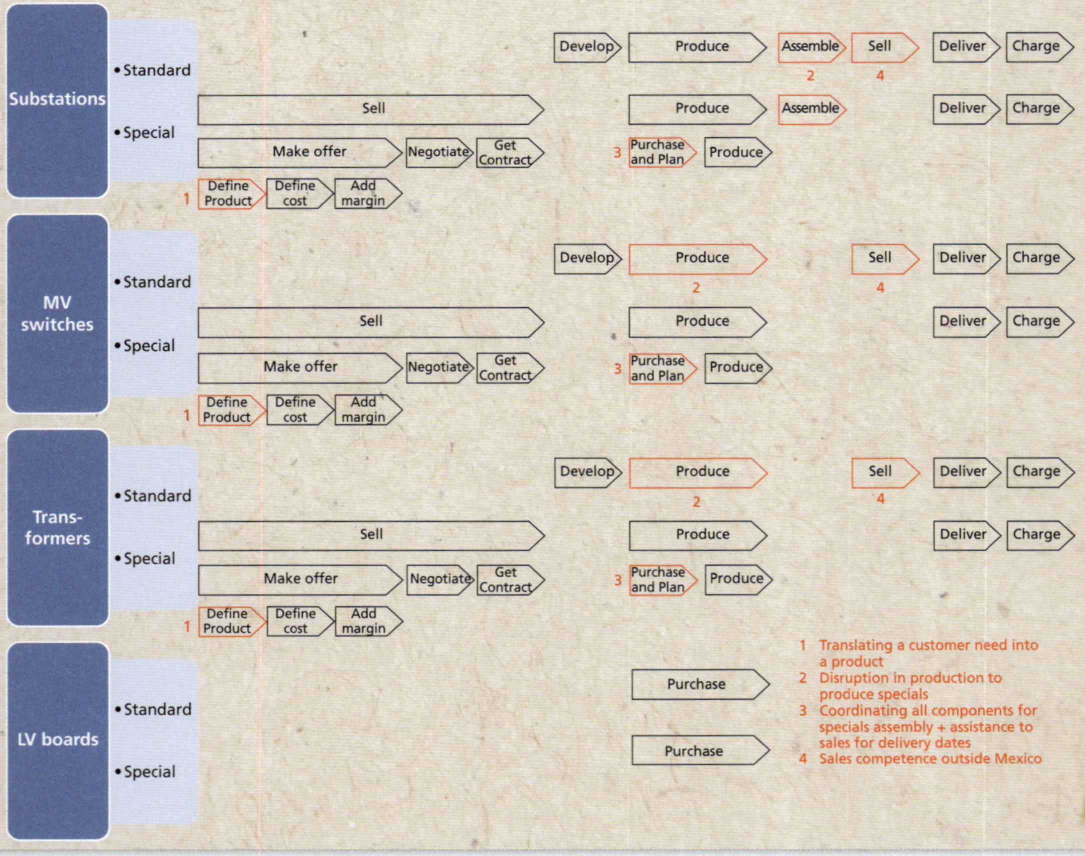

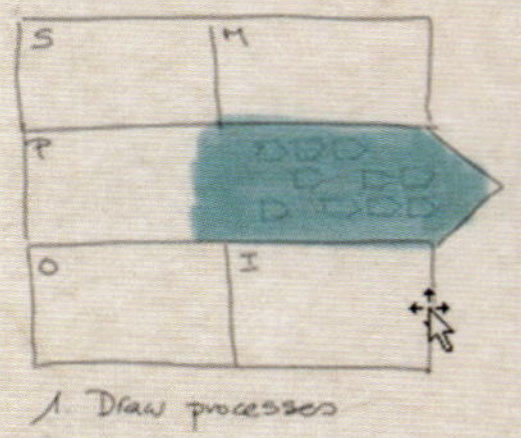

How many levels?

Only go into more detail where there are 'problems'. Then go down as many levels as needed to understand the root cause of the problem. In this case, three levels was enough in some places, and no extra detail was required in other places.

2. Analyze processes

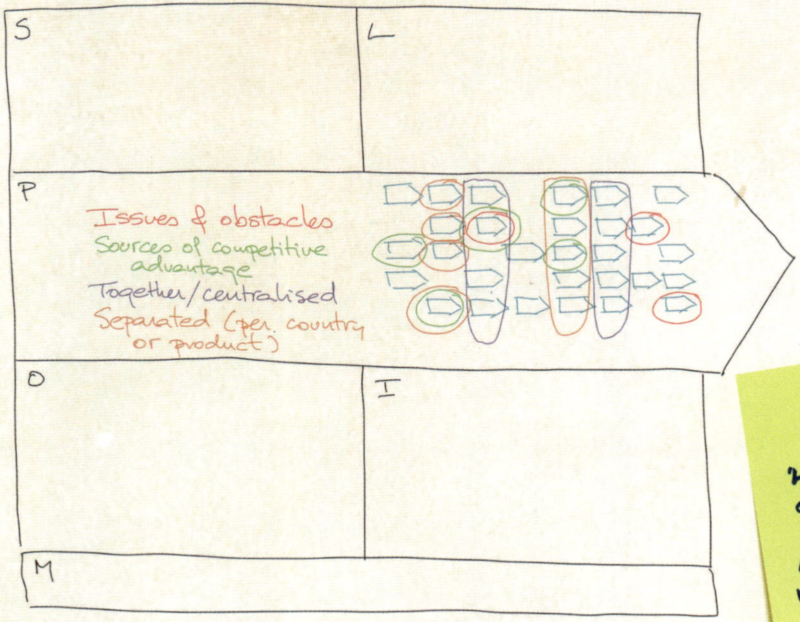

2. Analysis of the processes

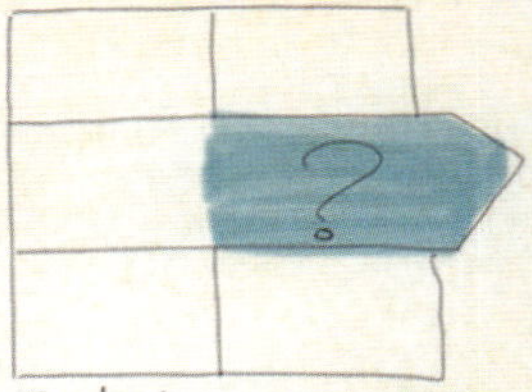

2. Analyse processes

> 'HAVING ALL STEPS IN A CHAIN FOCUSED ON THE VALUE PROPOSITION IS LIKELY TO DELIVER BEST VALUE TO THE CUSTOMER'

Identify the sources of competitive advantage or excellence

On the value chain map, the EEI team indicated in **GREEN** those steps that currently are, or could become, a source of advantage or excellence. These are the process steps that are 'critical success factors' or just the most important steps in terms of creating value for customers.

Where a source of advantage is also a problem (small **RED** circles) ... the step needs special attention

The steps that are critical to success, or those where the organization is not performing well, need special attention in the design process.

Consider which steps can be outsourced

It is helpful at this point to consider whether there are any steps in the value chains that could be better done by third parties. The EEI team did not do this analysis at this stage. Instead they did the analysis when thinking about suppliers.

Consider which steps can be combined, linked or need to be kept separate

Look across segments for process steps that can be combined (e.g. for economies of scale), linked (e.g. for good practice) or kept separate (e.g. to allow tailoring for a segment). If in doubt, keep separate. Having all steps focused on a segment is likely to deliver best value to the customer.

This analysis has important implications for the organization chart. But it can be done without the political concerns that are raised when an organization chart is being discussed.

Spend time on it.

EEI's value chain map analysis

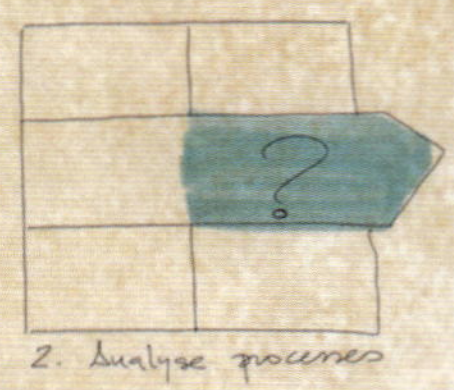

This marked-up map is the analysis done by EEI, including sources of advantage.

It gives one option. In this option 'Develop' remains a combined function where all product development reports to one boss. 'Produce' is split by product type. Each product leader being responsible for both standard and special products. 'Sell' is separated by country, but there is a central unit to define and schedule special products, once the local sales teams have identified the customer.

Other options are, of course, possible: a separate business unit for specials with its own production, or each product unit having its own sales team.

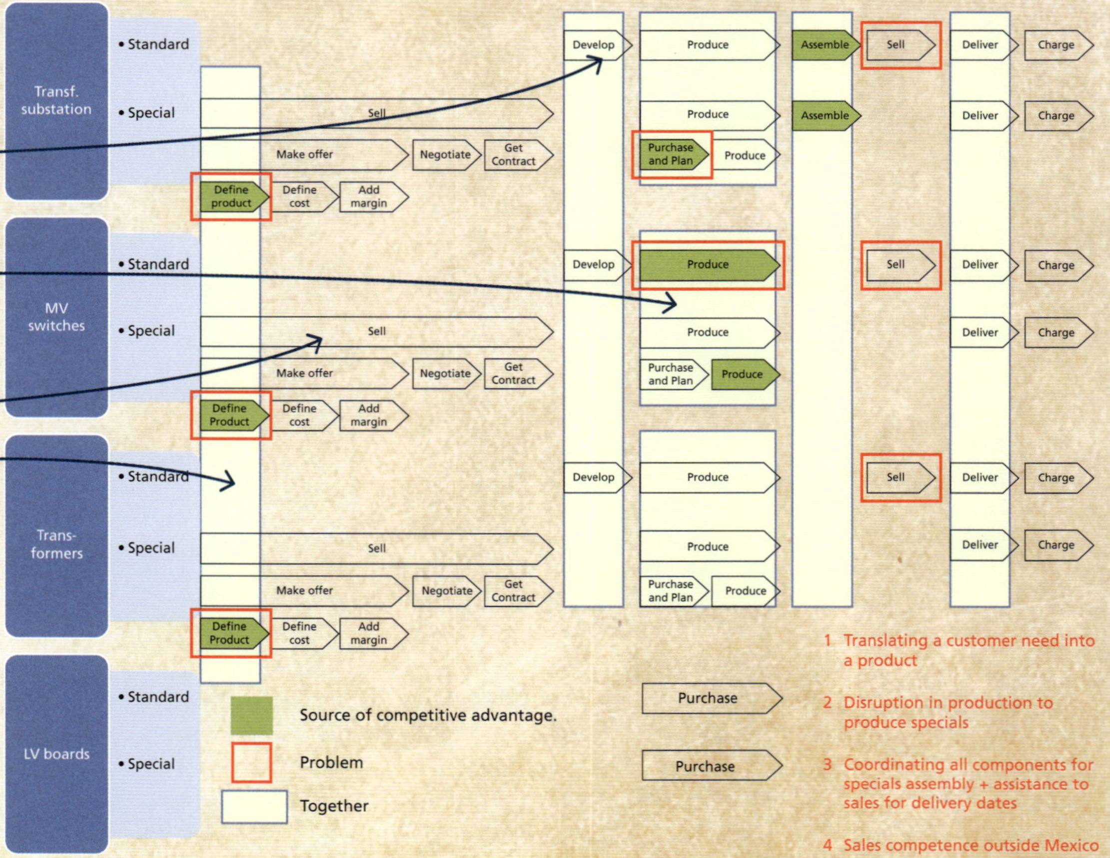

3. Organization chart

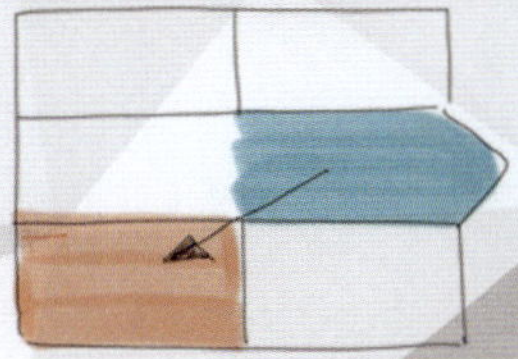

3. Organisation chart

The organization model is the most powerful tool for developing options for the organization structure

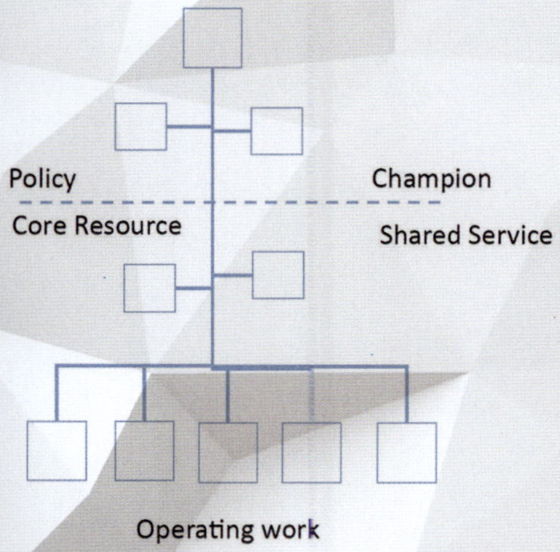

Four types of support work:

- Policy – sets rules;
- Champion – sells ideas or methods;
- Core resource – unique resource or capability;
- Shared service – service provided.

Three ways to structure operating work:

- Value chain;
- Units;
- Matrix.

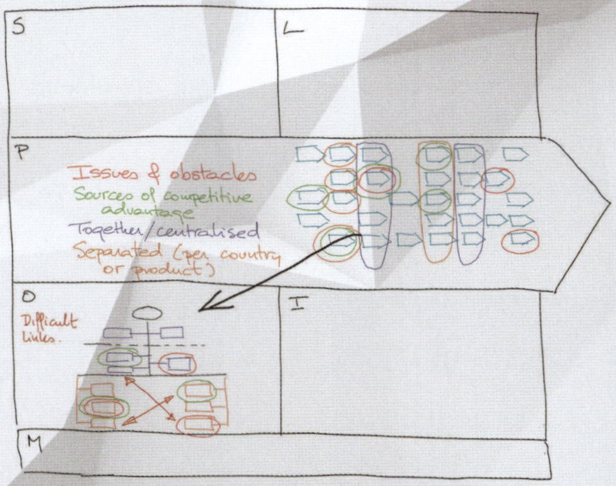

4. Organisation chart analysis

Analytical challenges

This tool has a few analytical challenges:

- What is operating work?
- How to allocate support work?

What is operating work?

- Operating work is the work required to complete the value delivery chains. The value chain map defines the operating work.
- The main structure aligns with the 'segements' unless all of the process steps have been 'combined/centralized' across the value chains.

How to allocate support work?

- Allocating roles for support work is a design choice
- Some 'functions', like HR, have multiple roles
- Policy and Champion are small units of 'experts'
- Core Resource and Shared Service are larger 'doing functions'

EEI's – organization

EEI considered four organization options for structuring the operating work.

Options

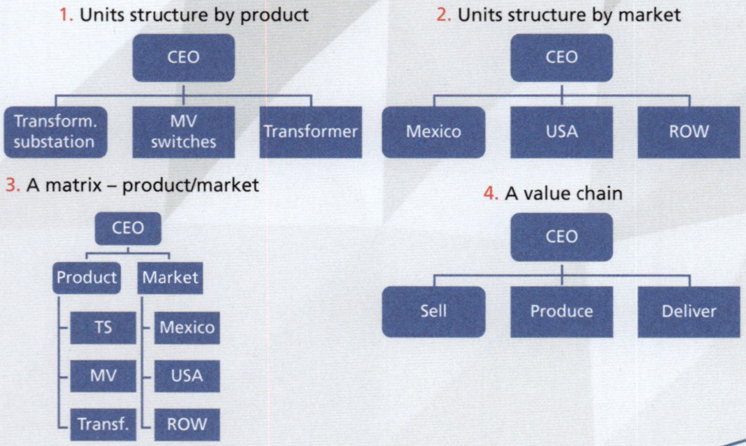

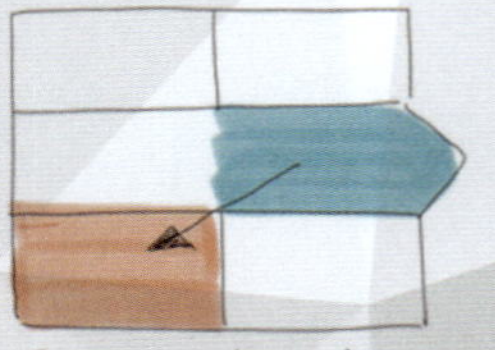

3. Organisation chart

The best option was chosen by comparing options against design principles

	Product	Market	Function	Matrix
Maintain Mexico	OK	Not good	OK	OK
Sell outside	Not good	Best	Not good	OK
Sell specials	Not good	Not good	Not good	OK – with Specials unit
Other	OK – with Develop unit OK – if profit centers	OK – with Develop unit OK – if profit centers	OK	OK – with Develop unit OK – if profit centers

Matrix was the chosen option

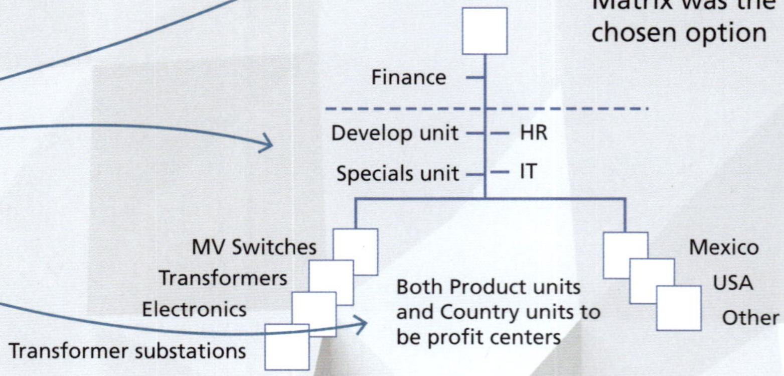

Once you have chosen a high-level option. You then add in support functions and make adjustments to deal with issues raised when comparing against design principles

CH4

4. Analyze organization chart

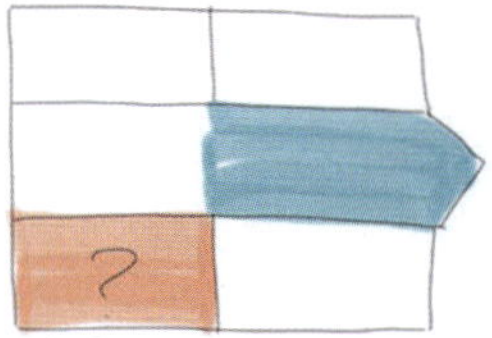

4. Org chart analysis

Identify the challenges

It is helpful to transfer the challenges identified in the value chain analysis onto the organization chart.

First, take the **RED** marks from the value chain map and mark the relevant boxes in the organization in **RED**. Then add additional **RED** marks if the box does not currently exist, or if there are other reasons suggesting that this box will need careful designing.

Second, take the **GREEN** marks from the value chain map – those identifying the critical steps – and mark the relevant boxes in the organization chart.

Third, draw **red arrows** between the important boxes where we know that the relationship is not going to be easy. In organization design work, these are referred to as the 'difficult links' : those relationships between different parts of the organization that are important to success, but will be difficult to get to work effectively.

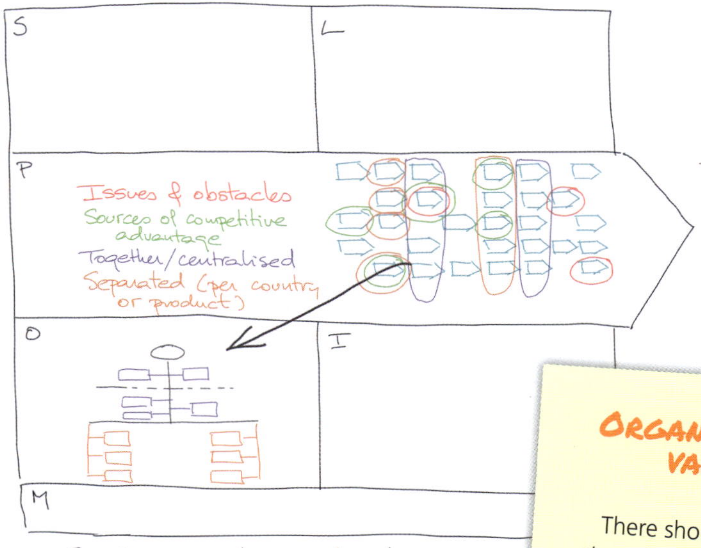

3. Organisation chart

Fourth identify in another color any important boxes on the chart that need to have specialist cultures: cultures that are different from the main culture. In this case the main culture is an engineering and production culture.

ORGANIZATION MODEL AND VALUE CHAIN MAP

There should be a correlation between the value chain map and the organization model. The primary structure of the organization will be by 'segment', unless many steps have been combined across segments so that the structure becomes a single value chain. This is why segmenting is such an important step.

Activities that have been combined across segments become central support functions as policy or champion or shared service or core resource.

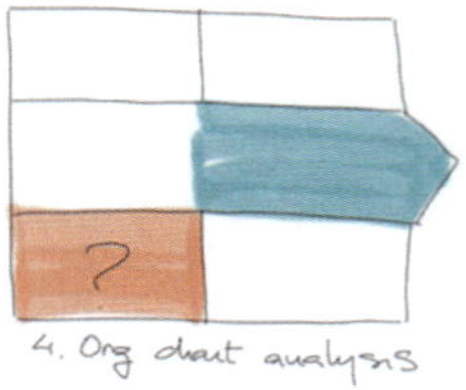

This is the analysis of the EEI organization model. It shows a lot of information. It shows the support functions and their roles and relationships to the operating units ('policy', 'service', etc.). It shows business units (both products and geographies). It also shows sources of advantage, problems areas, difficult links, and the areas that need to have specialist cultures.

The 'Develop' and 'Specials' units are sources of advantage. Both these units need cultures that are different from the predominant culture of the rest of the organization. So they need some separation.

The Specials unit is also a problem because it currently does not exist. Finding the people will not be easy.

The Specials unit is likely to have a difficult relationship with 'Product' because it will be requiring capacity for specials production. It will also have a difficult relationship with 'Sales' because it will be executing half of the sales task for specials and will need to interact with customers.

There is likely to be a difficult link between Product and Sales because both are business units but are dependent on each other (and hence can blame each other when performance is poor).

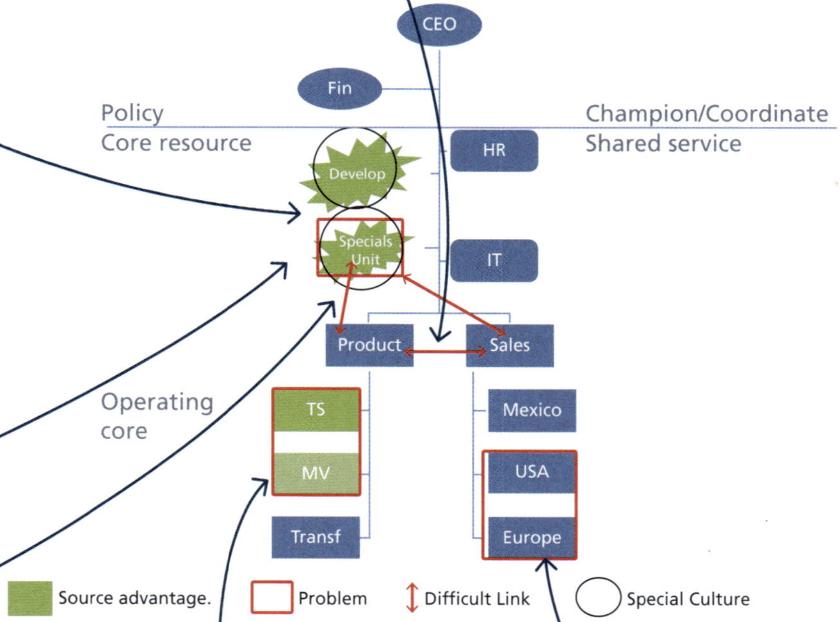

TS (the Substations unit) and MV (Medium Voltage switches) are sources of advantage. They are also a problem because of the rising costs of production and because they are not currently business units and need to become so in the new structure.

USA and Europe do not currently exist, so they are a problem.

5. Locations and assets

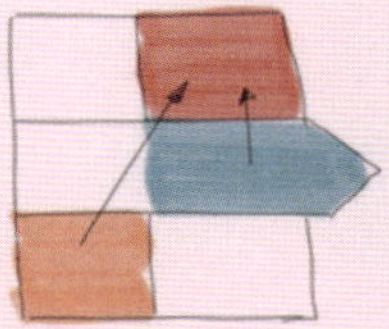

The "L" in POLISM

The 'Locations' element of an operating model covers:

- The allocation of activities or process steps to different geographic locations;
- The types of buildings, machinery and other assets needed in these locations;
- The allocation of activities or process steps to different buildings;
- The floor layout of important buildings.

The 'L' in POLISM is usually where the big money is. If significant changes are needed, sufficient money should be available to make the changes happen. Hence it is usually helpful to do some work on 'locations' early in the process.

There is no standard tool for helping with choices about 'locations' – other than a geographic map or a building layout plan. However, a stakeholder framework can help ensure that all aspects of the location choice have been considered.

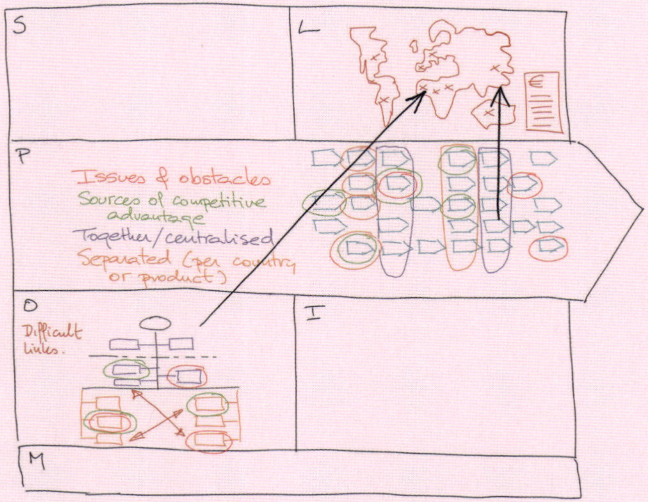

5. Locations & Assets

Activity or asset

Suppliers
- Where suppliers are skilled
- Where costs are lower
- To reduce transport cost

Government
- Laws/constraints
- Subsidies

Owner/investor
- Owner preference
- Location with good governacnce rulers
- Location with favorable tax treatment

Employee
- Where people with skills are
- Where people like to live
- Where labor/tax/union laws/norms are friendly
  Where labor is cheap
- To enable 24 hour coverage

Consumers
- Convenient for customer
- Same legal jurisdiction as customer

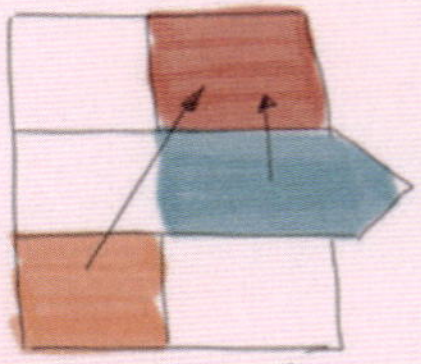

5. Locations & Assets

A table of locations

It is often helpful to use a table or tables to show the links between locations and processes, or locations and organizational units.

Org. Units \ Locations	Mexico	US	Spain	Brazil	Etc
Production	X				
Sales	X		X	X	
Develop	X				
Logistics	X				
etc					

Work on locations should continue throughout the design project

The order of POLISM suggests that work on 'locations' can be done after work on processes and organization. However, final decisions about locations are best taken after all the design work has been completed.

Decisions about suppliers and what activities are subcontracted and retained can affect locations choices.

Decisions about IT and the ownership of core processes can also affect locations.

It is for this reason that EEI included an additional step – 'review locations' – later in the design process.

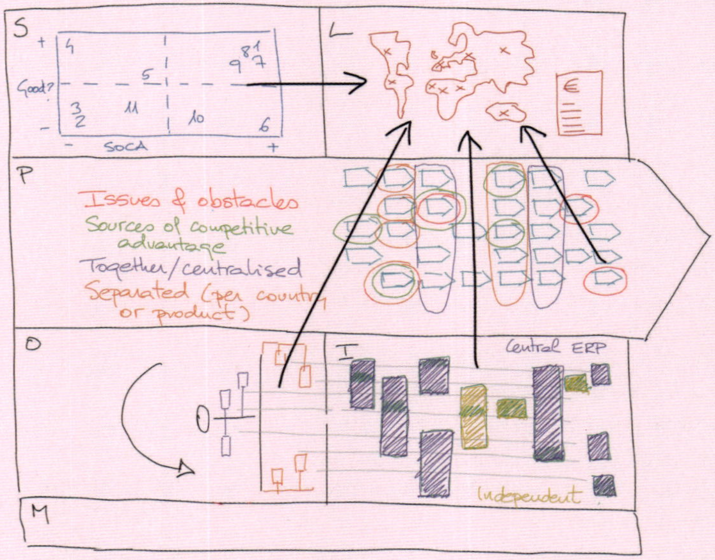

9. Re-visit Locations & Assets

EEI's Locations

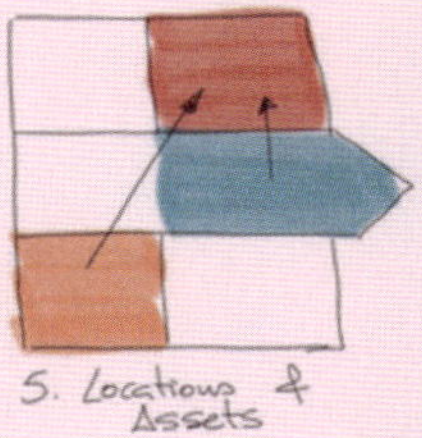

Locations issues for EEI

There were a number of important locations issues:

- Where to locate sales teams?
- Whether to separate specials manufacturing from standard products?
- Where to locate the Specials unit?
- Where to locate the Develop unit?

The CEO had already made some significant decisions expanding from one building to four. Because the current operations were already overcrowded and the business was growing fast, he had acquired a new factory building, identical to the existing building and on the same site.

The CEO had also acquired a small office building and decided to locate the Develop unit in a new laboratory in the countryside near an airport.

Options: There were two main options. First, use the new building for specials or use the new building for substations. In addition, there were three places where the Specials unit could be located: with the Develop unit, in the office building, or in one of the manufacturing plants.

As regards Sales, the sales people would need to be located in each geography where EEI would like to make direct sales.

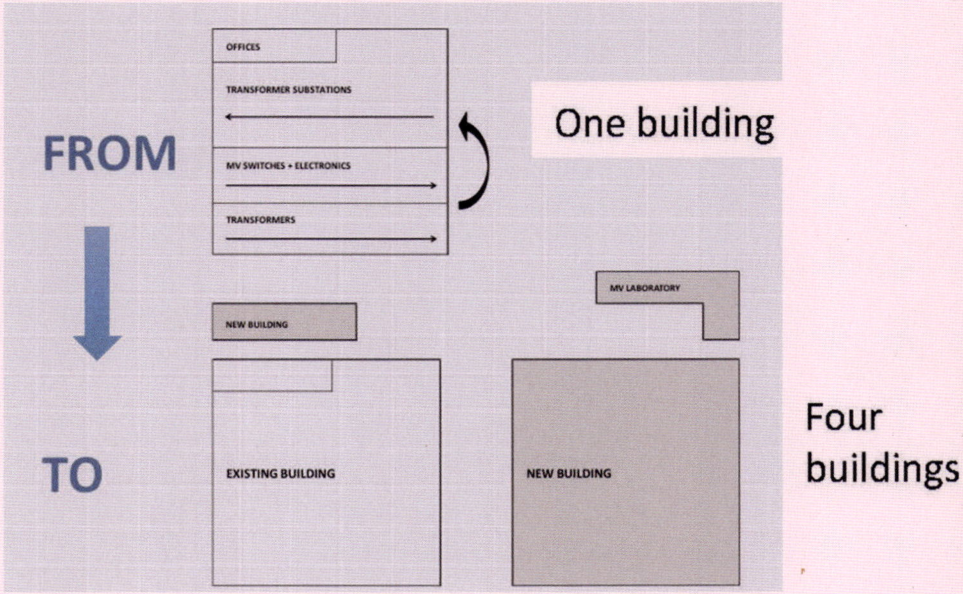

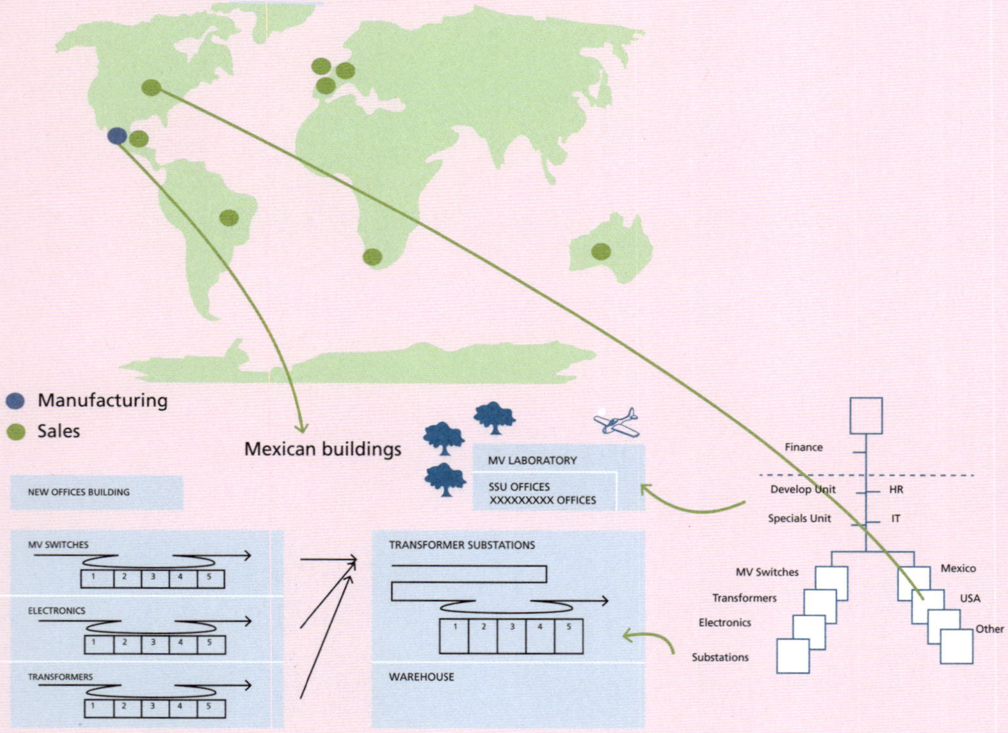

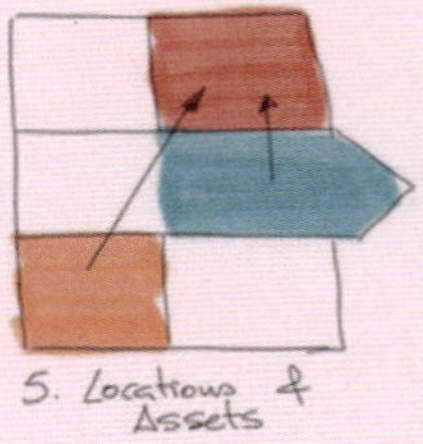

Sales

To achieve the objective of growing outside Mexico, it was decided that a sales presence would be needed in each major market.

Specials unit

The Specials unit was located with the Develop unit in the new laboratory building close to the airport.

This made it easy for them to interact with the technicians and the proximity of the airport was beneficial both for visiting customers and for receiving customer visits.

An additional benefit came from having customers visit the laboratory: they were impressed by the new building and the technology.

Specials manufacturing

Because of the high cost of the machinery on the production lines it was decided that it would not be cost effective to create separate production lines for special products. Specials would need to be manufactured on the same lines as standard products.

To reduce the disruption to manufacturing, special rooms were created so that special products could be taken out of the line when they were waiting for parts, or when they needed special attention.

6. Decision rights

Why focus on decisions?

The new organization allocated sales to the VP Sales and production to the VP Operations and specials configuration to the VP Specials. But this still left plenty of room for turf wars and disagreements. So it was important to clarify how decisions would be made in the new organization. Moreover, the CEO did not want all decisions landing on his desk.

One of the difficult steps in developing a decision grid is the choice of decisions to analyze. So some time was spent talking to the heads of each function to find out which decisions they wanted more clarity on.

The Grid opposite is not the complete Decision Grid. This was four pages long. The one shown here is an extract of some of the more contentious items.

For example, Sales retained authority on pricing because each country was a profit center. But the VP Specials had authority over product configuration (and hence the cost of the solution) that was offered to the customer.

The VP Specials had authority over the production schedule and hence the delivery times for special products. But the CEO retained authority over the allocation of capacity when capacity was limited. The CEO knew that Sales and Operations would fight over capacity as they attempted to maximize their separate profits.

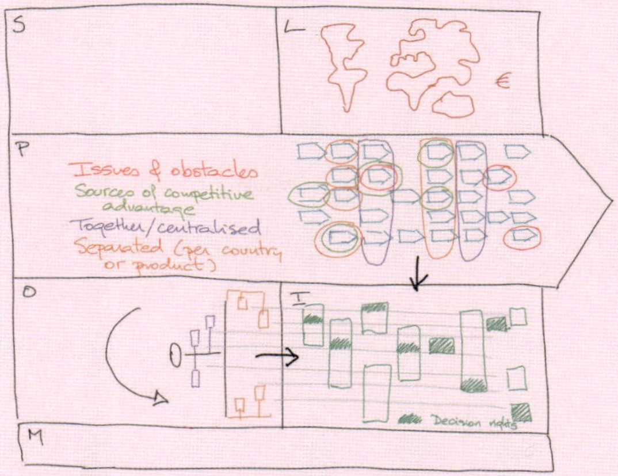

6. Processes vs. Organization: who is involved and who has the decision rights

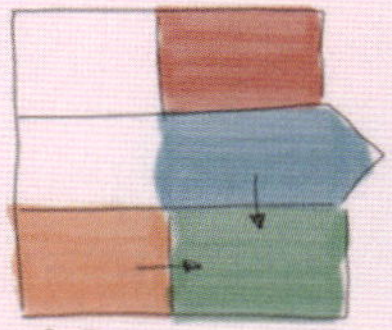

6. Decission rights

RAPID OR RACI?

EEI chose RAPID because the focus was on decisions. RAPID has an advantage in that one of the items is 'decide'. It was important to EEI to be clear about who had the appropriate authority in many areas of decision-making.

You will note on the grid that there are no 'A's. This was a deliberate part of the design. While the CEO retained ultimate 'Agree' rights on all decisions, he wanted his team to feel empowered to make decisions and ask forgiveness afterwards.

Why decision rights in the information box?

The EEI team decided that decision rights and process ownership were all part of the information box in the Canvas. More normally these are part of the organization box. But, as long as the important issues are addressed, it does not matter which box is linked to which item.

EEI's grid (focusing on specials)

Decisions	CEO	VP Sales	VP Specials	VP Tech	VP Ops	Other
Price for a special prod		D/P	I			
Special configuration offered to customer		R	D			
Allocation of capacity when limited	D	R	P		I	
Production schedule			D		R	
Transfer price from Ops to Sales					I	D-Finance P-Finance
What stock levels					D	I-Finance
Which new products/services	D	R	R	R/P		
What is on the scorecard	D	R		R		R-Finance P-Finance R-HR

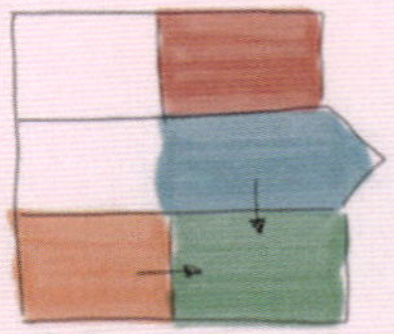

7. Process ownership and information

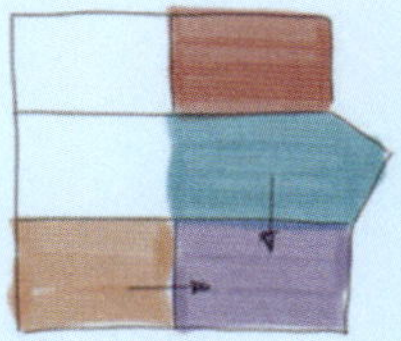

7. IT blueprint

The 'I' in POLISM

The 'I' in POLISM is about the IT blueprint. But, in the EEI project, the team worked on the IT blueprint and the process ownership grid at the same time. Moreover, they positioned the axes of the process ownership grid the same way as for the IT blueprint – process steps along the top and organization units down the side.

As the project leader pointed out, "if you list all the main organization units down the side and all the process steps across the top, one of the magic moments of operating model design occurs. You are exploring how the organization and the processes will work together, who will control the processes and what IT support is needed for each."

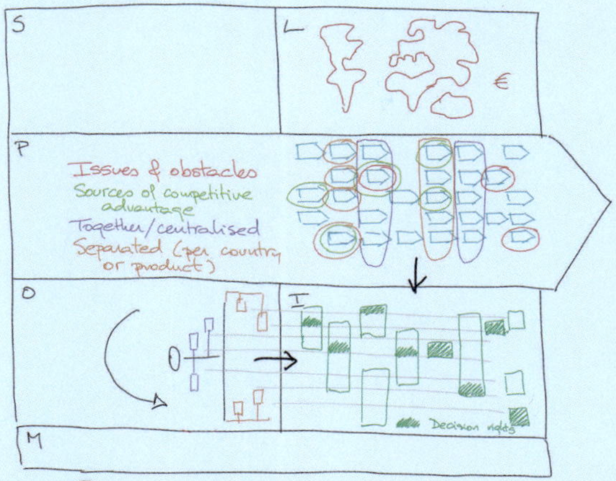

6. Processes vs. Organization: who is involved and who has the decision rights

Identify which organization units are involved in which processes

Start with each process step and mark those organization units that are involved in this process step. For example, product development (one of the process steps) involves the Develop unit, the Sales teams, the Specials unit, and the Produce unit.

Then consider who 'owns' this process step: whose responsibility is it to make sure that the process is well designed across all these units. There are two options – either one unit is responsible for the process (e.g. the Develop unit) or the responsibility for different parts of the process lie with different units. The latter option only makes sense if the hand-offs between units are simple. If they are complex, then one person needs to oversee the whole process.

Difficult links

It is normally helpful to revisit the earlier thinking about difficult links at this point. Consider each process step that crosses more than one organization unit and indicate with a **RED** connecting arrow, where you expect the working relationship will be difficult.

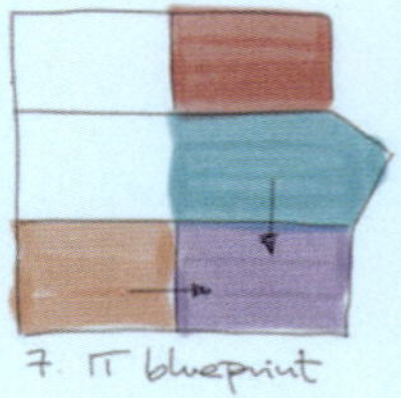

EEI's process ownership grid

EEI decided to make the Specials unit the process owner for many of the processes relating to specials – defining the product, costs, contract (other than price), and production plan and arranging delivery. 'Sales' retained process ownership over negotiating with customers and pricing.

The grid helped to expose some places where links were expected to be difficult. For example, the Specials unit now had ownership of the production schedule which had previously been owned by the manufacturing units. This would be likely to create tensions.

The grid was also used to highlight the different culture that would be required to make the Specials unit a success. This reinforced the benefit of locating the Specials unit with the Develop unit and away from the factories and offices. Of course the separate locations might also make the difficult links more difficult, so there was a good deal of debate about location.

EEI's process ownership grid for specials

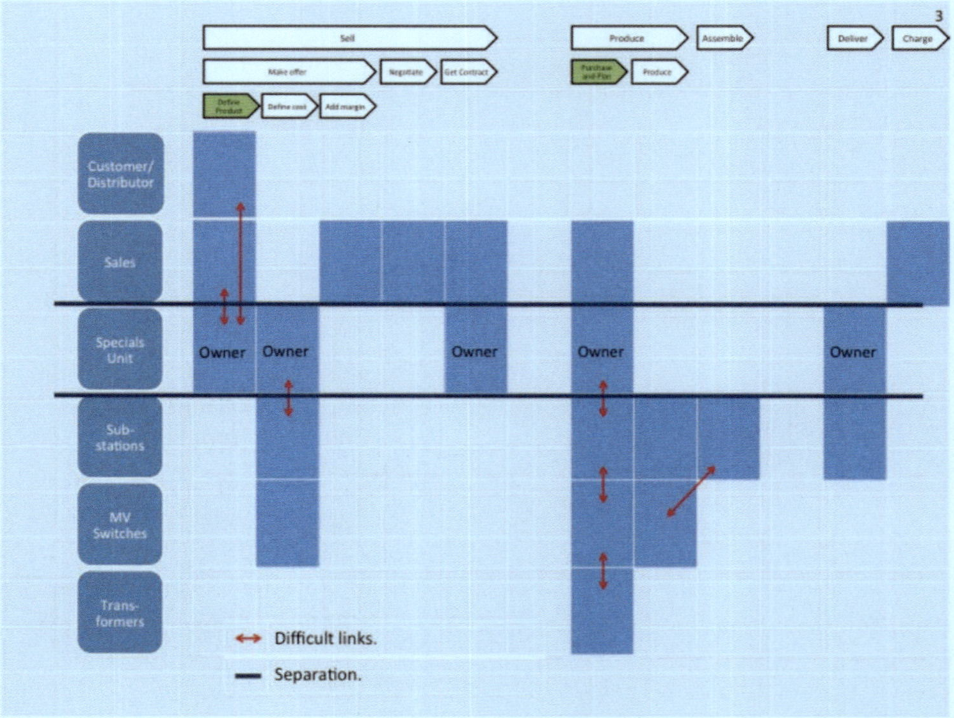

IT blueprint

IT applications

Information systems have become the backbone of most organizations. The enterprise system connects sales to finance, sales to production, supply chain to production and serves many more links. Traditionally these links have been provided through an ERP (enterprise resource planning) system containing standard modules from a provider, such as SAP. More recently, with cloud solutions, users are able to pick and choose standard modules in a less monolithic way. They are also able to plug-in bespoke modules in areas where the standard module is not adequate.

Either way, the big decision at this stage of an operating model design is about which software applications will be integrated into the enterprise system and which can be stand-alone. Also which will be standard and which bespoke. It is also helpful to identify the 'business owners' of the applications because, even if an application is developed and maintained by IT, it will be 'owned' by a function or business unit or committee of 'business responsible' managers.

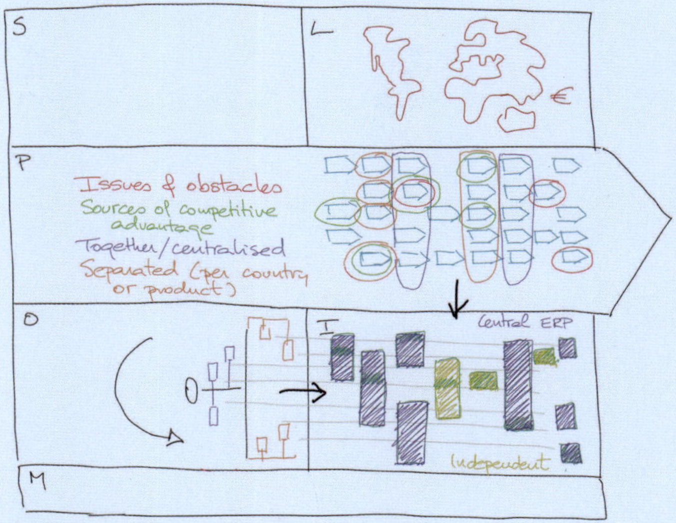

7. IT blueprint.

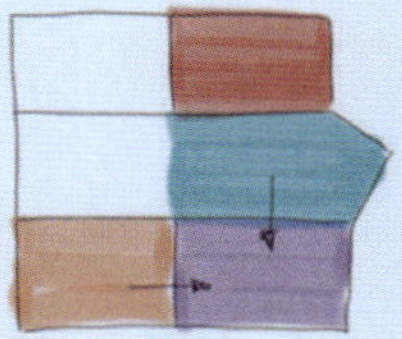

7. IT blueprint

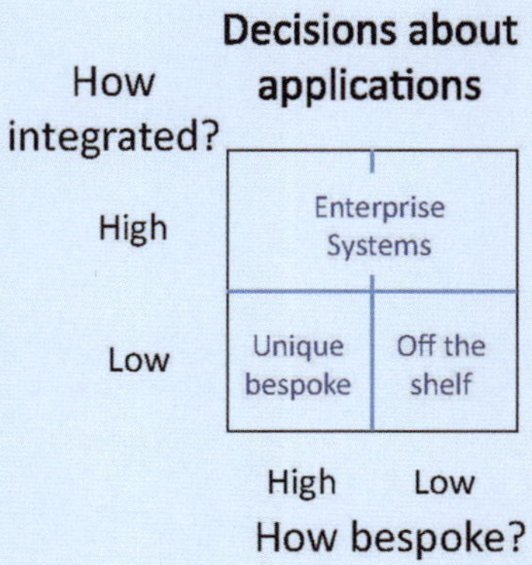

High-level IT blueprint

The table showing the main applications, indicating which of these are integrated into the enterprise system, which are bespoke and which are stand-alone, is a high-level IT blueprint. At this level of design, the operating model work is not trying to generate a complete IT blueprint, rather some high-level guidance for the more detailed work that will follow.

Typically, even at this high-level, more attention would be given to the critical data assets than was done in this project.

EEI's IT blueprint for specials

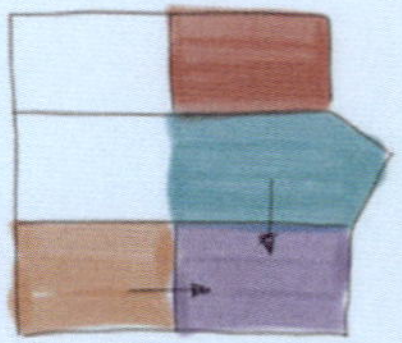

7. IT blueprint

EEI had a legacy portfolio of around 200 IT applications. This operating model project was an opportunity to convert to a single ERP system. To help reduce the number of applications, the CEO announced that the standard SAP modules (SAP had already been chosen as the supplier) would be used by all departments. Bespoke applications or modules would only be allowed when needed as an essential part of a source of advantage for the company.

So Finance, HR, Product and Sales used the standard modules in the SAP application. But the Specials unit and the Develop unit (not shown on this chart) were permitted to have bespoke applications because the standard SAP modules could not support their vital roles in creating competitive advantage for the company.

Repcon was the name of the application that was developed to help the Specials unit manage the 'define product' step of the sales process. The application made it possible to create a huge variety of special products from a defined range of options.

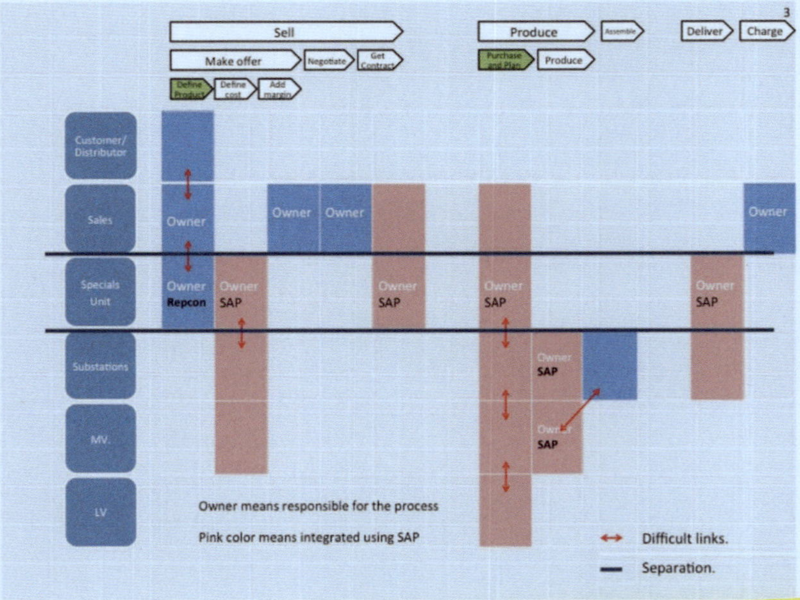

NOTE THAT IT IS THE LONG COLUMNS ON THE CHART THAT ARE PART OF THE ENTERPRISE SYSTEM. BECAUSE THESE PROCESSES TOUCH MANY ORGANIZATIONAL UNITS, AN INTEGRATED SYSTEM IS NEEDED.

ERP implementations are long, costly and complex projects. When faced with decisions during the project, it is helpful to have an agreed high-level blueprint as a reference to go back to. The blueprint links IT to both the strategy and the operating model. In this way, adjustments made during implementation are aligned with the original intent.

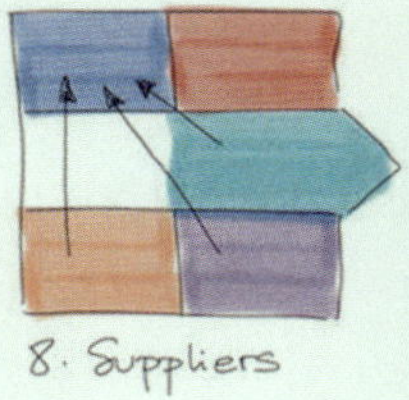

8. Supplier matrix

The 'S' in POLISM

Suppliers are an important part of any operating model. Deciding what to do in-house and what to outsource is one issue. Deciding what kind of relationship to have with each supplier is another issue.

The supplier matrix is a helpful tool for making these decisions.

Supplier issues at EEI

EEI faced a number of supplier issues:

- In countries where the company does not have its own sales force, what type of relationship should it have with distributors?
- In manufacturing, which components and products should EEI make itself versus outsource?
- What should be the relationship between EEI and SAP, the provider of the ERP system?
- What should the relationship be between EEI and the consultants working on Repcon, the bespoke software needed to support the configuration of specials.

Using the matrix

It is possible to plot any activity on the matrix, both operating work that is part of a value chain or support work, such as finance, or HR or IT.

There are four boxes in the matrix:

1. 'We do' means that this activity is a core part of the operating model and that the company should aim to be the best in its sector.
2. 'We do if it does not distract' means that this activity is not core, but we can still do the activity because we are good at it, unless it distracts from, or conflicts with, our ability to do core activities.
3. 'Outsource' means that we do not do this activity and we have a simple contract with the supplier.
4. 'Design a collaborative agreement' suggests that we need a joint venture (JV) or other similar type of relationship.

EEI's – supplier matrix

The **first step** was to place on the matrix the main activities of EEI and any more detailed activities that have significance, like the development of the Specials application software – Repcon.

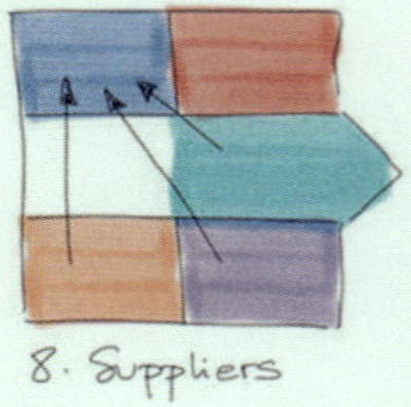

Selling was complicated.
EEI believed that Specials would be the company's biggest source of value in the future, and the company was determined to be the best competitor in selling and configuring special products. So this activity and the strong sales team in Mexico were considered 'core'.

The other sales activities could all be done by distributors. So the issue was about the nature of the relationship with these distributors – non-exclusive, exclusive or JV?

EEI decided that a JV was needed in the US because of the importance of the market. Exclusive relationships were needed in other important markets.

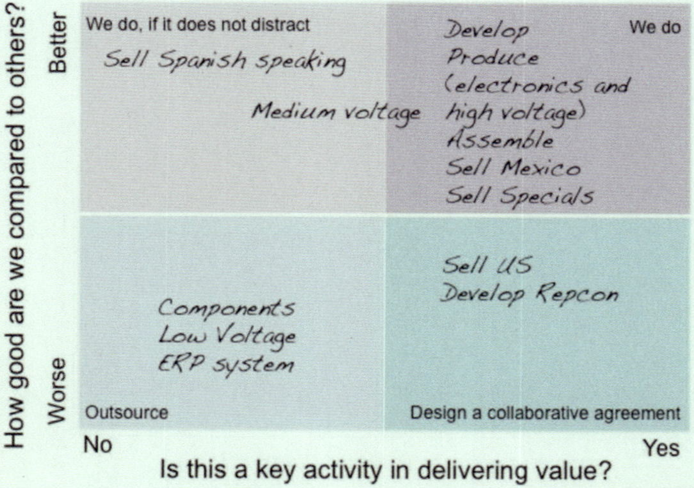

The **Specials software** – Repcon – was so important to success that a unique relationship was devised with the developers allowing them to work with other industries but not with direct competitors. The relationship with SAP on the **ERP system** could be a simple contract, because EEI was only using standard modules.

Developing technology, production and assembly were considered to be strengths of EEI and important for delivering value, with a couple of exceptions:

- Component production, and low voltage transformers were considered to be commodity items that could be outsourced to local suppliers
- Medium voltage transformers could also be outsourced if extra space was needed.

9. Revisit locations and assets

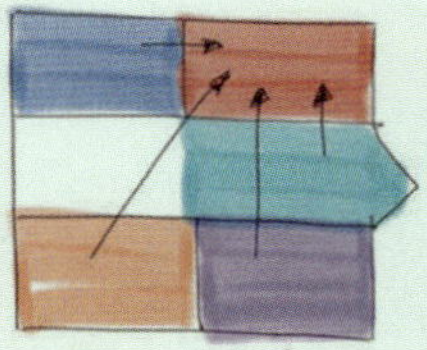

9. Re-visit locations & Assets

Why locations and assets again?

It is often helpful to revisit the locations and assets work after completing the IT blueprint, the process owner table/grid and the supplier matrix. This is because additional insights about locations and assets emerge after these other bits of work have been completed.

The 'L' comes early in POLISM because locations and assets involve significant amounts of money and often become a constraint on the design. Revisiting the work helps to ensure that something was not overlooked at the earlier step.

Of course revisiting every part of POLISM is theoretically advisable once all the sections of work have been completed. In practice, however, the work often proceeds more iteratively as the team adjusts different parts of the design and then loops back to previous steps. So do not treat the design process as being as linear as POLISM suggests.

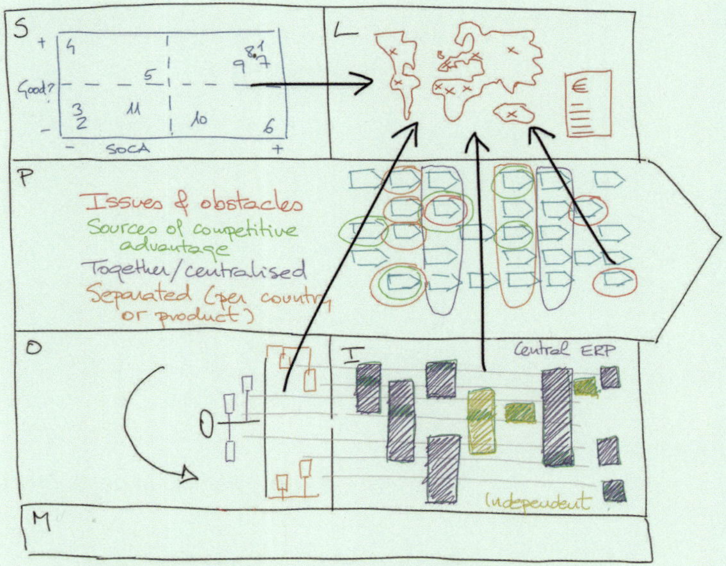

9. Re-visit Locations & Assets

Locations issues for EEI

There were a number of important locations issues:

- Where to locate sales teams?
- Whether to separate specials manufacturing from standard products?
- Where to locate the Specials unit?
- Where to locate the Develop unit?

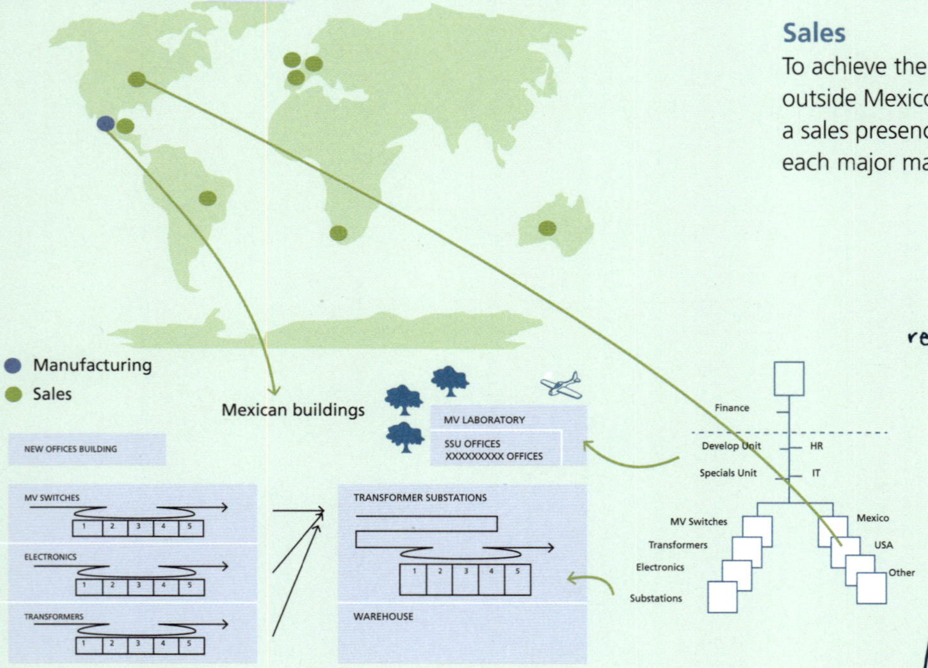

Sales

To achieve the objective of growing outside Mexico, it was decided that a sales presence would be needed in each major market.

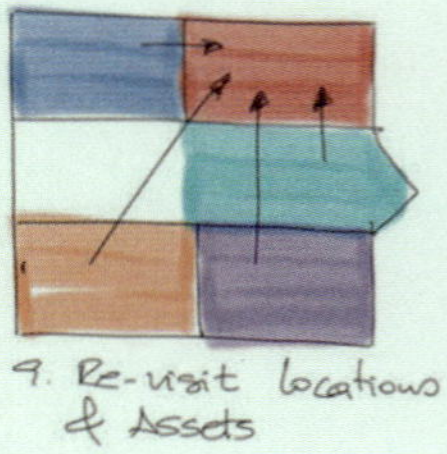

Decisions about using distributors reduced the number of countries where EEI needed a direct sales force

Specials Unit

The Specials unit was located with the Develop unit in the new laboratory building close to the airport.

This made it easy for them to interact with the technicians and the proximity of the airport was beneficial both visiting customers and for receiving customer visits.

An additional benefit came from having customers visit the laboratory: they were impressed by the new building and the technology.

The ERP system and bespoke software for configuring specials – Repcon – made it OK to locate the Specials unit away from both Production and Sales

Specials manufacturing

Because of the high cost of the machinery on the production lines it was decided that it would not be cost effective to create separate production lines for special products. Specials would need to be manufactured on the same lines as standard products.
To reduce the disruption to manufacturing, special rooms were created so that special products could be taken out of the line when they were waiting for parts or when they needed special attention.

The power given to the Specials unit over processes also meant that they did not need to be co-located with Production or Sales

10. Scorecards and management system

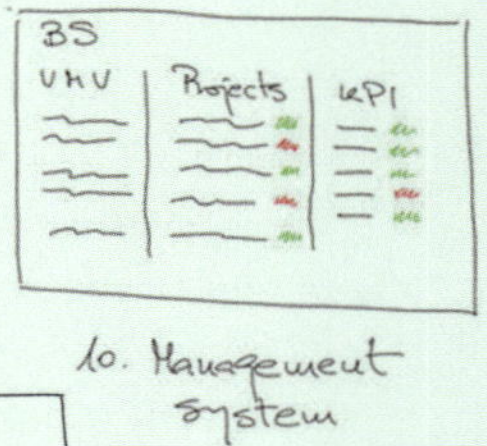

A scorecard is an essential tool within a management system. It helps managers know whether the organization is succeeding and whether any transformation efforts are on track.

The example on this page is a sketch of the EEI scorecard framework produced by the team. It was called a 'balanced scorecard' even though it is not the same as the more widely known tool 'The Balanced Scorecard' (see balancedscorecard.org)

The **first column** contains the vision, mission and values of the company. The time scale of this column is five to ten years. It defines the ambition. The text for this column comes from strategy.

The **second column** lists the projects that will deliver the Vision, Mission and Values. These projects come straight from the strategy, business model and operating model. These define the transformation work that needs to be done.

The **third column** lists the key performance indicators. They tell us how the company has done in the last month or quarter, assessed against the business plan.

Every month the scorecard can be completed with red or green colors for the projects and KPIs, and with supporting explanations.

Typically there is one scorecard for the whole organization, and one for each business unit and function.

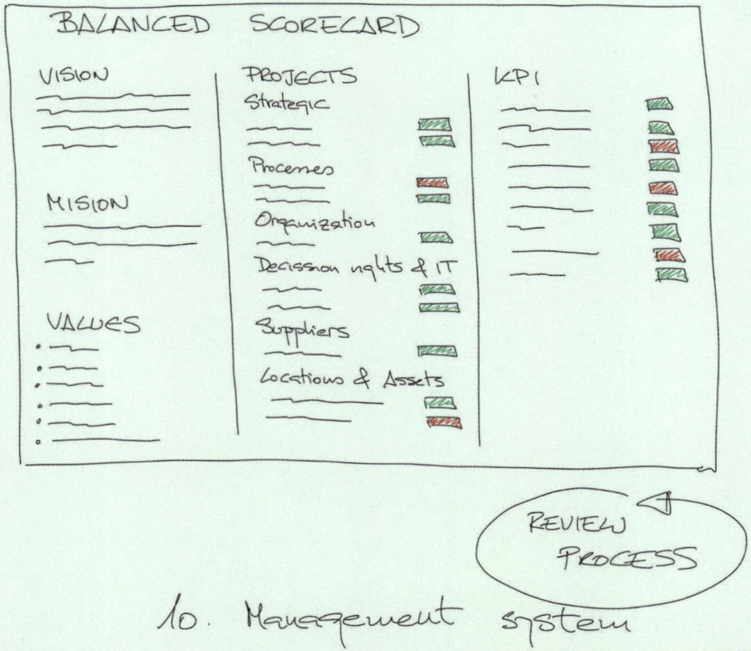

HOW OFTEN SHOULD THE SCORECARD CHANGE?

After every strategy change, review all elements of the scorecard.

After every period (often a year, but could be much less for a fast moving business – for example six weeks in an 'agile' process) set the targets and measures for each project and reset the KPIs for the business.

Projects

One of the issues on a scorecard is the choice of projects to include. In most companies there are tens of projects going on at any one time. So the scorecard should only include the most important projects: those that are transforming the company.

You can see the list of projects that came out of the operating model review of EEI.

You will notice that there are two types of projects. Those that answer the question WHAT we want to do, and those that answer the question HOW we want to do it.

The WHAT projects come from the strategic objectives. The HOW projects come from the 'to be' operating model design.

Where possible, projects should have numbers attached to them. This is not possible for all projects, but, a project with a number is much easier to monitor and manage and much more likely to happen than a project without a number.

WHAT

Sell 500 m€ outside Mexico in 2 years	
Sell 200 m€ in specials with 20% margin	

HOW

Create Specials Unit (1 m€/y)	Head Specials Unit + HR
New plant and layouts (10 m€/y)	Head Product
ERP (7 m€)	Head IT + Specials
Local sales capabilities (3 m€/y)	Head Sales
Re-adapt production lines to specials (2 m€)	Each BU GM
Organization design clarification	HR
Moving offices / office in the forest	HR

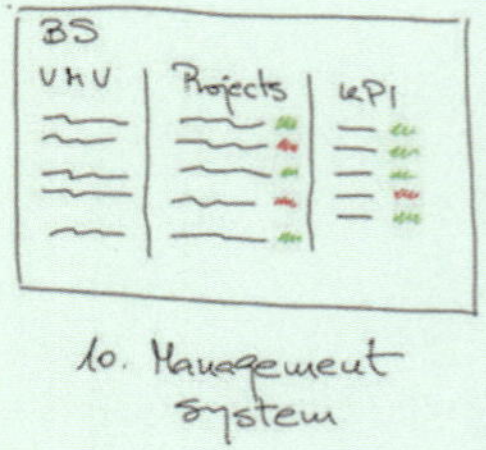

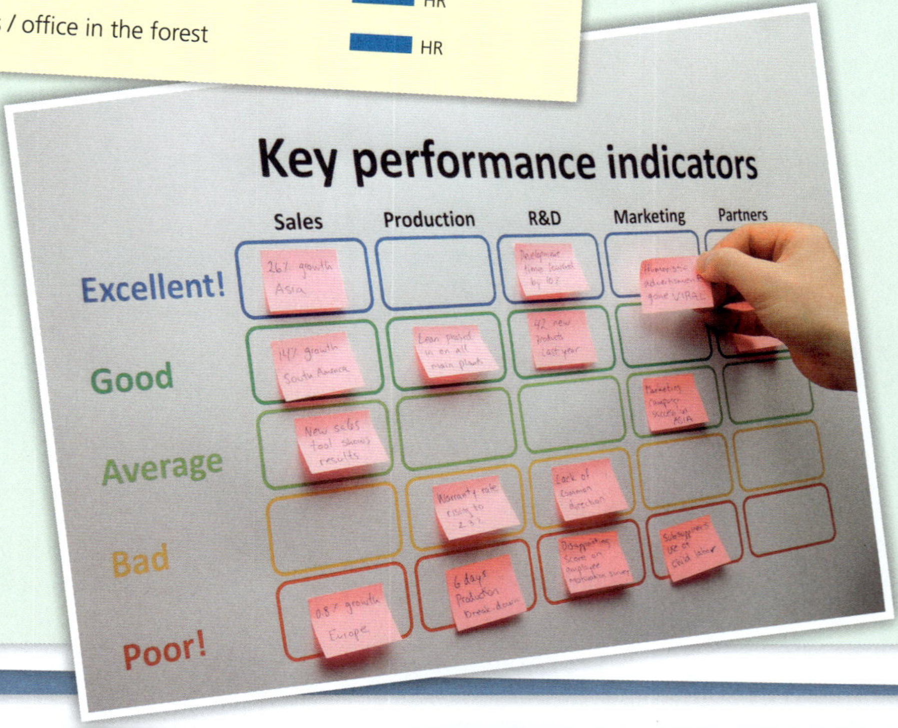

CH4

10. SCORECARDS

Management calendar

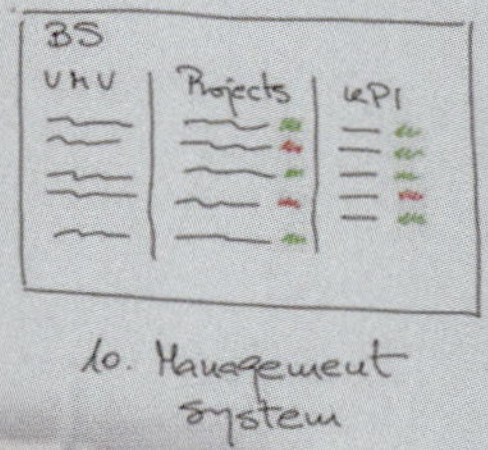

The 'M' in POLISM

Once all the other elements of the operating model have been designed, it is possible to design the management calendar of meetings and processes for planning and running the organization.

Management System issues at EEI

Given the changes that EEI was making, there were important management system issues:

- How to manage all the change projects needed to succeed in specials;
- How frequently to revisit strategy as information came in from market successes or failures;
- How to set targets and manage performance when sales in some countries were hard to predict;
- How to keep a focus on continuous improvement with so much change.

Management System	Jan	Feb	Mar	Apr	May	Jun	Jul	Aug	Sep	Oct	Nov	Dec
Board and Executive Committee	EC	ECB	EC	ECB	EC	ECB	EC		ECB	ECB	EC	ECB
Strategic Planning		——	*	——	——	——	*					
Budgets and Target Setting							*	——	——	——	*	
Performance Monitoring	P	P	P	P	P	P	P	P	P	P	P	P
People Review			——	*								
Major Project Reviews	MP	MP	MP	MP	MP	MP	MP	MP	MP	MP	MP	MP
Continuous Improvement	——	——	——	——	——	——	——	——	——	——	——	——

EEI DID NOT DESIGN A MANAGEMENT CALENDAR LIKE THIS AS PART OF THE OPERATING MODEL PROJECT. THE FOCUS WAS ON THE SCORECARD OPPOSITE.

EEI's - management system

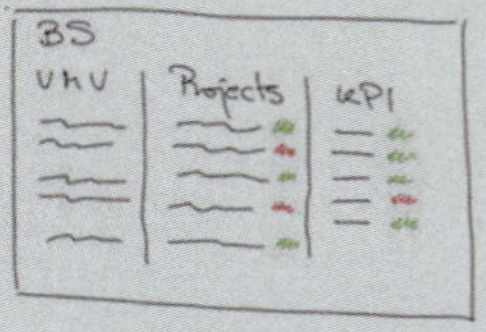

10. Management system

EEI decided to run its management system on a series of monthly meetings designed round a scorecard (shown below). Targets were set every six months. Strategy was debated whenever needed.

Six months was considered to be appropriate, because the company was making so much change. A year would have been too long a period to forecast.

Strategy needed to be under continuous review, because the company was exploring new markets.

Continuous improvement was driven by close monitoring of the key performance indicators.

Vision, mission and values reinforced every month

Color coded performance metrics for each project

Clear charter for every project

Monthly reports on each project reviewed by the CEO

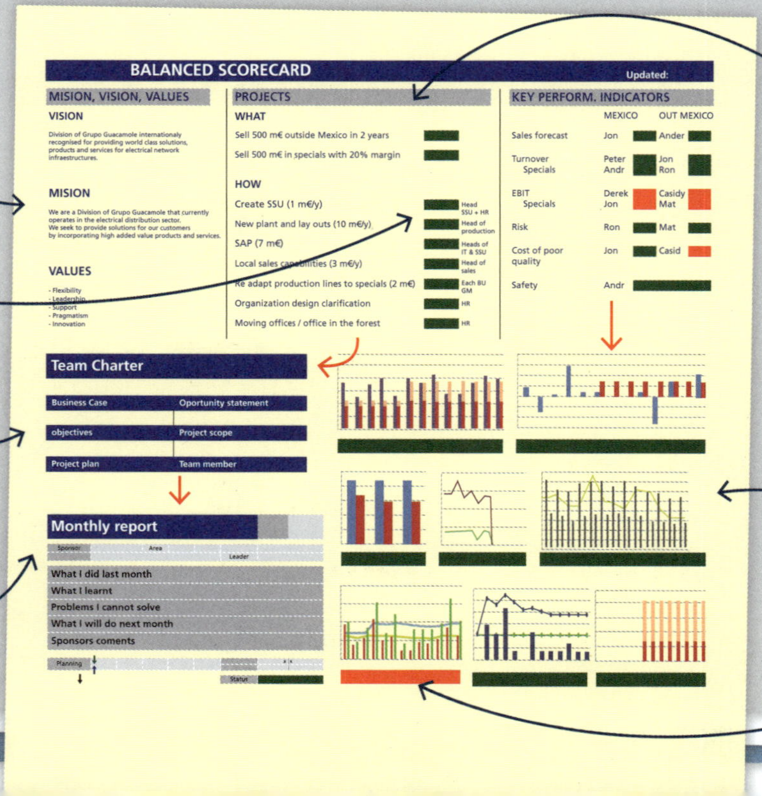

Projects come before key performance indicators because the company's survival depends on change

Charts for every key performance indicator showing continuous improvement over time, or red bars if no improvement

EEI succeeded

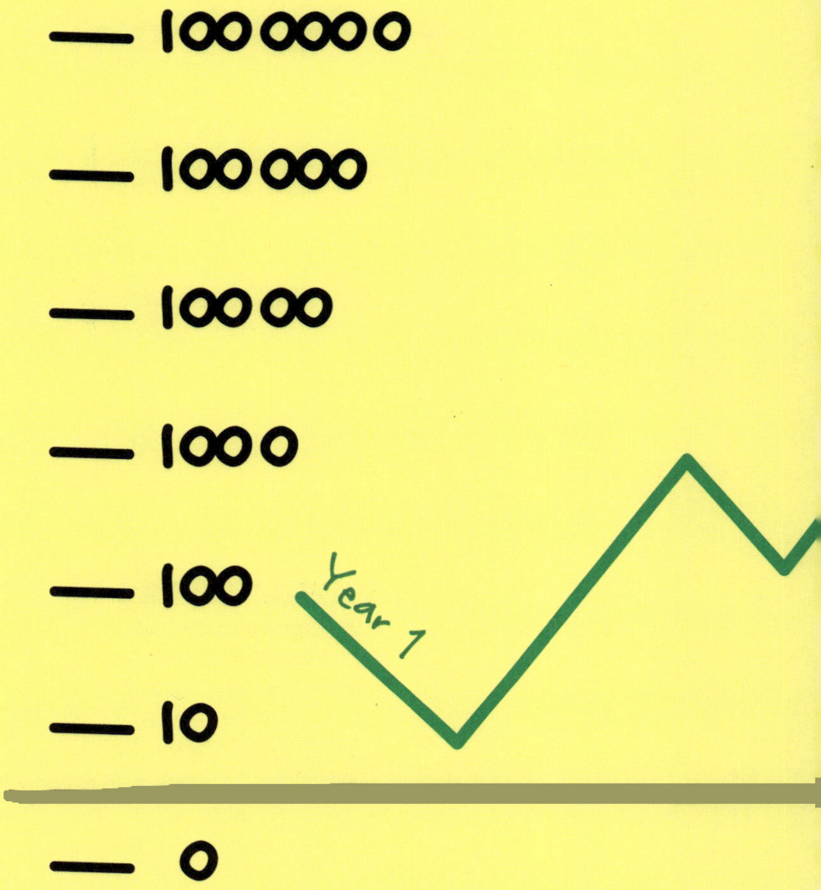

In the following six years:

- Sales tripled
- The number of employees doubled
- The number of countries with direct sales doubled
- The percent of international sales increased from 5% to 38%
- Profits tripled

But it was a lot of hard work and 25% of the top team were changed whilst more than 100 people lost their jobs or were sold/ outsourced

Gain rarely happens without pain

CHAPTER 5

CREATING AN OPERATING MODEL...

CH5

... FOR A FUNCTION

CH5

IT IN EEI

Operating model for a department

After using the operating model methodology to create a 'to be' model for EEI, one of the subsequent pieces of work was to develop an operating model for the IT function. This was a particularly important part of the work in EEI because of the history of the IT function.

History of IT in EEI

When EEI was a local company, based in one location, the IT services were relatively simple. The IT department was in charge of all that was called IT.

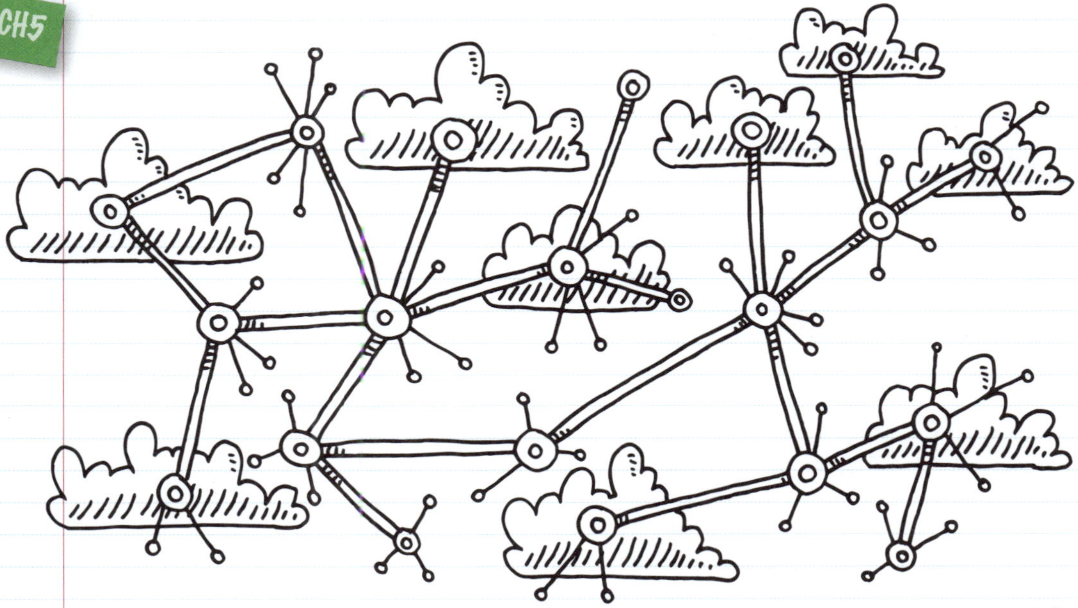

At a certain point in time, a member of the family that owned EEI took over this department, and created a separate company out of it, called TodoTIC (TT).

The objective was to continue to serve EEI, but also to offer services to other companies. The IT function was turned into an independent business. The expectation was that the IT staff would learn what standards were required in the market, and give a better service to EEI as a result.

With hindsight, this arrangement created a problem because there was no one left in EEI with the skills to act as a procurer of IT services. It was assumed that the new IT business would provide EEI with good value services.

But a conflict of interest arose, as the new IT business built up an external customer base: should it give preference to EEI or to its new clients?

Business case

At the same time as the new IT business was growing its external customer base, EEI was becoming a much more complex company: it was expanding into new countries and adding specials to its standard product line.

EEI decided that it needed an ERP system that would make it easier to coordinate across products and across countries. It also needed local applications in some countries providing local language interfaces. TodoTIC could not provide all this support.

As a result, the CEO asked the manager in charge of business process improvement to develop an operating model for a new IT function, within EEI.

The pages that follow summarize the work that he led. He chose to use the Operating Model Canvas as his guide, but did not follow a standard approach.

THE WORK STEPS TO DEVELOP AN ...

WHY THIS PROCESS?

You will see from this example that it is not helpful to be dogmatic about the order of the process steps needed to design an operating model.

In this example, the order of analysis and design followed the issues that were most pressing at each stage. The work started with a value chain map. The focus then moved to the supplier box, because a critical issue was about how much of the value chain map EEI should do in-house. At that time this was the core of the discussion within EEI. And, as you will see later, the decisions were not easy to take.

The work then focused on locations because of the importance of having a solution that could serve the new countries EEI was entering.

Then the work focused on organization: what people and structure would the IT department need to have in place in order to both define its requirements and manage its suppliers.

The leader of the project, then examined who in the IT organization would own which processes and who would make which decisions.

Attention then reverted to locations, in order to make a list of all the investments that would be needed to set up this new function.

Finally, an IT scorecard was developed, with vision, mission and values statements, a list of the main projects, and a list of the measures that would be used to assess the performance of the IT team.

WHERE WERE THE DESIGN PRINCIPLES?

As you read on, you will note that the design work on EEI's IT function proceeded without any formal design principles. This is not recommended. But it can work. Informally the design principles were pretty clear in the head of the project leader. The principles included thoughts such as 'one ERP system', 'outsource where possible', 'consider TodoTIC', 'bespoke applications only where an advantage can be gained'.

...OPERATING MODEL FOR EEI'S IT FUNCTION

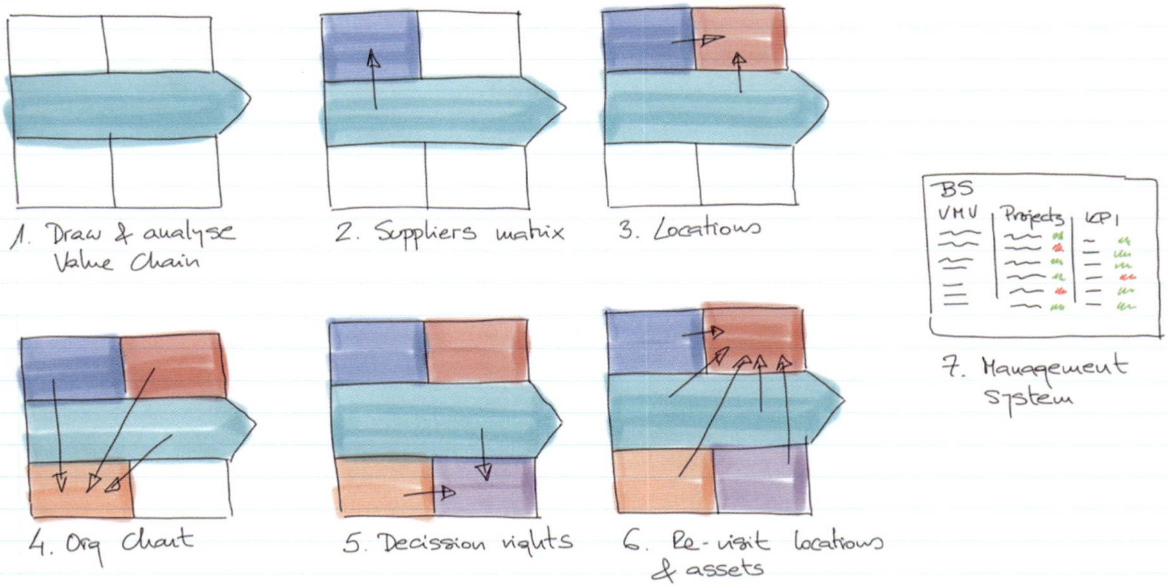

1. VALUE CHAIN MAP

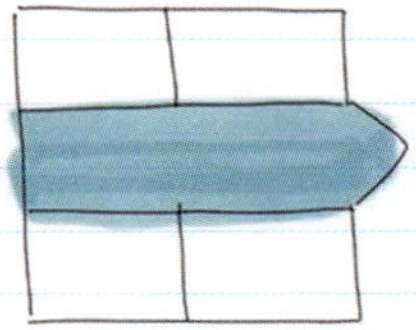

CH5

SEGMENTING EEI'S IT FUNCTION

The first challenge was to segment the IT function by the different services that IT would provide. Four services were identified:

- ERP management;
- Communications management;
- Office systems management;
- IT Infrastructure.

ERP management included all the activities related to defining, optimizing and automating the company's business processes. This value chain involved choosing a suitable ERP system, developing a budget/business case, defining the projects needed to customize and install the system, running and maintaining it once installed, measuring performance and handling user requests and issues.

Communication management included all the activities needed for the company's intranet and extranet. This value chain involved defining what was needed, developing a business case, defining projects, running and maintaining the system, assessing its performance and handling issues that arose.

Office systems management included, selection, installation and maintenance of the company's standard office-based applications - email, Word, Excel, Internet, etc…

IT infrastructure included the selection and management of PCs, servers, routers, and other devices needed to support the ERP system, the communications systems and the office applications.

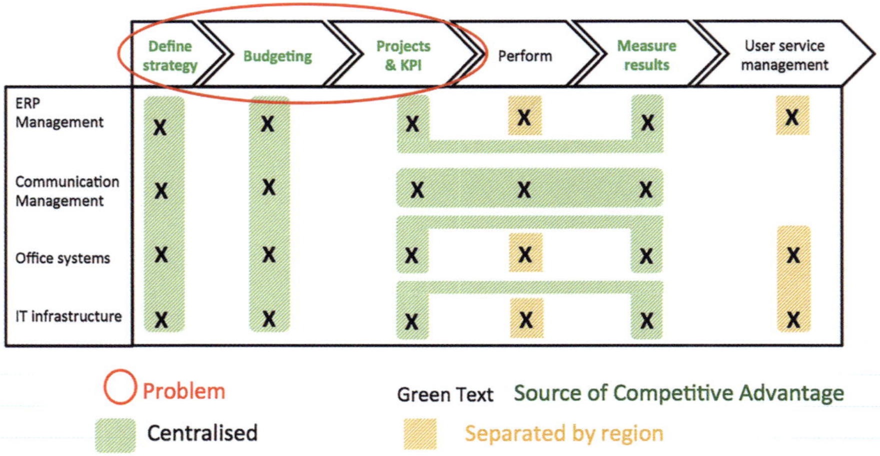

VALUE CHAIN MAP

After drawing out the value chains for each of the four segments, the team decided that the steps in the value chains were similar:

- Define strategy;
- Budgeting/Business Case;
- Projects & KPIs;
- Perform and Maintain;
- Measure results;
- User service management.

Define strategy meant selecting the solutions and defining the five year vision. **Budgeting** meant developing the business cases to support the strategy and preparing year-on-year budgets. **Projects & KPIs** meant defining and setting up the projects needed to achieve the objectives. It also meant defining the KPIs that would need to be achieved. **Perform and maintain** meant executing the projects, and running and maintaining the systems (likely to be outsourced). **Measure results** meant measuring with data how good the performance had been compared to the KPIs. **User service management** refers to call centers and user interface.

PROBLEMS AND EXCELLENCE

Problems. Because EEI had little IT expertise and needed to change its way of operating, the problems were at the beginning of the value chain: *define strategy, budgeting, projects & KPIs*. It was clear that these activities could not be done by the existing supplier. *Perform* and *user management* steps were in general not a problem. They were being done well by the existing supplier (with the exception of ERP management).

Sources of advantage/excellence. The IT function would become a source of advantage or excellence if it effectively supported EEI's moves into new countries and into specials. So IT needed to choose the right solutions, define the right projects, identify the right KPIs, and measure them properly. These were all areas where problems also existed.

TOGETHER/SEPARATED

Together refers to those activities that could be centralized within the IT function, across the four different services. *Defining strategy and Budgeting/business case* were both activities that would be best done together and probably by the head of the IT function.

User service needed to be separated by region because it would be provided locally (and probably outsourced). There was also an important local element in *Perform*, in most service areas.

Defining projects and *measuring results* needed to be done centrally in Mexico, but by different specialists in each of the four services.

CH5

2. Suppliers Matrix

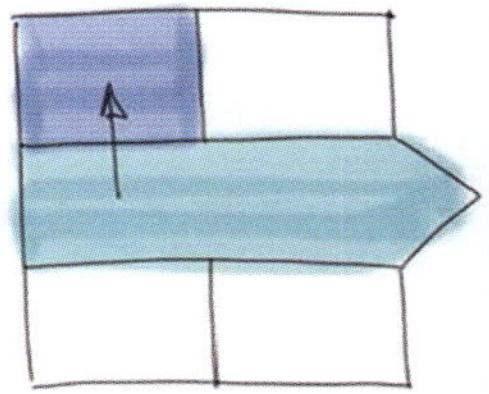

WHY SUPPLIERS AT THIS POINT, AND NOT AFTER ORGANIZATION, LOCATIONS AND IT?

The question ***"What should we do and what should others do?"*** became the next most important topic following the value chain map. As the team considered the 'problem areas' and the 'sources of excellence', they realized that they had a big problem. External suppliers might not do these steps well because of conflicts of interest, yet EEI did not have the skills to do them well either.

SUPPLIER MATRIX (SEE OPPOSITE)

The supplier matrix was used to examine this issue. The process steps were plotted on the matrix. On the axis '***How good are we compared to others?***' the answer was easy. EEI did not have the skills, so the company was worse than others for all steps.

On the axis '***Is it a source of competitive advantage?***' the answer was also easy. The analysis from the value chain map could be used.

ANALYSIS OF THE CHART

The orange steps are in the 'outsource' part of the chart, while the green steps are in the 'design a collaborative agreement' part of the chart.

Since the orange steps are already subcontracted, the chart suggests that nothing needs to change.

The problem comes with the green steps. How could EEI design a collaborative agreement for such activities? The team decided that it would be too difficult to develop a suitable collaborative agreement for these steps. They needed to have the skills in-house. This meant building up the skills in EEI so that EEI would be better than suppliers at these steps, as shown by the arrows on the chart.

ACTIONS DERIVED FROM THE CHART

EEI concluded that it would take too long to develop internal people with the relevant skills. So it needed to hire from outside. The existing supplier – TodoTIC - was approached, but was unwilling to release people because these people were needed to develop its own business.

So EEI decided to search externally for the relevant skills.

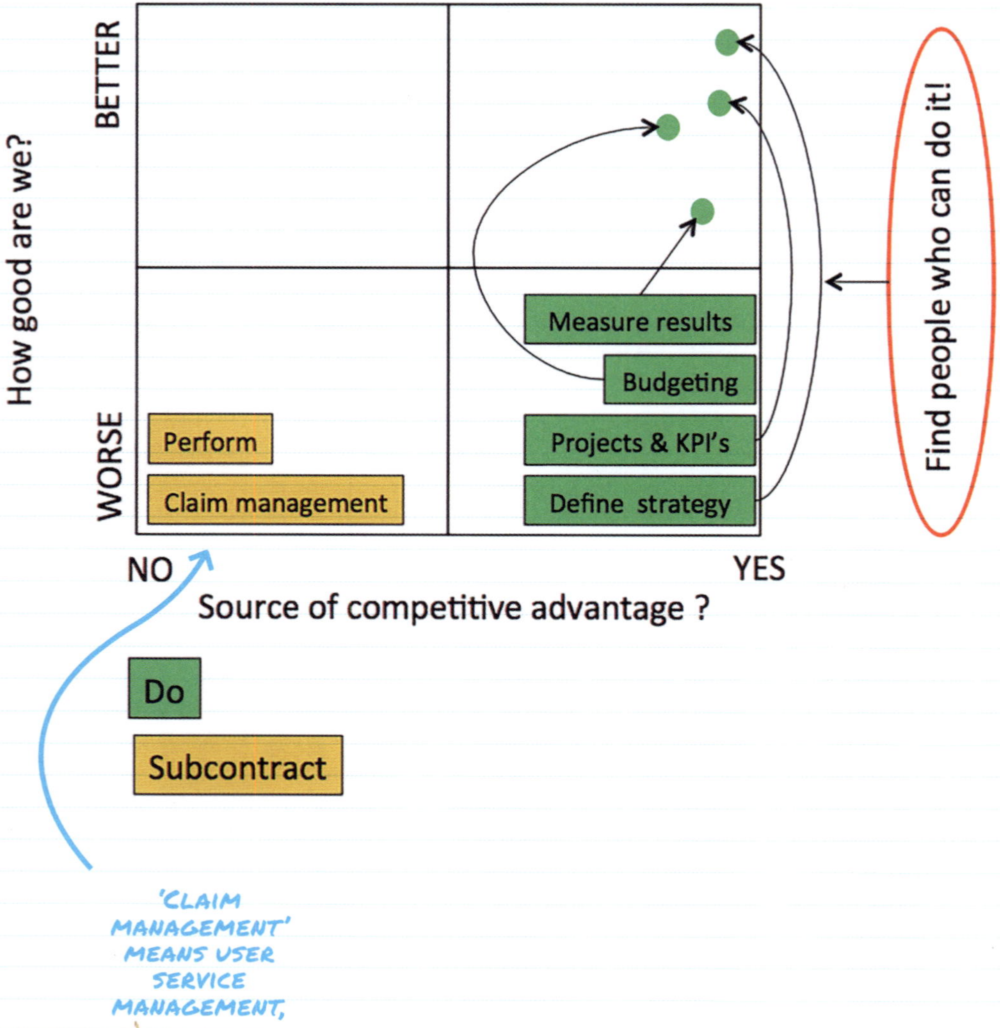

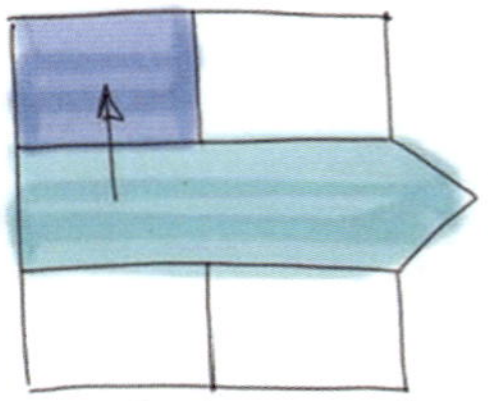

2. Suppliers matrix

CH5

3. Locations

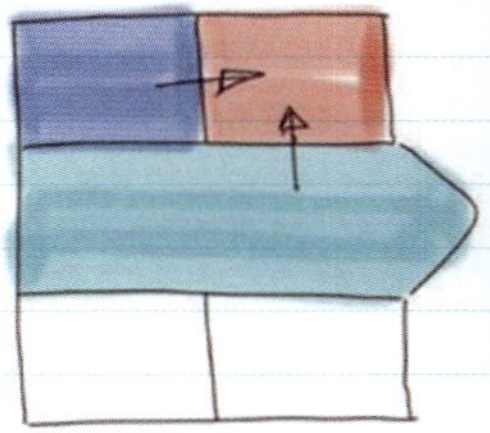

3. Locations

> **WHY LOCATIONS AT THIS POINT, AND NOT AFTER ORGANIZATION?**
> In the value chain map, the team decided that *perform* and *user service* should be 'separated by region' (at least the ERP and office systems). Both activities were ones that could be subcontracted (see supplier matrix). Unfortunately the current supplier did not have the capability to provide these services outside of Mexico.
>
> So, before considering organization, the team had a discussion about what 'separated by region' actually meant in terms of resources and whether it was still OK to outsource these activities. The locations chart proved helpful.

CH5

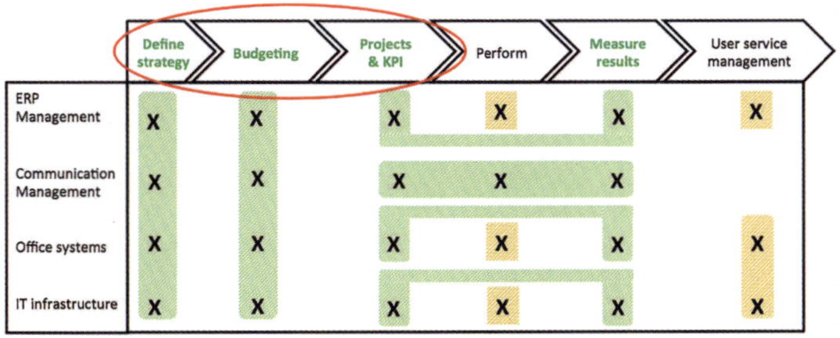

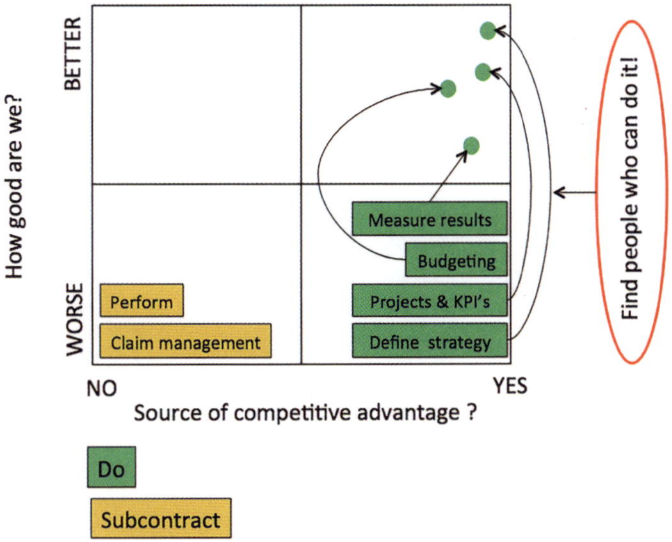

LOCATIONS CHART

The world map on the opposite page shows the locations where IT support in the local language could be needed. There are more spots on this chart than on the locations chart for the EEI operating model because the IT team felt that they needed to look further ahead.

A central team in Mexico would take care of the *strategy, budgeting, projects* and *measures* part of the value chain. But there would be around 15 additional locations where IT *perform* and *user service* could be needed.

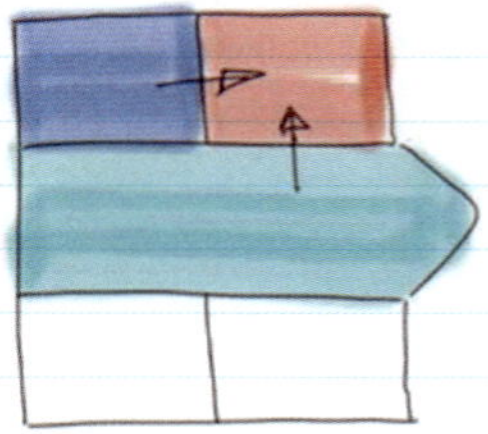

3. Locations

SUBCONTRACTING ARRANGEMENTS

It became clear that 90% of the work, in terms of man hours, would be done in the orange locations.

The existing supplier could cover Mexico and three Latin American countries. So the initial idea was to hire an additional subcontractor to cover the other countries.

But EEI did not have the skills to identify and hire a good supplier. So it was decided to give the world-wide contract to the existing supplier – TodoTIC - who would then find local subcontractors to work with. The existing supplier had the skills to identify appropriate subcontractors.

EEI had performance KPIs and penalties with the existing supplier, who was responsible for managing all the sub-contractors.

Since this was a development opportunity for the existing supplier (and remembering that the owner of this existing supplier was a member of the same family who owned EEI), EEI was able to negotiate a good deal for the provision of these *perform* and *user service* activities.

4. ORGANIZATION CHART

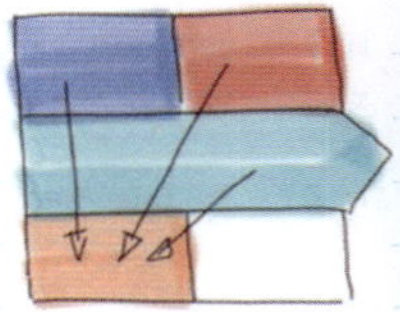

THE ORGANIZATION MODEL

The first decision taken by the BPI director, even before starting the project, was to hire an IT director. He needed someone to help with the operating model design who understood IT issues. It was difficult to convince the existing supplier - TodoTIC - that EEI needed to define its own IT strategy and operating model. But the BPI director was convinced that it would be better for both in the medium and long term.

Fortunately, it was clear to TodoTIC, that the objective was not to create a large IT department in EEI. So cooperation was good.

The work on the value chain map, had convinced the BPI director that EEI must have control of IT *strategy* and *business case*. This would be the main work for the IT director. It is represented on the organization chart as a centralized activity, but was not intended as a separate person.

Projects, KPIs and *measure results* needed to be done by specialists in each area, so it was decided to have one person for each service line – ERP, communications, infrastructure and office systems. These individuals would work with the IT director on the strategies and business cases for their areas and then define and manage projects and overall performance through the suppliers.

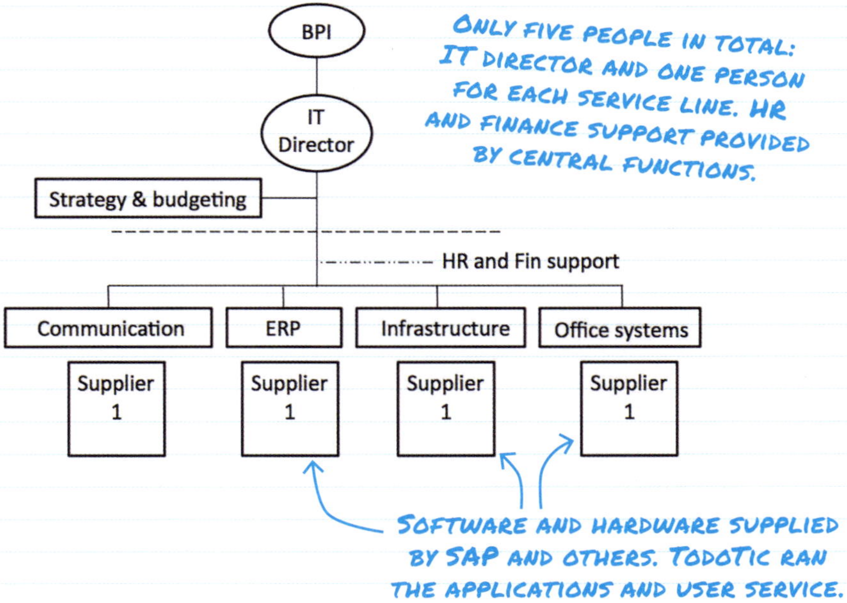

ANALYSIS OF THE ORGANIZATION MODEL

Issues & obstacles. All boxes on the organization chart were a problem, because, with the exception of the IT director, the people did not exist. Moreover, EEI needed to find people who had the technical knowledge to define and manage projects, were capable of discussing strategy, and were able to build a relationship with TodoTIC, while being strong enough to tell TodoTIC what to do.

Difficult links. The main difficult links were expected to be with TodoTIC.

Sources of competitive advantage. All of the roles in this small IT function were considered to be sources of excellence.

Separation. By having a separate individual managing each service, EEI was recognizing the benefits of separating the services rather than managing them as one.

CH5

5. Decision rights

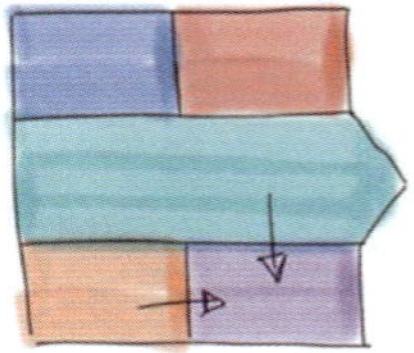

RAPID analysis

The team did a RAPID analysis to confirm the different roles in this five-person IT function.

The BPI director retained decision rights over the IT budget, with the IT director expected to make a recommendation. Of course, the BPI director's decision could be challenged by EEI's executive committee and the CEO. But in terms of the IT function, the BPI director had the final say on budget.

	Define strategy	Budgeting	Projects & KPI	Perform	Measure results	Decision rights
BPI director	A	D				
IT director	D	R			A	
ERP lead	R		D		D	
Comm. lead	R		D		D	
Infra. lead	R		D		D	
Office lead	R		D		D	
Suppliers				P		P

Recommend
Agree
Perform
Input
Decide

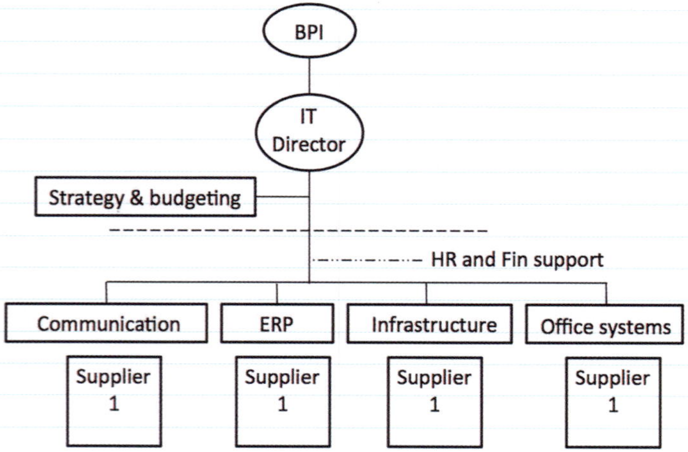

The IT director had the decision rights over IT strategy, in all four service areas. The service leads being expected to make recommendations to him.

The head of each service had decision rights for defining projects, KPIs and monitoring supplier performance in their service areas. The delivery of projects and of IT performance was all outsourced to suppliers.

6. Revisit Locations & Assets

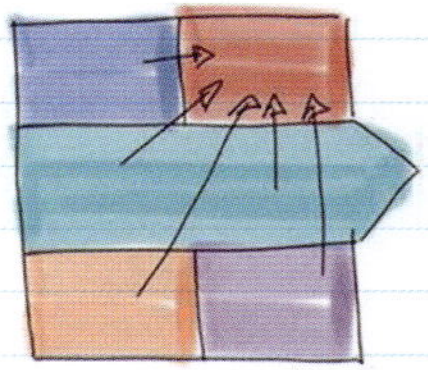

What assets to own?

The BPI director revisited the locations topic in order to define the investment that would be needed in each location to support this transformation.

After some discussion, it was decided that it would be best if EEI owned as few IT assets as possible. The BPI director took the view that EEI did not have enough capability to look after IT equipment. The head of infrastructure should have the capability to advise on strategy and select equipment, but not be responsible for 'up time' and 'maintenance'. As a result all assets were leased.

Nevertheless there were still expensive projects to be costed (see opposite). The total capital cost was expected to be $7 million, with a running cost of $2.6 million per year.

PROJECTS

Find people with knowledge	HR dir	0'3m€/y
ERP implementation	ERP resp	7m€ + 1m€/y
Communications definition + implem	Comm resp	0'2m€/y
Infraestructures	Infr def	0'4m€/y
Offimatic	off resp	0'7m€/y
Define strategy	IT resp	
		7m€ + 2'6m€/y

CH5

7. MANAGEMENT SYSTEM

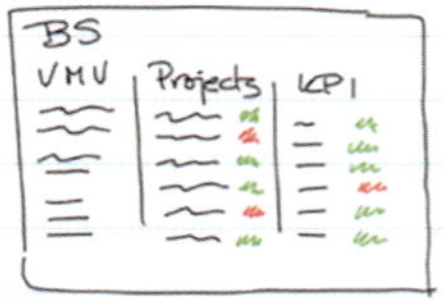

7. Management system

WE HAVE NOT INCLUDED SOME OF THE DETAILS IN THIS CHART FOR CONFIDENTIALITY REASONS.

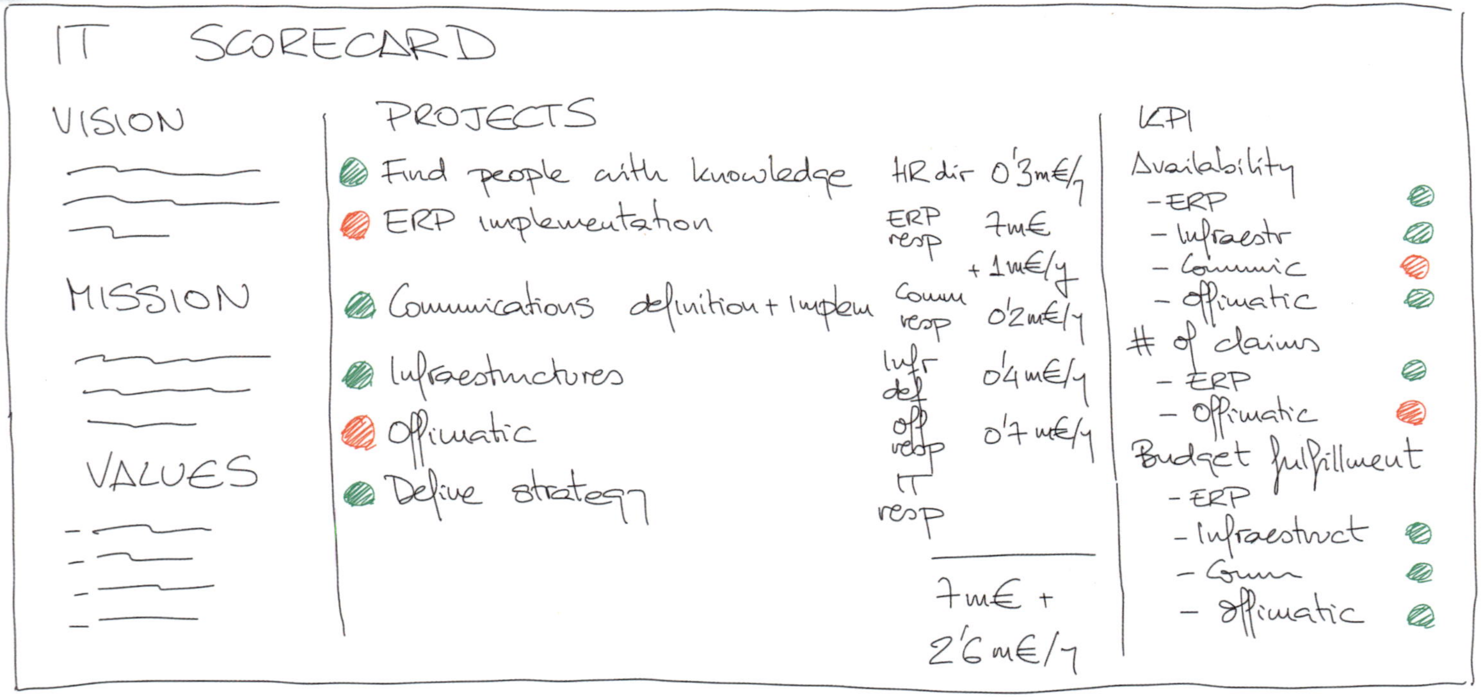

CH5

AND THERE YOU HAVE 'IT' ... IN SIX CHARTS

DEVELOPING AN OPERATING MODEL EVEN FOR A FIVE PERSON FUNCTION IS STILL QUITE A BIT OF WORK.

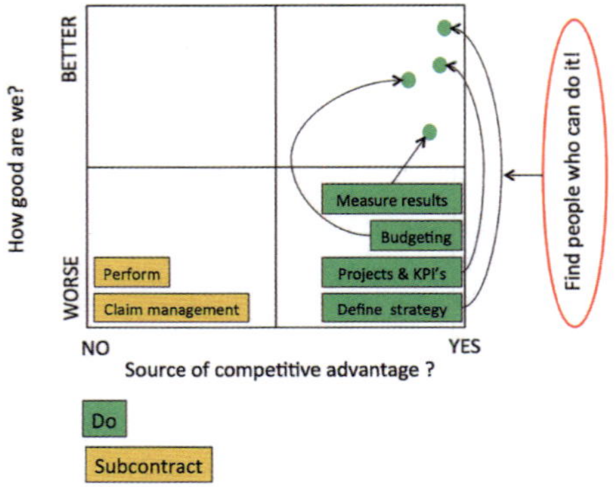

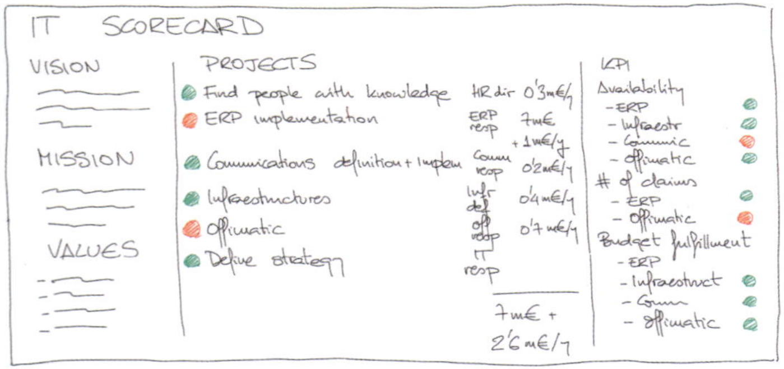

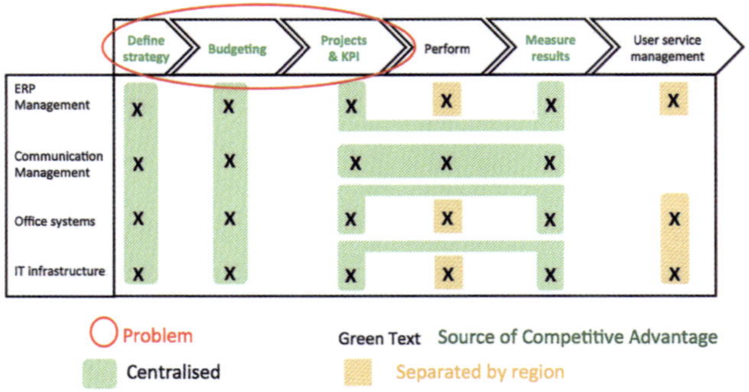

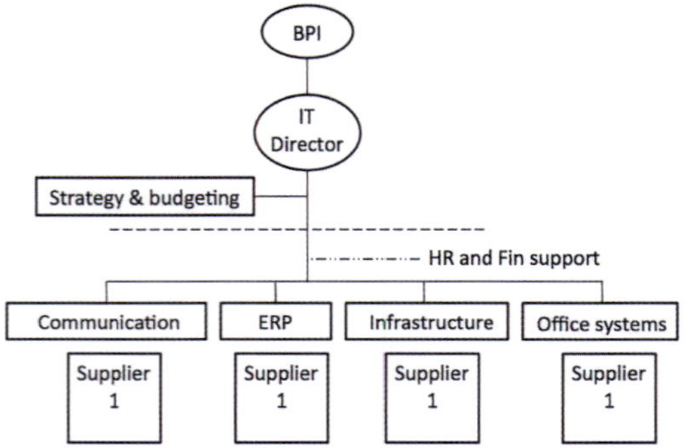

	Define strategy	Budgeting	Projects & KPI	Perform	Measure results	Decision rights
BPI director	A	D				
IT director	D	R			A	
ERP lead	R		D		D	
Comm. lead	R		D		D	
Infra. lead	R		D		D	
Office lead	R		D		D	
Suppliers				P		P

SOME THOUGHTS FOR IT EXPERTS

IT REFERENCE ARCHITECTURE

The Open Group (see page 131) has created a reference value chain map for the IT function (see below). You will see in the value chain map on page 185 some similarities – at least with the plan, build, deliver, run sequence. The differences though are also interesting.

The EEI map focuses more attention on the different services – ERP, office systems, etc. This raises the interesting question of whether it is more helpful to think of IT as one value chain or many, with consequences for the operating model, particularly the organization structure and people models.

The argument for thinking of IT as multiple value chains comes from the market place of suppliers, most of which specialize or at least have sub-units that specialize. EEI's structure may have been influenced by this.

CH5

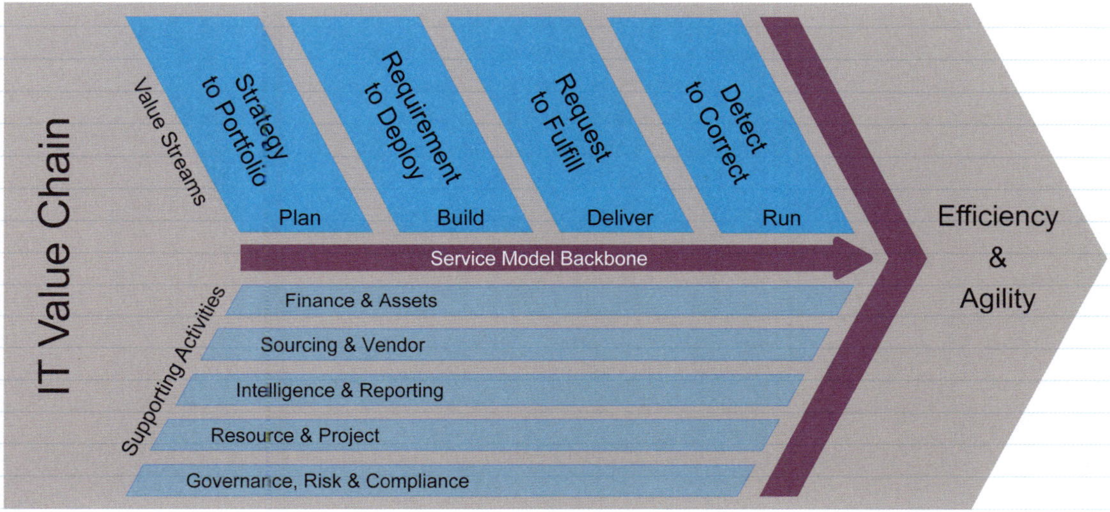

REFERENCE ARCHITECTURES

The Open Group and many consultants are enthusiastically creating reference architectures for different functions and types of business. The example below is taken from a consultancy called BiZZdesign. It is a capability reference map for the insurance industry provided by Marc Lankhorst, one of the founders.

The benefit of these reference architectures is that they save work. A team can take the reference as a starting point for their work. The danger is that it reduces the likelihood that the team will start with the customers and the value propositions and work backwards into value chains and value chain maps.

So we are slightly in two minds about these aids to operating model work, particularly for high-level work where strategic thinking is most valuable. References and benchmarks are helpful. However, they are no substitute for starting with first principles: what are you trying to do, for whom and why?

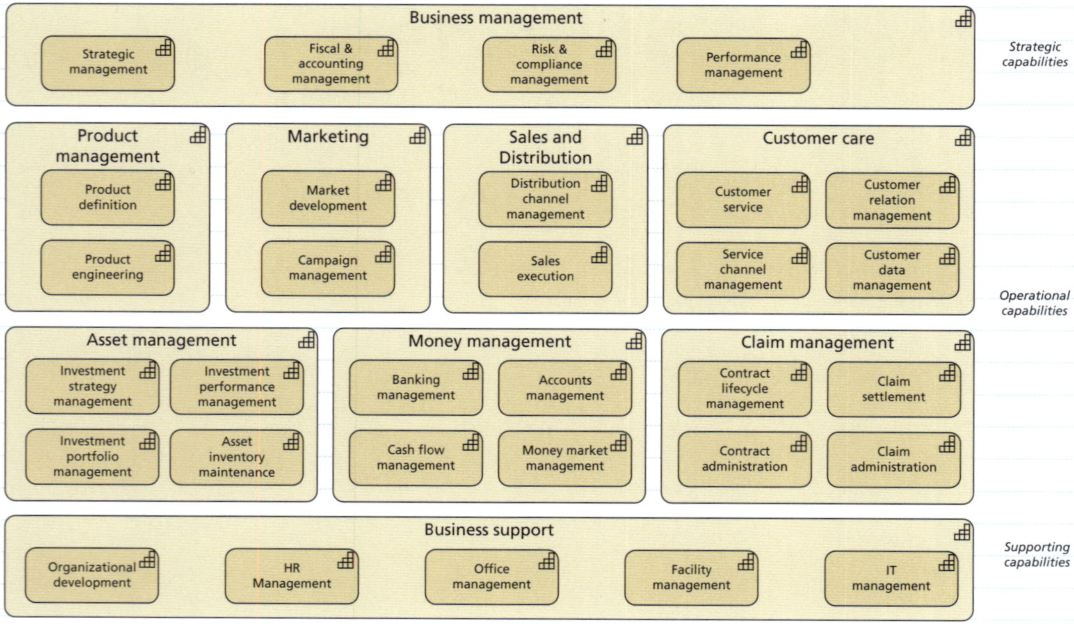

CH5

CHAPTER 6

CH6

Examples... ... of operating model change

E-MAIL
CONTENT
PEOPLE RESOURCE
Leader
TEAM
Risk
RESPONSIVE WEB DESIGN
WEB

Strategic change management ...

A large Life and Pensions company wanted to improve its ability to respond to change. At the time there were separate teams for each area of expertise: strategy, business model, transformation, lean and technology. As change projects moved from one team to the next, there was significant documentation, signing-off processes and hand-over requirements. Because change took so long, adjustments were needed to the original plan as circumstances changed, creating extensive re-work and re-documentation. The result was slow and expensive change.

The organization identified some design principles:

- Provide a faster and more responsive change capability;
- Move from a philosophy of doing everything 100% correct to delivering quick functionality;
- Deliver change in "sprints" to allow for changing requirements;
- Reduce time spent on documentation;
- Share skills across teams.

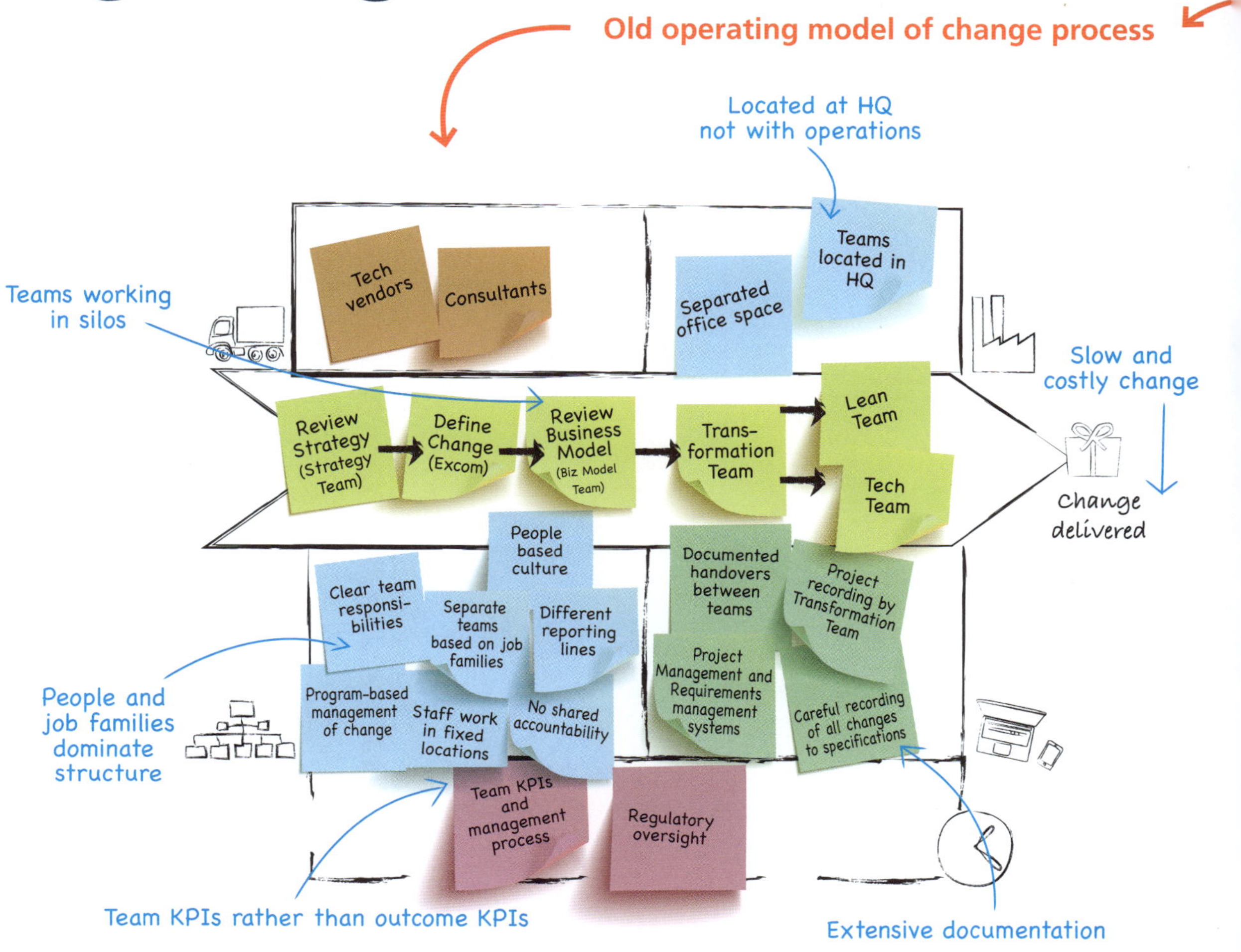

... in an insurance company

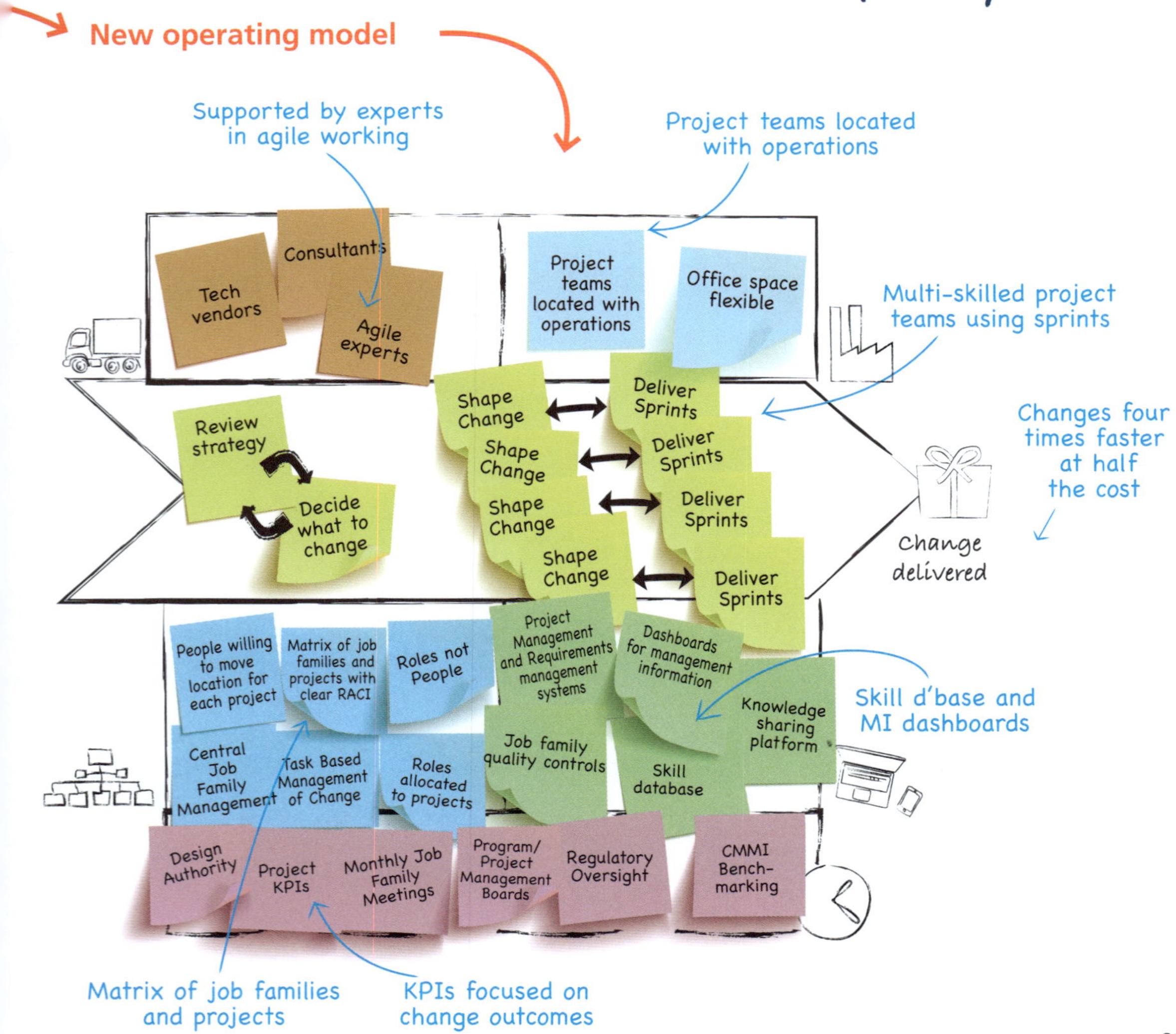

Processes

Moved from functional silos, with documented hand-offs, to multi-skilled teams focused on change projects using agile methods.

Organization

A matrix structure with functions acting as job family leaders and Transformation leading day-to-day management of projects. Transformation is accountable for change outcomes; functions for competence and people development. Career path based on professional competencies, values and willingness to work in multiple roles and locations. Some people not suitable so counseled out of the organization.

Locations

Projects now co-located with the business area concerned. Function heads co-located at HQ to promote process development and collaboration.

Information

Skills database, project-based information system and knowledge platform, all open access.

Suppliers

Suppliers that have a proven record in Agile working.

Management processes

Design Authority to ensure that multiple projects advance the overall organizational development.

Project-based KPIs.

Strong regulatory oversight.

Benchmarking of capabilities with CMMI.

Addressing complexity caused by...

A US company with three product divisions was suffering from some performance issues. Certain segments were not being well served. The product divisions were slow to react to market changes. Margins were not increasing despite rising volumes.

A few years earlier, to save costs, the company had created a multi-product sales function, across its three product divisions. As the product divisions grew, managers had been complaining that the complexities created by this shared sales force were slowing down decisions, increasing costs and making it hard for product divisions to keep in touch with their customers. The managers in sales were critical of slow product development in product Divisions, unclear objectives and exhausting planning and target-setting processes.

The chief executive decided to review the operating model because he wanted to accelerate growth and profits.

CH6

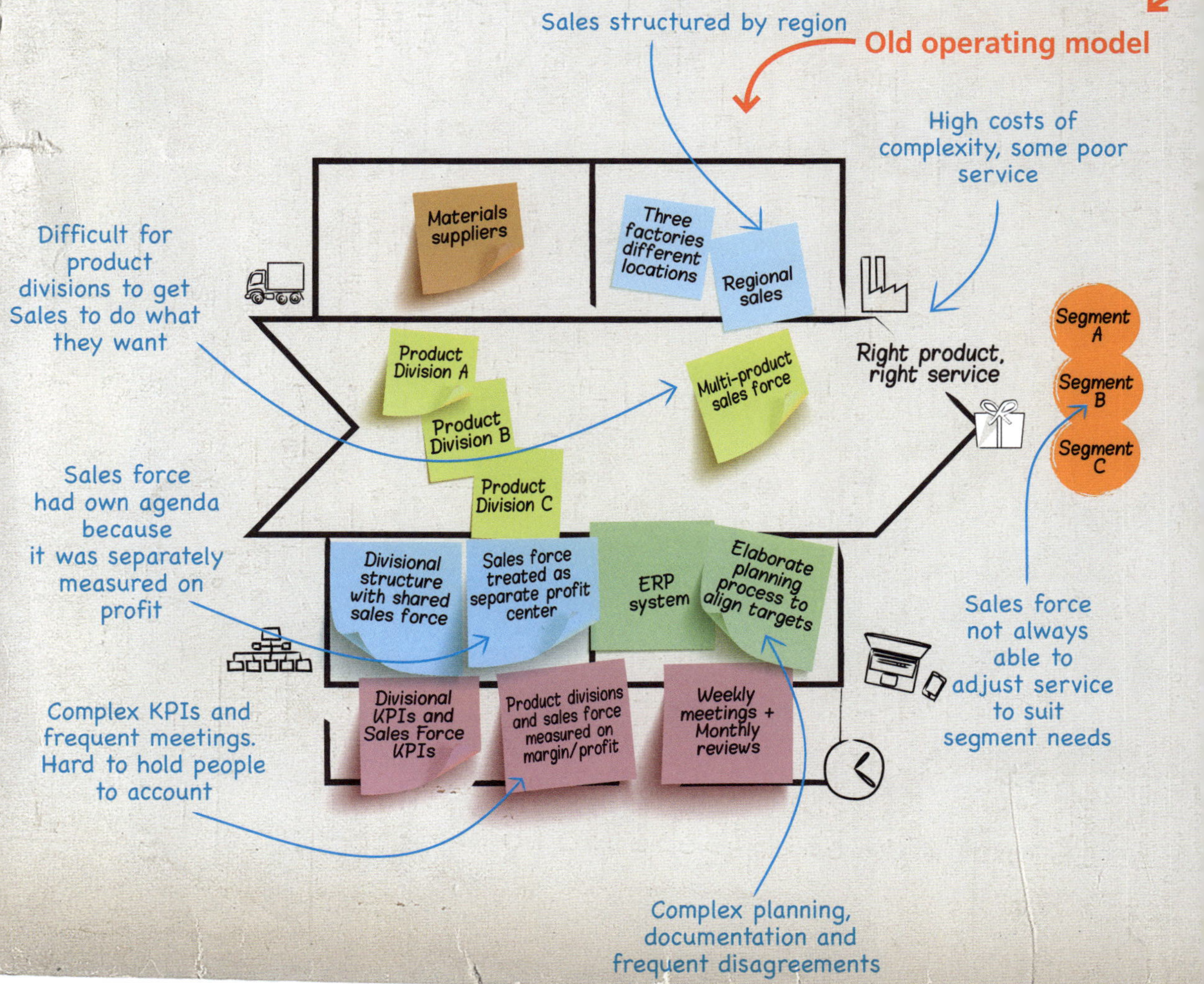

... a shared sales force

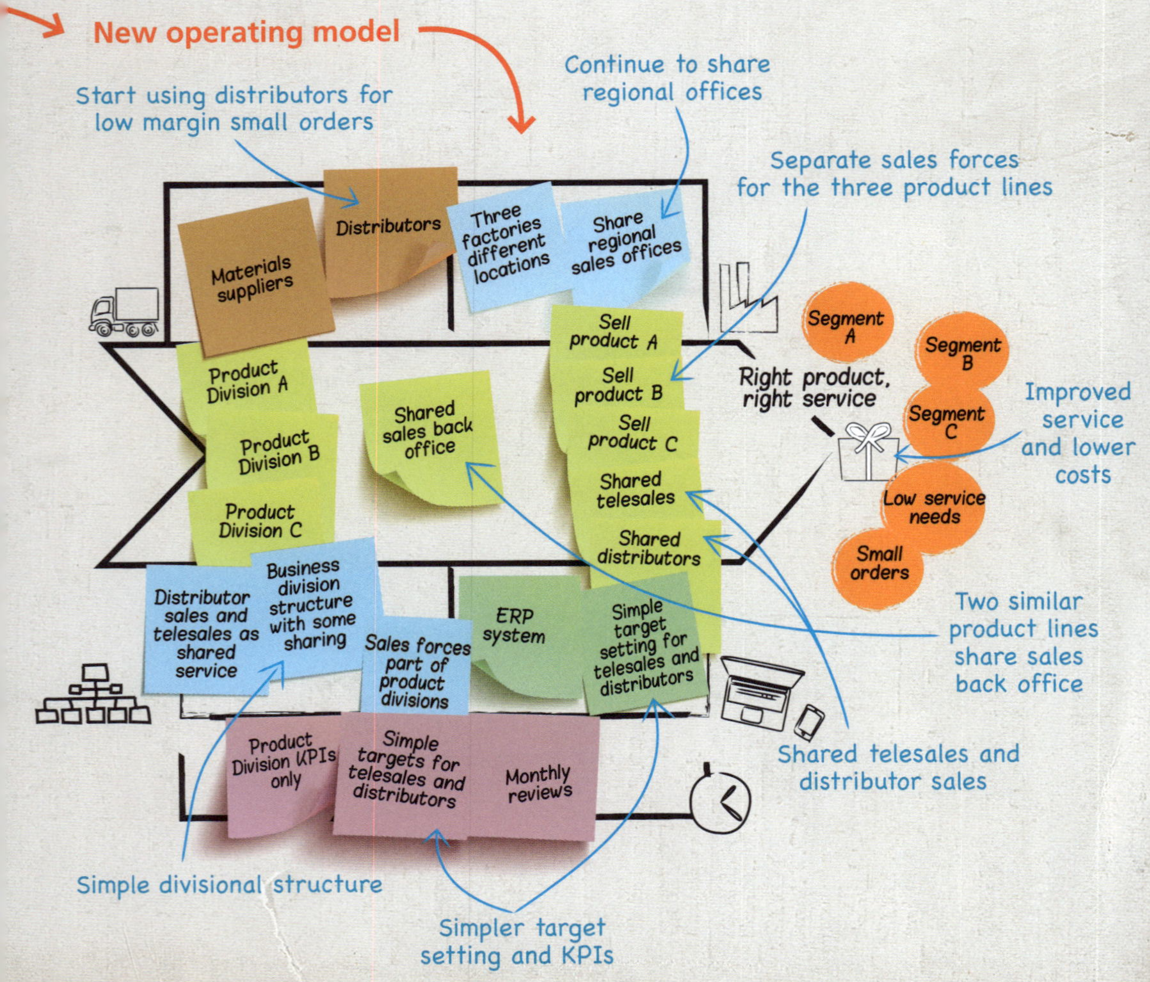

Processes
Moved from shared sales force to sales forces aligned with product divisions, but retained some overhead sharing as well as shared telesales for customers with low service needs and shared distributors for small orders.

Organization
Simplify the organization so that the product divisions are fully accountable. Shared elements are 'shared services'.

Locations
No location changes.

Information
Reduce the coordination needed across products lines.

Suppliers
Use distributors for small orders.

Management processes
Simplified accountabilities.
Decisions made by product divisions
Shared elements set up as cost centers.
Monthly rather than weekly management meetings.

Speeding up the custom design ...

A company was losing market share and profitability in its custom design business. Competitors were faster at designing products for their customers and appeared to have lower design costs.

The company was confident that it had good designers and leading technology. It was also proud of its robust design process that ensured designs were fully compliant and tested before they were offered to the customer.

Analysis of the custom design team, suggested that the problem could be the large number of designers involved in each project. Data showed that the more designers involved, the longer the design work took.

In addition, customers suggested that the products were sometimes over-engineered. They contained features and technologies that were not needed by the customer.

Another problem was the number of approval steps required before a design could be offered to the customer. Bottlenecks were causing delays.

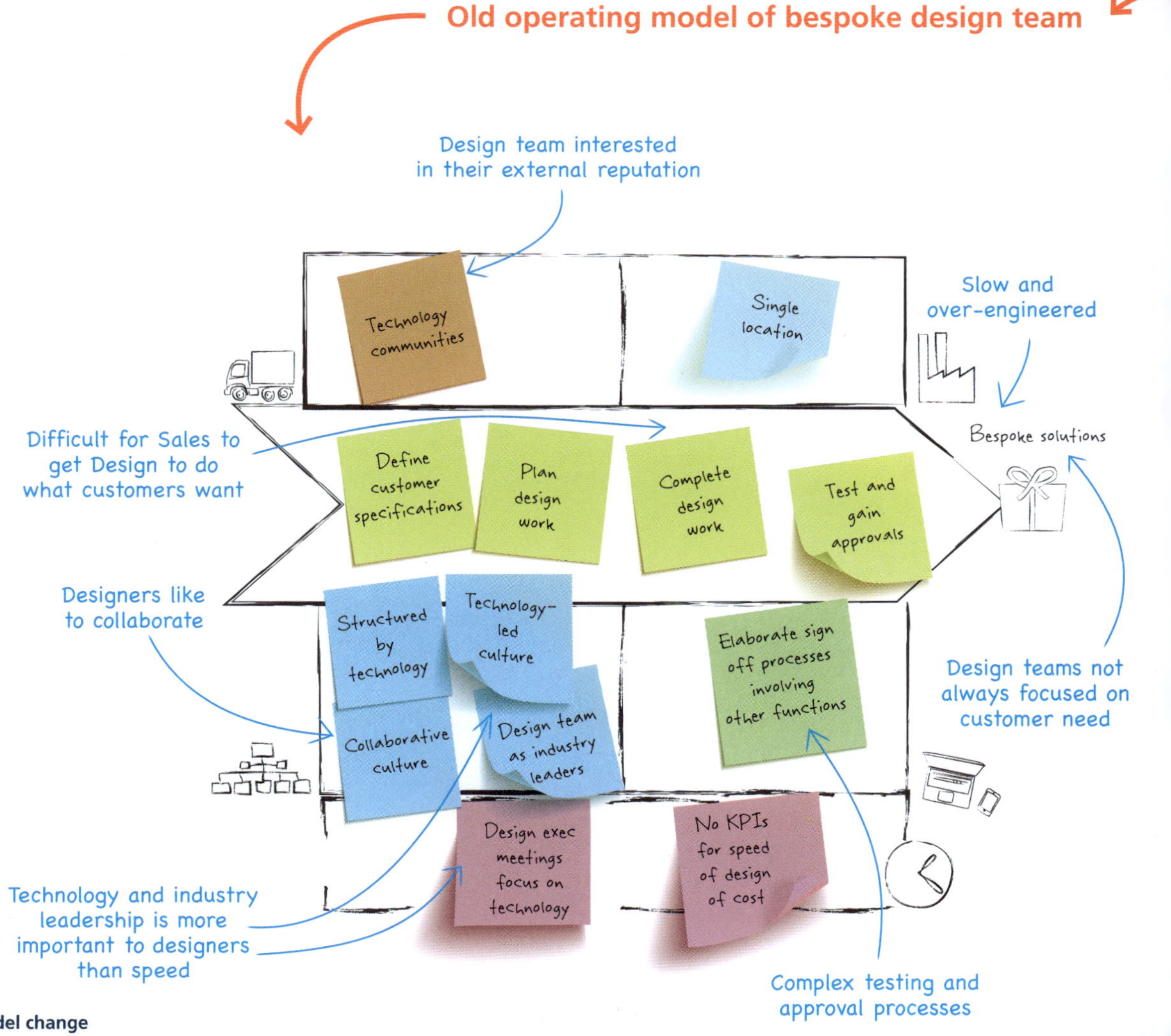

CH6

... team for bespoke products

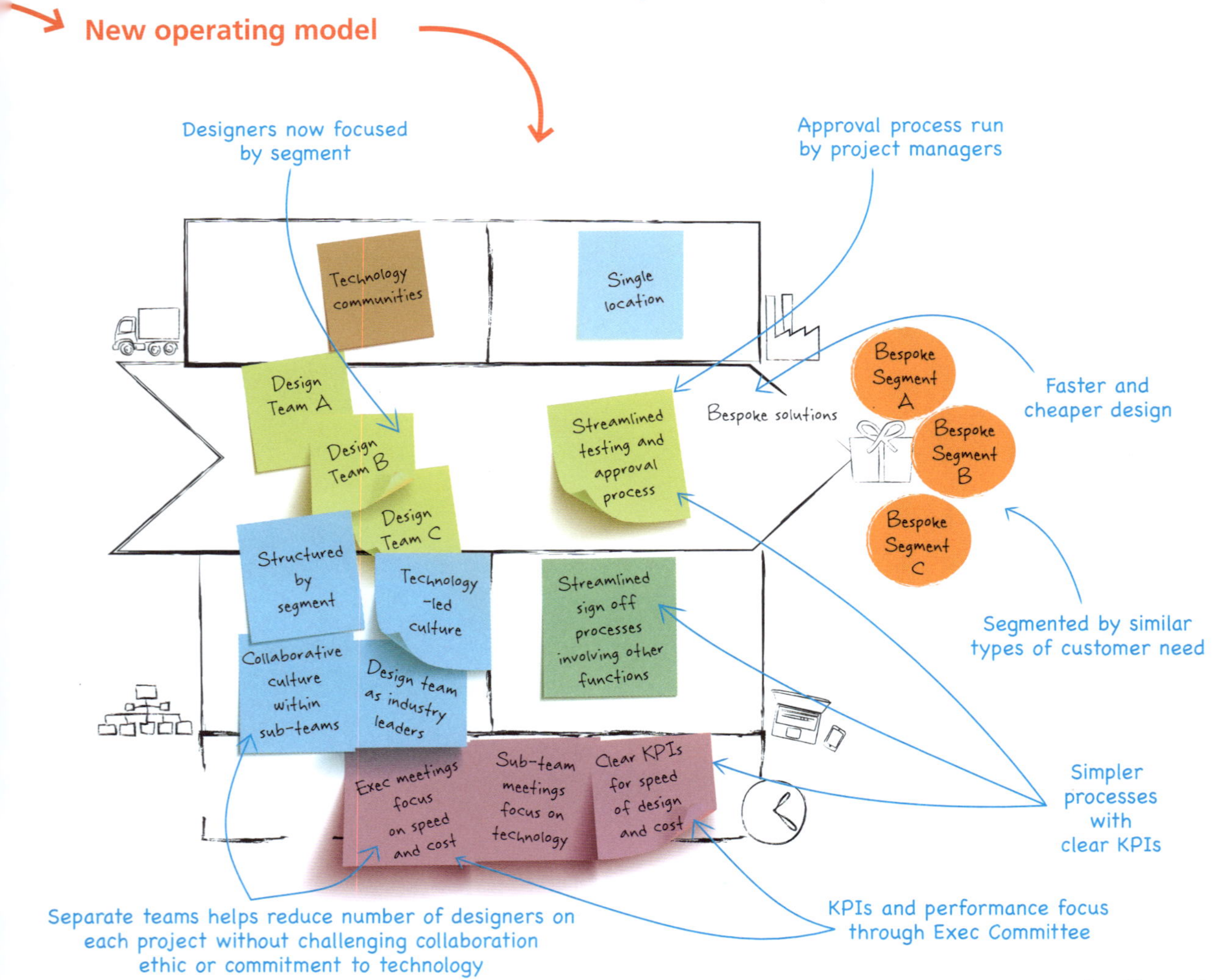

Processes
No change in design process steps but fewer designers involved by limiting team size. Streamlined approval process.

Organization
No change in people model. Create smaller teams focused on different segments. Create separate team responsible for approvals.

Locations
No location changes.

Information
Streamlined links with other functions.

Suppliers
No changes.

Management Processes
Two levels of meeting allow for a focus on both technology and performance.
Clear KPIs create a focus on speed and cost.
Some team comparisons help motivate more attention to speed and cost.

Remodeling the HR function ...

The company has two retailing brands: a grocery business unit and a fashion and homewares business unit. Both BUs have online businesses.

The culture is paternalistic and supportive of employees, resulting in a large HR function involved in employee development, benefits management, talent, corporate social responsibility and other areas.

The problem was multi-dimensional. The HR function was perceived to be too costly, so there was a desire to simplify and cut costs, especially in the management structure of HR and in the cost of employee development. Because each division had different views, training programmes were often being redesigned at significant expense to accommodate minor preferences.

There was also a desire to reallocate some HR cost to areas such as 'analytics' and 'diversity and inclusion', as well as to be more strategic and less reactive.

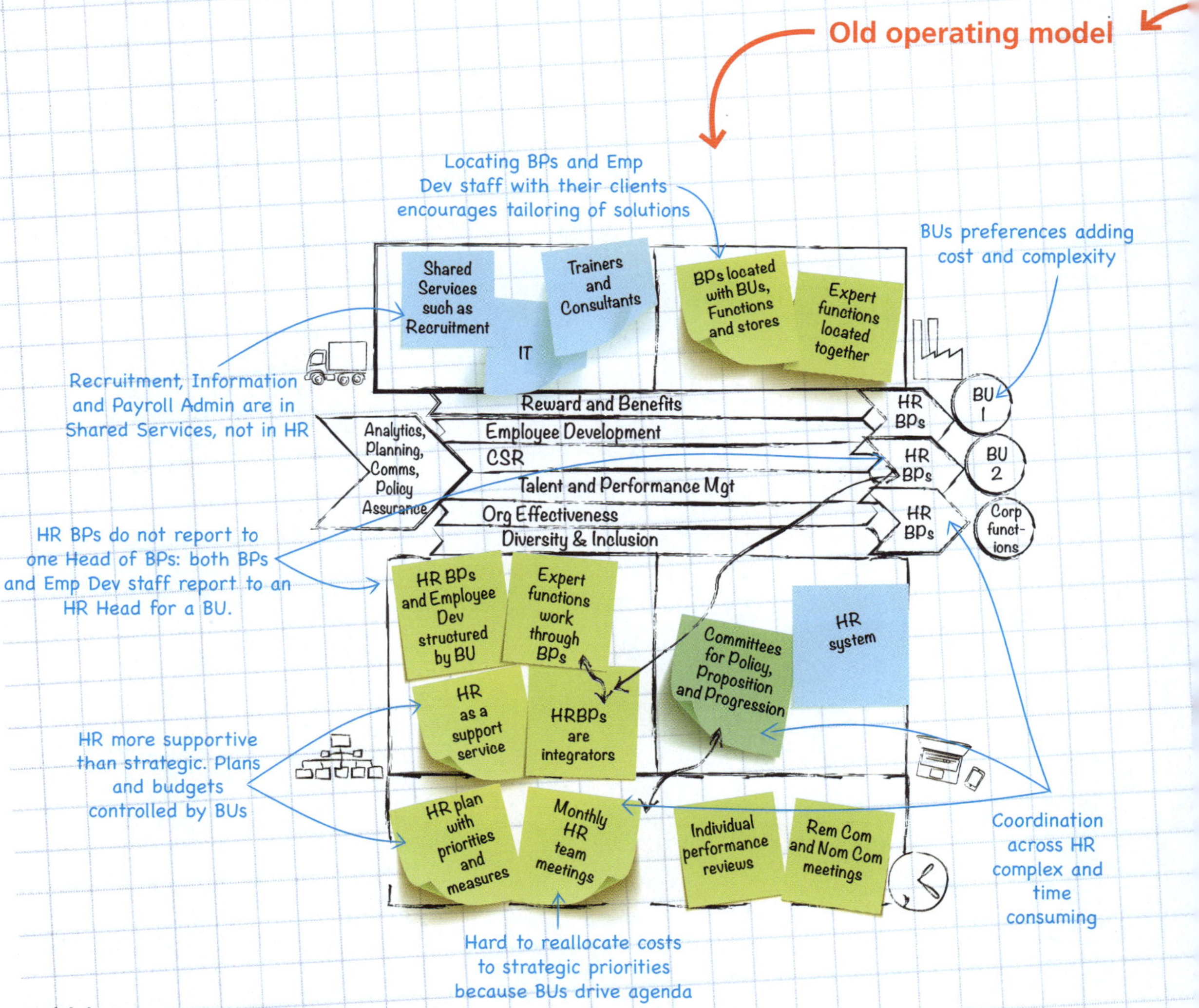

... of a European retailer

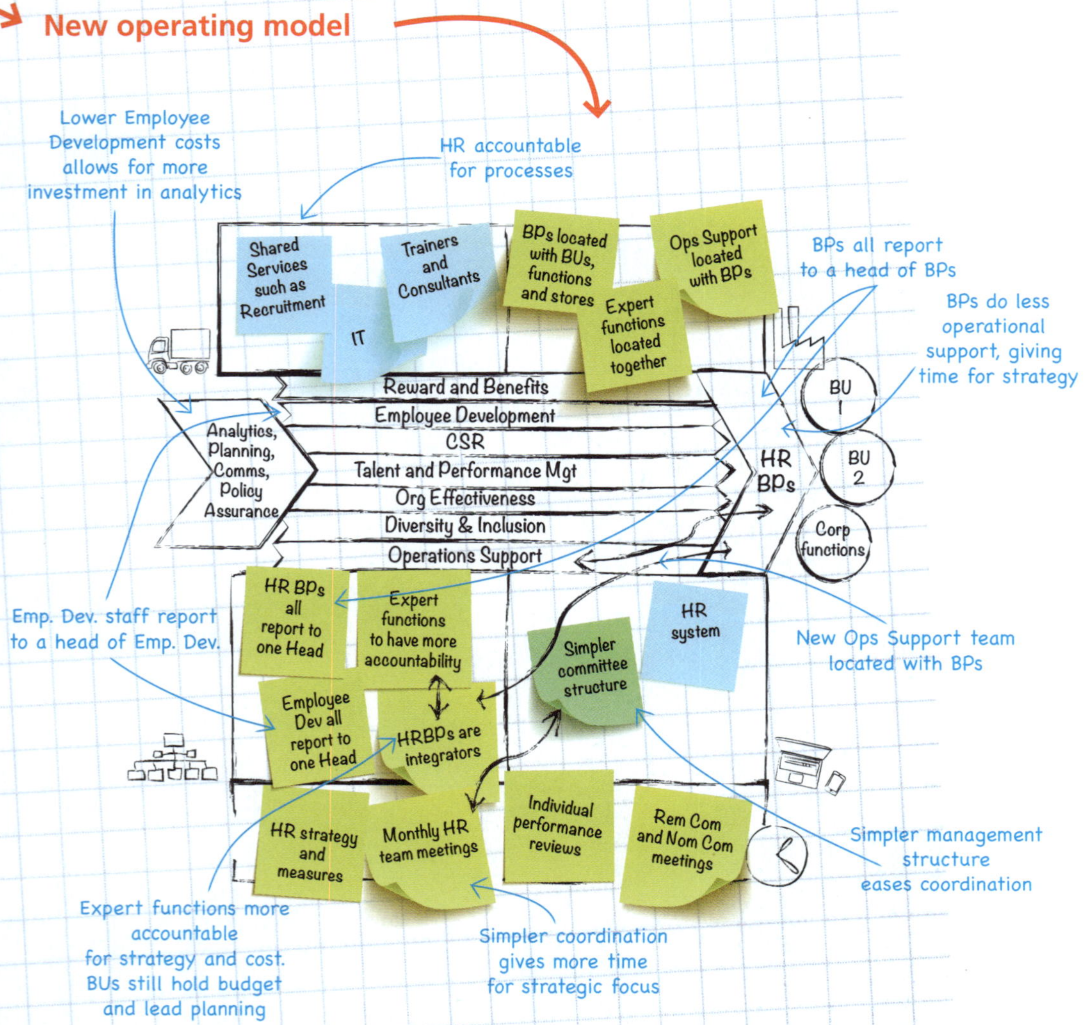

Processes
No change in process steps. Less cost in employee development due to standardization across BUs. More investment in diversity, analytics and strategy.

Organization
Change in reporting structure for BPs and employee development. New operations support team to release BP time for strategic work. Fewer layers of BP management.

Locations
Ops Support located close to businesses, like BPs.

Information
Simpler coordination.

Suppliers
HR now accountable for processes, including those performed by shared services.

Management processes
Clearer HR strategy gives more accountability to expert functions. Simpler coordination means more time for strategic dialog.

Result
Reduced costs. Other Impacts not yet clear.

Changing the operating model ...

The organization is a department of government that provides unemployment benefits, such as out-of-work payments, in-work payments for low paid workers, and payments to single parents.

The benefits are delivered through 'employment offices' located all round the country. Claimants go to an employment office or call a help line. Their claims are assessed before being passed to the 'benefits team'. The benefits team make a further assessment and issue preliminary benefit papers. The papers are sent to the local office where the claimant has an interview and further assessment. The papers then go back to the benefits team for finalization. There can be appeals and legal challenges. Payments are made by bank transfer.

Change was needed because unemployment benefits were to be combined with housing benefits and tax relief benefits into a single 'combined benefit' which would be administered through the 'employment offices'. There was also a need to achieve greater efficiency savings.

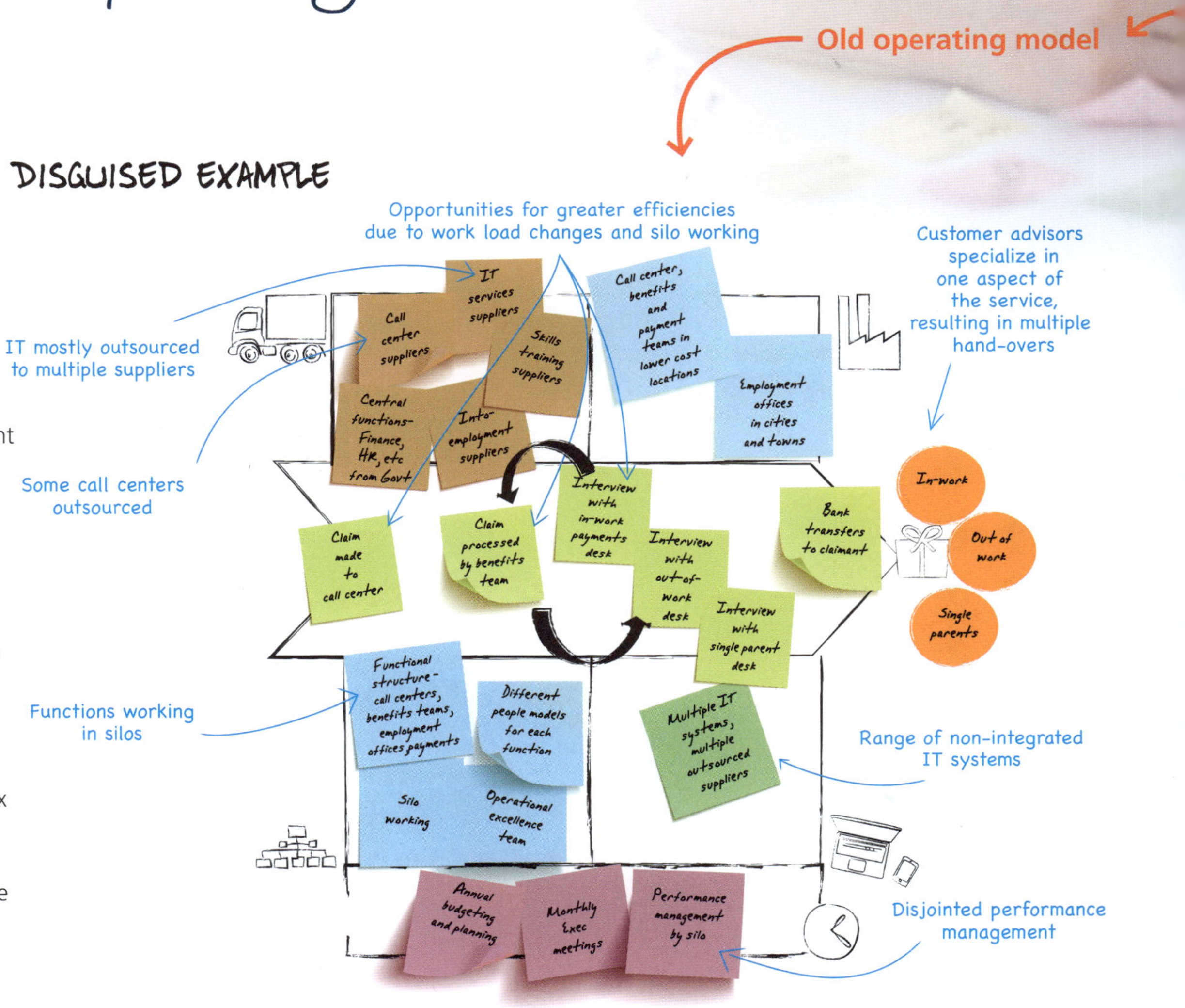

... for unemployment benefit

New operating model

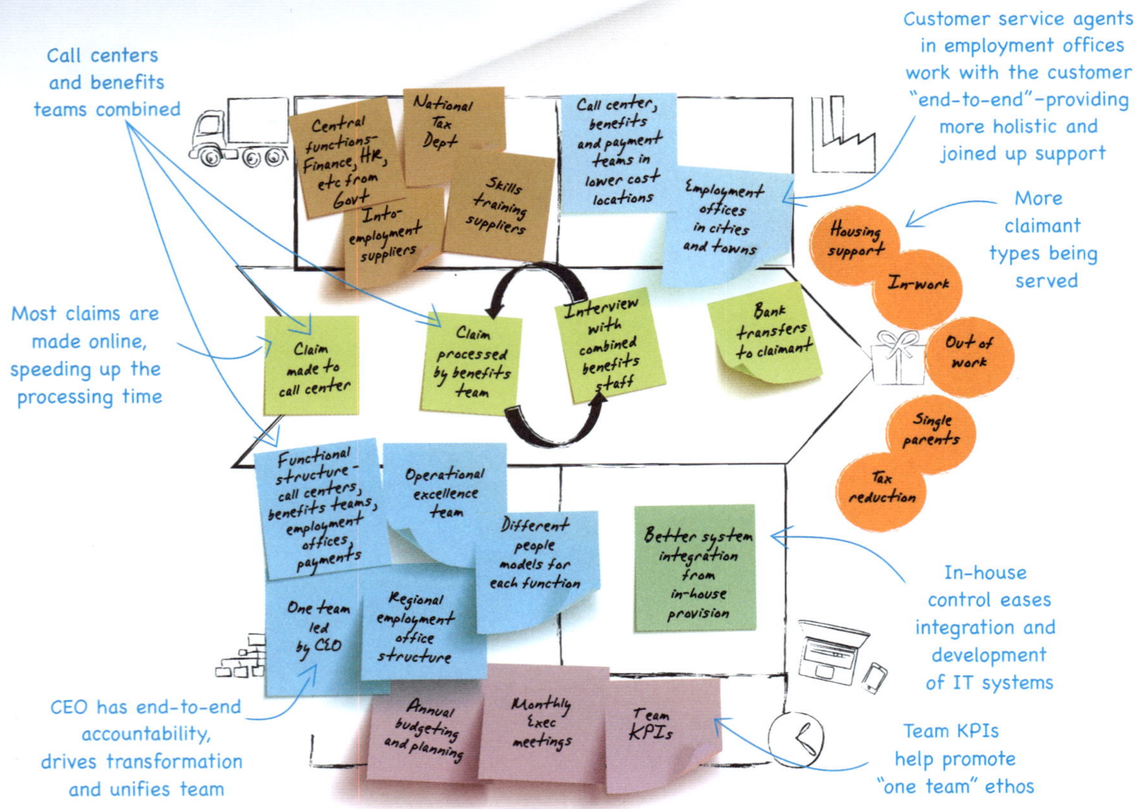

Processes
The basic value chain stays the same, but the organization processes more types of claimant. Call centers and IT services in-sourced. Employment centers only have one 'desk'.

Organization
Call centers and benefits team are combined to enable workload sharing. CEO appointed to provide a single point of accountability, to drive transformation and pull the team together.

Locations
No change to locations.

Information
In-house provision makes integration and system development easier.

Suppliers
National tax department provides income tax information.

Management processes
Better performance management due to team KPIs.

Result
Reduced costs, better outcomes for citizens and the taxpayer (more people into work and working longer hours).